The Chinese Fairy Book

Richard Wilhelm

In the interest of creating a more extensive selection of rare historical book reprints, we have chosen to reproduce this title even though it may possibly have occasional imperfections such as missing and blurred pages, missing text, poor pictures, markings, dark backgrounds and other reproduction issues beyond our control. Because this work is culturally important, we have made it available as a part of our commitment to protecting, preserving and promoting the world's literature. Thank you for your understanding.

THE
CHINESE FAIRY
BOOK

EDITED BY
DR. R. WILHELM

TRANSLATED AFTER ORIGINAL SOURCES BY
FREDERICK H. MARTENS

WITH SIX ILLUSTRATIONS IN COLOR BY
GEORGE W. HOOD

NEW YORK
FREDERICK A. STOKES COMPANY
PUBLISHERS

Copyright, 1921, by
Frederick A. Stokes Company

All Rights Reserved

Printed in the U. S. of America

PREFACE

The fairy tales and legends of olden China have in common with the "Thousand and One Nights" an oriental glow and glitter of precious stones and gold and multicolored silks, an oriental wealth of fantastic and supernatural action. And yet they strike an exotic note distinct in itself. The seventy-three stories here presented after original sources, embracing "Nursery Fairy Tales," "Legends of the Gods," "Tales of Saints and Magicians," "Nature and Animal Tales," "Ghost Stories," "Historic Fairy Tales," and "Literary Fairy Tales," probably represent the most comprehensive and varied collection of oriental fairy tales ever made available for American readers. There is no child who will not enjoy their novel color, their fantastic beauty, their infinite variety of subject. Yet, like the "Arabian Nights," they will amply repay the attention of the older reader as well. Some are exquisitely poetic, such as "The Flower-Elves," "The Lady of the Moon" or "The Herd Boy and the Weaving Maiden"; others like "How Three Heroes Came By Their Deaths Because Of Two Peaches", carry us back dramatically and powerfully to the Chinese age of Chivalry. The summits of fantasy are scaled in the quasi-religious dramas of "The Ape Sun Wu Kung" and "Notcha," or the wierd sorceries unfolded in "The Kindly Magician". Delightful ghost stories, with happy endings, such as "A Night on the Battlefield" and "The Ghost Who Was Foiled," are paralleled

PREFACE

with such idyllic love-tales as that of "Rose of Evening, or such Lilleputian fancies as "The King of the Ants" and "The Little Hunting Dog". It is quite safe to say that these Chinese fairy tales will give equal pleasure to the old as well as the young. They have been retold simply, with no changes in style or expression beyond such details of presentation which differences between oriental and occidental viewpoints at times compel. It is the writer's hope that others may take as much pleasure in reading them as he did in their translation.

Fredrick H. Martens.

CONTENTS

		PAGE
PREFACE	. . . .	v

NURSERY FAIRY TALES

CHAPTER		
I	WOMEN'S WORDS PART FLESH AND BLOOD	1
II	THE THREE RHYMSTERS	4
III	HOW GREED FOR A TRIFLING THING LED A MAN TO LOSE A GREAT ONE	6
IV	WHO WAS THE SINNER?	9
V	THE MAGIC CASK	10
VI	THE FAVORITE OF FORTUNE AND THE CHILD OF ILL LUCK	11
VII	THE BIRD WITH NINE HEADS	13
VIII	THE CAVE OF THE BEASTS	17
IX	THE PANTHER	20
X	THE GREAT FLOOD	24
XI	THE FOX AND THE TIGER	27
XII	THE TIGER'S DECOY	28
XIII	THE FOX AND THE RAVEN	29
XIV	WHY DOG AND CAT ARE ENEMIES . . .	30

LEGENDS OF THE GODS

XV	HOW THE FIVE ANCIENTS BECAME MEN . .	35
XVI	THE HERD BOY AND THE WEAVING MAIDEN .	37
XVII	YANG OERLANG	42

CONTENTS

CHAPTER		PAGE
XVIII	Notscha	44
XIX	The Lady of the Moon	53
XX	The Morning and the Evening Star . .	55
XXI	The Girl with the Horse's Head or the Silkworm Goddess	56
XXII	The Queen of Heaven	58
XXIII	The Fire-God	61
XXIV	The Three Ruling Gods	62
XXV	A Legend of Confucius	64
XXVI	The God of War	66

TALES OF SAINTS AND MAGICIANS

XXVII	The Halos of the Saints	71
XXVIII	Laotsze	73
XXIX	The Ancient Man	75
XXX	The Eight Immortals (I)	76
XXXI	The Eight Immortals (II)	82
XXXII	The Two Scholars	84
XXXIII	The Miserly Farmer	88
XXXIV	Sky O'Dawn	90
XXXV	King Mu of Dschou	95
XXXVI	The King of Huai Nan	99
XXXVII	Old Dschang	102
XXXVIII	The Kindly Magician	107

NATURE AND ANIMAL TALES

XXXIX	The Flower-Elves	119
XL	The Spirit of the Wu-Lian Mountain . .	124

CONTENTS

CHAPTER		PAGE
XLI	The King of the Ants	125
XLII	The Little Hunting Dog	127
XLIII	The Dragon After His Winter Sleep	130
XLIV	The Spirits of the Yellow River	131
XLV	The Dragon-Princess	137
XLVI	Help in Need	142
XLVII	The Disowned Princess	151
XLVIII	Fox-Fire	161

GHOST STORIES

XLIX	The Talking Silver Foxes	165
L	The Constable	168
LI	The Dangerous Reward	174
LII	Retribution	177
LIII	The Ghost Who Was Foiled	180
LIV	The Punishment of Greed	184
LV	The Night on the Battlefield	186
LVI	The Kingdom of the Ogres	189
LVII	The Maiden Who Was Stolen Away	196
LVIII	The Flying Ogre	199
LIX	Black Arts	201

HISTORIC LEGENDS

LX	The Sorcerer of the White Lotus Lodge	209
LXI	The Three Evils	212
LXII	How Three Heroes Came By Their Deaths Because of Two Peaches	215
LXIII	How the River God's Wedding Was Broken Off	218

CONTENTS

CHAPTER		PAGE
LXIV	Dschang Liang	220
LXV	Old Dragonbeard	223
LXVI	How Molo Stole the Lovely Rose-Bed	231
LXVII	The Golden Canister	235
LXVIII	Yang Gui Fe	240
LXIX	The Monk of the Yangtze-Kiang	243

LITERARY FAIRY TALES

LXX	The Heartless Husband	251
LXXI	Giauna the Beautiful	261
LXXII	The Frog Princess	271
LXXIII	Rose of Evening	280
LXXIV	The Ape Sun Wu Kung	288

LIST OF ILLUSTRATIONS

"The crows come flying and form a bridge over which the Weaving Maiden crosses the Silver River" *Frontispiece*

FACING PAGE

"Beside it stood a Cassia-tree" 54

" 'And I crossed the water on the shoe' " 90

"A fisherboy dived into the water and brought up a pearl from beneath the chin of a black dragon" 138

"Tsian Tang brought out a platter of red amber on which lay a carbuncle" 156

"Then he took his master and Rose-Red upon his back and flew with them over the steep walls" 234

NURSERY FAIRY TALES

THE CHINESE FAIRY BOOK

I

WOMEN'S WORDS PART FLESH AND BLOOD

ONCE upon a time there were two brothers, who lived in the same house. And the big brother listened to his wife's words, and because of them fell out with the little one. Summer had begun, and the time for sowing the high-growing millet had come. The little brother had no grain, and asked the big one to loan him some, and the big one ordered his wife to give it to him. But she took the grain, put it in a large pot and cooked it until it was done. Then she gave it to the little fellow. He knew nothing about it, and went and sowed his field with it. Yet, since the grain had been cooked, it did not sprout. Only a single grain of seed had not been cooked; so only a single sprout shot up. The little brother was hard-working and industrious by nature, and hence he watered and hoed the sprout all day long. And the sprout grew mightily, like a tree, and an ear of millet sprang up out of it like a canopy, large enough to shade half an acre of ground. In the fall the ear was ripe. Then the little brother took his ax and chopped it down. But no sooner had the ear fallen to the ground, than an enormous Roc came rushing down, took the ear in his beak and flew away. The little brother ran after him as far as the shore of the sea.

Then the bird turned and spoke to him like a human being, as follows: "You should not seek to harm me! What is this one ear worth to you? East of the sea is the isle of gold and silver. I will carry you across. There you may take whatever you want, and become very rich."

The little brother was satisfied, and climbed on the bird's back, and the latter told him to close his eyes. So he only heard the air whistling past his ears, as though he were driving through a strong wind, and beneath him the roar and surge of flood and waves. Suddenly the bird settled on a rock: "Here we are!" he said.

Then the little brother opened his eyes and looked about him: and on all sides he saw nothing but the radiance and shimmer of all sorts of white and yellow objects. He took about a dozen of the little things and hid them in his breast.

"Have you enough?" asked the Roc.

"Yes, I have enough," he replied.

"That is well," answered the bird. "Moderation protects one from harm."

Then he once more took him up, and carried him back again.

When the little brother reached home, he bought himself a good piece of ground in the course of time, and became quite well to do.

But his brother was jealous of him, and said to him, harshly: "Where did you manage to steal the money?"

So the little one told him the whole truth of the matter. Then the big brother went home and took counsel with his wife.

"Nothing easier," said his wife. "I will just cook grain again and keep back one seedling so that it is not done. Then you shall sow it, and we will see what happens."

No sooner said than done. And sure enough, a single sprout shot up, and sure enough, the sprout bore a single ear of millet, and when harvest time came around, the Roc again appeared and carried it off in his beak. The big brother was pleased, and ran after him, and the Roc said the same thing he had said before, and carried the big brother to the island. There the big brother saw the gold and silver heaped up everywhere. The largest pieces were like hills, the small ones were like bricks, and the real tiny ones were like grains of sand. They blinded his eyes. He only regretted that he knew of no way by which he could move mountains. So he bent down and picked up as many pieces as possible.

The Roc said: "Now you have enough! You will overtax your strength."

"Have patience but a little while longer," said the big brother. "Do not be in such a hurry! I must get a few more pieces!"

And thus time passed.

The Roc again urged him to make haste: "The sun will appear in a moment," said he, "and the sun is so hot it burns human beings up."

"Wait just a little while longer," said the big brother. But that very moment a red disk broke through the clouds with tremendous power. The Roc flew into the sea, stretched out both his wings, and beat the water with them in order to escape the heat. But the big brother was shrivelled up by the sun.

Note: This fairy-tale is traditionally narrated. The Roc is called *pong* in Chinese, and the treasures on the island are spoken of as "all sorts of yellow and white objects" because the little fellow does not know that they are gold and silver.

II

THE THREE RHYMSTERS

ONCE there were three daughters in a family. The oldest one married a physician, the second one married a magistrate; but the third, who was more than usually intelligent and a clever talker, married a farmer.

Now it chanced, once upon a time, that their parents were celebrating a birthday. So the three daughters came, together with their husbands, to wish them long life and happiness. The parents-in-law prepared a meal for their three sons-in-law, and put the birthday wine on the table. But the oldest son-in-law, who knew that the third one had not attended school, wanted to embarrass him.

"It is far too tiresome," said he, "just to sit here drinking: let us have a drinking game. Each one of us must invent a verse, one that rimes and makes sense, on the words: 'in the sky, on the earth, at the table, in the room,' And whoever cannot do so, must empty three glasses as a punishment."

All the company were satisfied. Only the third son-in-law felt embarrassed and insisted on leaving. But the guests would not let him go, and obliged him to keep his seat.

Then the oldest son-in-law began: "I will make a start with my verse. Here it is:

> "In the sky the phenix proudly flies,
> On the earth the lambkin tamely lies,
> At the table through an ancient book I wade,
> In the room I softly call the maid."

The second one continued: "And I say:

> "In the sky the turtle-dove flies round,
> On the earth the ox paws up the ground,
> At the table one studies the deeds of yore,
> In the room the maid she sweeps the floor."

But the third son-in-law stuttered, and found nothing to say. And when all of them insisted, he broke out in rough tones of voice:

> "In the sky—flies a leaden bullet
> On the earth—stalks a tiger-beast,
> On the table—lies a pair of scissos,
> In the room—I call the stable-boy."

The other two sons-in-law clapped their hands and began to laugh loudly.

"Why the four lines do not rhyme at all," said they, "and, besides they do not make sense. A leaden bullet is no bird, the stable-boy does his work outside, would you call him into the room? Nonsense, nonsense! Drink!"

Yet before they had finished speaking, the third daughter raised the curtain of the women's room, and stepped out. She was angry, yet she could not suppress a smile.

"How so do our lines not make sense?" said she. "Listen a moment, and I'll explain them to you: In the sky our leaden bullet will shoot your phenix and your turtle-dove. On the earth our tiger-beast will devour your sheep and your ox. On the table our pair of scissors will cut up all your old books. And finally, in the room—well, the stable-boy can marry your maid!"

Then the oldest son-in-law said: "Well scolded! Sister-in-law, you know how to talk! If you were a man you would have had your degree long ago. And, as a punishment, we will empty our three glasses."

Note: This is also a fairy-tale traditionally handed down.

III

HOW GREED FOR A TRIFLING THING LED A MAN TO LOSE A GREAT ONE

ONCE upon a time there was an old woman, who had two sons. But her older son did not love his parents, and left his mother and brother. The younger one served her so faithfully, however, that all the people spoke of his filial affection.

One day it happened that there was a theatrical performance given outside the village. The younger son started to carry his mother there on his back, so that she might look on. But there was a ravine before the village, and he slipped and fell down in the middle of it. And his mother was killed by the rolling stones, and her blood and flesh were sprinkled about everywhere. The son stroked his mother's corpse, and wept bitterly. He was about to kill himself when, suddenly, he saw a priest standing before him.

The latter said: "Have no fear, for I can bring your mother back to life again!" And as he said so, he stooped, gathered up her flesh and bones, and laid them together as they should be. Then he breathed upon them, and at once the mother was alive again. This made the son very happy, and he thanked the priest on his knees. Yet on a sharp point of rock he still saw a bit of his mother's flesh hanging, a bit about an inch long.

"That should not be left hanging there either," said he, and hid it in his breast.

"In truth, you love your mother as a son should," said the priest. Then he bade the son give him the bit of flesh, kneaded a manikin out of it, breathed upon it, and in a minute there it stood, a really fine-looking little boy.

"His name is Small Profit," said he, turning to the son, "and you may call him brother. You are poor and have not the wherewithal with which to nourish your mother. If you need something, Small Profit can get it for you."

The son thanked him once more, then took his mother on his back again, and his new little brother by the hand, and went home. And when he said to Small Profit: "Bring meat and wine!" then meat and wine were at hand at once, and steaming rice was already cooking in the pot. And when he said to Small Profit: "Bring money and cloth!" then his purse filled itself with money, and the chests were heaped up with cloth to the brim. Whatever he asked for that he received. Thus, in the course of time, they came to be very well off indeed.

But his older brother envied him greatly. And when there was another theatrical performance in the village, he took his mother on his back—by force—and went to it. And when he reached the ravine, he slipped purposely, and let his mother fall into the depths, only intent to see that she really was shattered into fragments. And sure enough his mother had such a bad fall that her limbs and trunk were strewn around in all directions. He then climbed down, took his mother's head in his hands, and pretended to weep.

And at once the priest was on hand again, and said: "I can wake the dead to life again, and surround white bones with flesh and blood!"

Then he did as he had done before, and the mother came to life again. But the older brother already had hidden one of her ribs on purpose. He now pulled it out and said to the priest: "Here is a bone left. What shall I do with it?"

The priest took the bone, enclosed it in lime and earth, breathed upon it, as he had done the other time, and it became a little man, resembling Small Profit, but larger in stature.

"His name is Great Duty," he told his older brother, "if you stick to him he will always lend you a hand."

The son took his mother back again, and Great Duty walked beside him.

When he came to their courtyard door, he saw his younger brother coming out, holding Small Profit in his arms.

"Where are you going?" he said to him.

His brother answered: "Small Profit is a divine being, who does not wish to dwell for all time among men. He wants to fly back to the heavens, and so I am escorting him."

"Give Small Profit to me! Don't let him get away!" cried the older brother.

Yet, before he had ended his speech, Small Profit was rising in the air. The older brother then quickly let his mother drop on the ground, and stretched out his hand to catch Small Profit. But he did not succeed, and now Great Duty, too, rose from the ground, took Small Profit's hand, and together they ascended to the clouds and disappeared.

Then the older brother stamped on the ground, and said with a sigh: "Alas, I have lost my Great Duty because I was too greedy for that Small Profit!"

Note: In China—usually on festive days or because of some religious celebration—a provisional stage is erected before the village or temple, and a play given. Permanent theaters are to be found only in the large cities.

IV

WHO WAS THE SINNER?

ONCE upon a time there were ten farmers, who were crossing a field together. They were surprised by a heavy thunder-storm, and took refuge in a half-ruined temple. But the thunder drew ever nearer, and so great was the tumult that the air trembled about them, while the lightning flew around the temple in a continuous circle. The farmers were greatly frightened, and thought that there must be a sinner among them, whom the lightning would strike. In order to find out who it might be, they agreed to hang their straw hats up before the door, and he whose hat was blown away was to yield himself up to his fate.

No sooner were the hats outside, than one of them was blown away, and the rest thrust its unfortunate owner out of doors without pity. But as soon as he had left the temple the lightning ceased circling around, and struck it with a crash.

The one whom the rest had thrust out, had been the

only righteous one among them, and for his sake the lightning had spared the temple. So the other nine had to pay for their hardheartedness with their lives.

Note: A traditionally narrated fairy-tale.

V

THE MAGIC CASK

ONCE upon a time there was a man who dug up a big, earthenware cask in his field. So he took it home with him and told his wife to clean it out. But when his wife started brushing the inside of the cask, the cask suddenly began to fill itself with brushes. No matter how many were taken out, others kept on taking their place. So the man sold the brushes, and the family managed to live quite comfortably.

Once a coin fell into the cask by mistake. At once the brushes disappeared and the cask began to fill itself with money. So now the family became rich; for they could take as much money out of the cask as ever they wished.

Now the man had an old grandfather at home, who was weak and shaky. Since there was nothing else he could do, his grandson set him to work shoveling money out of the cask, and when the old grandfather grew weary and could not keep on, he would fall into a rage, and shout at him angrily, telling him he was lazy and did not want to work. One day, however, the old man's strength gave out, and he fell into the cask and died. At once the money disappeared, and the whole cask began to fill itself with dead grandfathers.

Then the man had to pull them all out and have them buried, and for this purpose he had to use up again all the money he had received. And when he was through, the cask broke, and he was just as poor as before.

Note: "The Magic Cask" is a traditionally narrated tale. In Northern China wooden casks or barrels are unknown. Large vessels, open at the top, of earth or stone are used to hold water and other liquids.

VI

THE FAVORITE OF FORTUNE AND THE CHILD OF ILL LUCK

ONCE upon a time there was a proud prince who had a daughter. But the daughter was a child of ill luck. When it came time for her to marry, she had all her suitors assemble before her father's palace. She was going to throw down a ball of red silk among them, and whoever caught it was to be her husband. Now there were many princes and counts gathered before the castle, and in their midst there was also a beggar. And the princess could see dragons crawling into his ears and crawling out again from his nostrils, for he was a child of luck. So she threw the ball to the beggar and he caught it.

Her father asked angrily: "Why did you throw the ball into the beggar's hands?"

"He is a favorite of Fortune," said the princess, "I will marry him, and then, perhaps, I will share in his good luck."

But her father would not hear of it, and since she insisted, he drove her from the castle in his rage. So the princess had to go off with the beggar. She dwelt with him in a little hut, and had to hunt for herbs and roots, and cook them herself, so that they might have something to eat; and often they both went hungry.

One day her husband said to her: "I will set out and seek my fortune. And when I have found it, I will come back again and fetch you." The princess was willing, and he went away, and was gone for eighteen years. Meanwhile the princess lived in want and affliction, for her father remained hard and merciless. If her mother had not secretly given her food and money, no doubt she would have starved to death during all that time.

But the beggar found his fortune, and at length became emperor. He returned and stood before his wife. She however, no longer recognized him: She only knew that he was the powerful emperor.

He asked her how she were getting along.

"Why do you ask me how I am getting along?" she replied. "I am too far beneath your notice."

"And who may your husband be?"

"My husband was a beggar. He went away to seek his fortune. That was eighteen years ago, and he has not yet returned."

"And what have you done during all those long years?"

"I have been waiting for him to return."

"Do you wish to marry some one else, seeing that he has been missing so long?"

"No, I will remain his wife until I die."

When the emperor saw how faithful his wife was, he told her who he was, had her clothed in magnificent garments, and took her with him to his imperial palace. And there they lived in splendor and happiness.

After a few days the emperor said to his wife: "We

spend every day in festivities, as though every day were New Year."

"And why should we not celebrate," answered his wife, "since we have now become emperor and empress?"

Yet his wife was a child of ill luck. When she had been empress no more than eighteen days, she fell sick and died. But her husband lived for many a long year.

Note: "The Favorite of Fortune and the Child of Ill Luck" is a traditionally narrated fairy-tale. The dragon is the symbol of imperial rule, and the New Year's feasts, which old and young celebrate for weeks, is the greatest of Chinese festivals.

VII

THE BIRD WITH NINE HEADS

LONG, long ago, there once lived a king and a queen who had a daughter. One day, when the daughter went walking in the garden, a tremendous storm suddenly came up and carried her away with it. Now the storm had come from the bird with nine heads, who had robbed the princess, and brought her to his cave. The king did not know whither his daughter had disappeared, so he had proclaimed throughout the land: "Whoever brings back the princess may have her for his bride!"

Now a youth had seen the bird as he was carrying the princess to his cave. This cave, though, was in the middle of a sheer wall of rock. One could not climb up to it from below, nor could one climb down to it from above. And as the youth was walking around the rock, another youth came along and asked him what he was doing there. So the first youth told him that the bird with nine heads had carried off the king's daughter, and had brought her up to his cave. The other chap knew what he had to do. He called together his friends, and they lowered the youth to the cave in a basket. And when he went into the cave, he saw the king's daughter sitting there, and washing the wound of the bird with nine heads; for the hound of heaven had bitten off his tenth head, and his wound was still bleeding. The princess, however, motioned to the youth to hide, and he did so. When the king's daughter had washed his wound and bandaged it, the bird with nine heads felt so comfortable, that one after another, all his nine heads fell asleep. Then the youth stepped forth from his hiding-place, and cut off his nine heads with a sword. But the king's daughter said: "It would be best if you were hauled up first, and I came after."

"No," said the youth. "I will wait below here, until you are in safety." At first the king's daughter was not willing; yet at last she allowed herself to be persuaded, and climbed into the basket. But before she did so, she took a long pin from her hair, broke it into two halves and gave him one and kept the other. She also divided her silken kerchief with him, and told him to take good care of both her gifts. But when the other man had drawn up the king's daughter, he took her along with him, and left the youth in the cave, in spite of all his calling and pleading.

The youth now took a walk about the cave. There he saw a number of maidens, all of whom had been carried off by the bird with nine heads, and who had perished there of hunger. And on the wall hung a fish, nailed against it with four nails. When he touched the fish, the latter turned into a handsome youth, who thanked him for delivering him, and they agreed to regard each other as brothers. Soon the first youth grew very hungry. He stepped out in front of the cave to search for food, but only stones were lying there. Then, suddenly, he saw a great dragon, who was licking a stone. The youth imitated him, and before long his hunger had disappeared. He next asked the dragon how he could get away from the cave, and the dragon nodded his head in the direction of his tail, as much as to say he should seat himself upon it. So he climbed up, and in the twinkling of an eye he was down on the ground, and the dragon had disappeared. He then went on until he found a tortoise-shell full of beautiful pearls. But they were magic pearls, for if you flung them into the fire, the fire ceased to burn and if you flung them into the water, the water divided and you could walk through the midst of it. The youth took the pearls out of the tortoise-shell, and put them in his pocket. Not long after he reached the sea-shore. Here he flung a pearl into the sea, and at once the waters divided and he could see the sea-dragon. The sea-dragon cried: "Who is disturbing me here in my own kingdom?" The youth answered: "I found pearls in a tortoise-shell, and have flung one into the sea, and now the waters have divided for me."

"If that is the case," said the dragon, "then come into the sea with me and we will live there together." Then the youth recognized him for the same dragon whom he had seen in the cave. And with him was the youth with whom he had formed a bond of brotherhood: He was the dragon's son.

"Since you have saved my son and become his brother, I am your father," said the old dragon. And he entertained him hospitably with food and wine.

One day his friend said to him: "My father is sure

to want to reward you. But accept no money, nor any jewels from him, but only the little gourd flask over yonder. With it you can conjure up whatever you wish."

And, sure enough, the old dragon asked him what he wanted by way of a reward, and the youth answered: "I want no money, nor any jewels. All I want is the little gourd flask over yonder."

At first the dragon did not wish to give it up, but at last he did let him have it, after all. And then the youth left the dragon's castle.

When he set his foot on dry land again he felt hungry. At once a table stood before him, covered with a fine and plenteous meal. He ate and drank. After he had gone on a while, he felt weary. And there stood an ass, waiting for him, on which he mounted. After he had ridden for a while, the ass's gait seemed too uneven, and along came a wagon, into which he climbed. But the wagon shook him up too, greatly, and he thought: "If I only had a litter! That would suit me better." No more had he thought so, than the litter came along, and he seated himself in it. And the bearers carried him to the city in which dwelt the king, the queen and their daughter.

When the other youth had brought back the king's daughter, it was decided to hold the wedding. But the king's daughter was not willing, and said: "He is not the right man. My deliverer will come and bring with him half of the long pin for my hair, and half my silken kerchief as a token." But when the youth did not appear for so long a time, and the other one pressed the king, the king grew impatient and said: "The wedding shall take place to-morrow!" Then the king's daughter went sadly through the streets of the city, and searched and searched in the hope of finding her deliverer. And this was on the very day that the litter arrived. The king's daughter saw the half of her silken handkerchief in the youth's hand, and filled with joy, she led him to her father. There he had to show his half of the long pin, which fitted the other exactly, and then the king was convinced that he was the right, true deliverer. The false bridegroom was now punished, the wedding celebrated, and they lived in peace and happiness till the end of their days.

Note: "The Bird With Nine Heads" is a traditionally narrated fairy-tale. The long hair needle is an example of the halved jewel sed as a sign of recognition by lovers (see No. 67, "Yang-Gui Fee"). The "Fish" in the cave is the dragon's son, for like East Indian *Nagaradjas*, the Chinese dragons are often sea-gods. Gourd flasks often occur as magic talismans in Chinese fairy-tales, and spirits who serve their owners are often imprisoned in them. See No. 81.

VIII

THE CAVE OF THE BEASTS

ONCE upon a time there was a family in which there were seven daughters. One day when the father went out to gather wood, he found seven wild duck eggs. He brought them home, but did not think of giving any to his children, intending to eat them himself, with his wife. In the evening the oldest daughter woke up, and asked her mother what she was cooking. The mother said: "I am cooking wild duck eggs. I will give you one, but you must not let your sisters know." And so she gave her one. Then the second daughter woke up, and asked her mother what she was cooking. She said: "Wild duck eggs. If you will not tell your sisters, I'll give you one." And so it went. At last the daughters had eaten all the eggs, and there were none left.

In the morning the father was very angry with the children, and said: "Who wants to go along to grandmother?" But he intended to lead the children into the mountains, and let the wolves devour them there. The older daughters suspected this, and said: "We are not going along!" But the two younger ones said: "We will go with you." And so they drove off with their father. After they had driven a good ways, they asked: "Will we soon get to grandmother's house?" "Right away," said their father. And when they had reached the mountains he told them: "Wait here. I will drive into the village ahead of you, and tell grandmother that you are coming." And then he drove off with the donkey-cart. They waited and waited, but their father did not come. At last they decided that their father would not come back to fetch them, and that he had left them alone in the mountains. So they went further and further into the hills seeking a shelter for the night. Then they spied a great stone. This they selected for a pillow, and rolled it over to the place where they were going to lie down to sleep. And then they saw that the stone was the door to a cave. There was a light in the cave, and they went into it. The light they had seen came from the many precious stones and jewels of every sort in the cave, which belonged to a wolf and a fox. They had a number of jars of precious stones and pearls that shone by night. The girls said: "What a lovely cave this is! We will lie right down and go to bed." For there stood two golden beds with gold-embroidered covers. So they lay down and fell asleep. During the night the wolf and fox came home. And the wolf said: "I smell human flesh!" But the fox replied: "Oh, nonsense! There are no human beings who can enter our cave. We lock it up too well for that." The wolf said: "Very well, then let us lie down in our beds and sleep." But the fox answered: "Let us curl up in the kettles on the hearth. They still hold a little warmth from the fire." The one kettle was of gold and the other of silver, and they curled up in them.

When the girls rose early in the morning, they saw the wolf and the fox lying there, and were much frightened. And they put the covers on the kettles and heaped a number of big stones on them, so that the wolf and the fox could not get out again. Then they made a fire. The wolf and the fox said: "Oh, how nice and warm it is this morning! How does that happen?" But at length it grew too hot for them. Then they noticed that the two girls had kindled a fire and they cried: "Let us out! We will give you lots of precious stones, and lots of gold, and will do you no harm!" But the girls would not listen to them, and kept on making a bigger fire. So that was the end of the wolf and the fox in the kettles.

Then the girls lived happily for a number of days in the cave. But their father was seized with a longing for his daughters, and he went into the mountains to look for them. And he sat right down on the stone in front of the cave to rest, and tapped his pipe against it to empty the ashes. Then the girls within called out: "Who is knocking at our door?" And the father said: "Are those not my daughters' voices?" While the daughters replied: "Is that not our father's voice?" Then they pushed aside the stone and ·aw that it was their father, and their father was glad to see them once more. He was much surprised to think that they should have chanced on this cave full of precious stones, and they told him the whole story. Then their father fetched people to help him carry home the jewels. And when they got home, his wife wondered where he had obtained all these treasures. So the father and daughters told her everything, and they became a very wealthy family, and lived happily to the end of their days.

Note: "The Cave of the Beasts" is traditionally narrated.

IX

THE PANTHER

ONCE upon a time there was a widow who had two daughters and a little son. And one day the mother said to her daughters: "Take good care of the house, for I am going to see grandmother, together with your little brother!" So the daughters promised her they would do so, and their mother went off. On her way a panther met her, and asked where she were going.

She said: "I am going with my child to see my mother."

"Will you not rest a bit?" asked the panther.

"No," said she, "it is already late, and it is a long road to where my mother lives."

But the panther did not cease urging her, and finally she gave in and sat down by the road side.

"I will comb your hair a bit," said the panther. And the woman allowed the panther to comb her hair. But as he passed his claws through her hair, he tore off a bit of her skin and devoured it.

"Stop!" cried the woman, "the way you comb my hair hurts!"

But the panther tore off a much larger piece of skin. Now the woman wanted to call for help, but the panther seized and devoured her. Then he turned on her little son and killed him too, put on the woman's clothes, and laid the child's bones, which he had not yet devoured, in her basket. After that he went to the woman's home, where her two daughters were, and called in at the door: "Open the door, daughters! Mother has come home!" But they looked out through a crack and said: "Our mother's eyes are not so large as yours!"

Then the panther said: "I have been to grandmother's house, and saw her hens laying eggs. That pleases me, and is the reason why my eyes have grown so large."

"Our mother had no spots in her face such as you have."

"Grandmother had no spare bed, so I had to sleep on the peas, and they pressed themselves into my face."

"Our mother's feet are not so large as yours."

"Stupid things! That comes from walking such a distance. Come, open the door quickly!"

Then the daughters said to each other: "It must be our mother," and they opened the door. But when the panther came in, they saw it was not really their mother after all.

At evening, when the daughters were already in bed, the panther was still gnawing the bones he had brought with him.

Then the daughters asked: "Mother, what are you eating?"

"I'm eating beets," was the answer.

Then the daughters said: "Oh, mother, give us some of your beets, too! We are so hungry!"

"No," was the reply, "I will not give you any. Now be quiet and go to sleep."

But the daughters kept on begging until the false mother gave them a little finger. And then they saw that it was their little brother's finger, and they said to each other: "We must make haste to escape else he will eat us as well." And with that they ran out of the door, climbed up into a tree in the yard, and called down to the false mother: "Come out! We can see our neighbor's son celebrating his wedding!" But it was the middle of the night.

Then the mother came out, and when she saw that they were sitting in the tree, she called out angrily: "Why, I'm not able to climb!"

The daughters said: "Get into a basket and throw us the rope and we will draw you up!"

The mother did as they said. But when the basket was half-way up, they began to swing it back and forth, and bump it against the tree. Then the false mother had to turn into a panther again, lest she fall down. And the panther leaped out of the basket, and ran away.

Gradually daylight came. The daughters climbed down, seated themselves on the doorstep, and cried for their mother. And a needle-vender came by and asked them why they were crying.

"A panther has devoured our mother and our brother," said the girls. "He has gone now, but he is sure to return and devour us as well."

Then the needle-vender gave them a pair of needles, and said: "Stick these needles in the cushion of the arm chair, with the points up." The girl thanked him and went on crying.

Soon a scorpion-catcher came by; and he asked them why they were crying. "A panther has devoured our mother and brother," said the girls. "He has gone now, but he is sure to return and devour us as well."

The man gave them a scorpion and said: "Put it behind the hearth in the kitchen." The girls thanked him and went on crying.

Then an egg-seller came by and asked them why they were crying. "A panther has devoured our mother and our brother," said the girls. "He has gone now, but he is sure to return and devour us as well."

So he gave them an egg and said: "Lay it beneath the ashes in the hearth." The girls thanked him and went on crying.

Then a dealer in turtles came by, and they told him their tale. He gave them a turtle and said: "Put it in the water-barrel in the yard." And then a man came by who sold wooden clubs. He asked them why they were crying. And they told him the whole story. Then he gave them two wooden clubs and said: "Hang them up over the door to the street." The girls thanked him and did as the men had told them.

In the evening the panther came home. He sat down in the armchair in the room. Then the needles in the cushion stuck into him. So he ran into the kitchen to light the fire and see what had jabbed him so; and then it was that the scorpion hooked his sting into his hand. And when at last the fire was burning, the egg burst and spurted into one of his eyes, which was blinded. So he ran out into the yard and dipped his hand into the water-barrel, in order to cool it; and then the turtle bit it off. And when in his pain he ran out through the door into the street, the wooden clubs fell on his head and that was the end of him.

Note: "The Panther" in this tale is in reality the same beast as "the talking silver fox" in No. 48, and the fairy-tale is made up of motives to be found in "Little Red Riding-Hood," "The Wolf and the the Seven Kids," and "The Vagabonds."

X

THE GREAT FLOOD

ONCE upon a time there was a widow, who had a child. And the child was a kind-hearted boy of whom every one was fond. One day he said to his mother: "All the other children have a grandmother, but I have none. And that makes me feel very sad!"

"We will hunt up a grandmother for you," said his mother. Now it once happened that an old beggar-woman came to the house, who was very old and feeble. And when the child saw her, he said to her: "You shall be my grandmother!" And he went to his mother and said: "There is a beggar-woman outside, whom I want for my grandmother!" And his mother was willing and called her into the house; though the old woman was very dirty. So the boy said to his mother: "Come, let us wash grandmother!" And they washed the woman. But she had a great many burrs in her hair, so they picked them all out and put them in a jar, and they filled the whole jar. Then the grandmother said: "Do not throw them away, but bury them in the garden. And you must not dig them up again before the great flood comes."

"When is the great flood coming?" asked the boy.

"When the eyes of the two stone lions in front of the prison grow red, then the great flood will come," said the grandmother.

So the boy went to look at the lions, but their eyes were not yet red. And the grandmother also said to him: "Make a little wooden ship and keep it in a little box." And this the boy did. And he ran to the prison every day and looked at the lions, much to the astonishment of the people in the street.

One day, as he passed the chicken-butcher's shop, the butcher asked him why he was always running to the lions. And the boy said: "When the lions' eyes grow red then the great flood will come." But the butcher laughed at him. And the following morning, quite early, he took some chicken-blood and rubbed it on the lions' eyes. When the boy saw that the lions' eyes were red he ran swiftly home, and told his mother and grandmother. And then his grandmother said: "Dig up the jar quickly, and take the little ship out of its box." And when they dug up the jar, it was filled with the purest pearls and the little ship grew larger and larger, like a real ship. Then the grandmother said: "Take the jar with you and get into the ship. And when the great flood comes, then you may save all the animals that are driven into it; but human beings, with their black heads, you are not to save." So they climbed into the ship, and the grandmother suddenly disappeared.

Now it began to rain, and the rain kept falling more and more heavily from the heavens. Finally there were no longer any single drops falling, but just one big sheet of water which flooded everything.

Then a dog came drifting along, and they saved him in their ship. Soon after came a pair of mice, with their little ones, loudly squeaking in their fear. And these they also saved. The water was already rising to the roofs of the houses, and on one roof stood a cat, arching her back and mewing pitifully. They took the cat into the ship, too. Yet the flood increased and rose to the tops of the trees. And in one tree sat a raven, beating his wings and cawing loudly. And him, too, they took in. Finally a swarm of bees came flying their way. The little creatures were quite wet, and could hardly fly. So they took in the bees on their ship. At last a man with black hair floated by on the waves. The boy said: "Mother, let us save him, too!" But the mother did not want to do so. "Did not grandmother tell us that we must save no black-headed human beings?" But the boy answered: "We will save the man in spite of that. I feel sorry for him, and cannot bear to see him drifting along in the water." So they also saved the man.

Gradually the water subsided. Then they got out of their ship, and parted from the man and the beasts. And the ship grew small again and they put it away in its box.

But the man was filled with a desire for the pearls. He went to the judge and entered a complaint against the boy and his mother, and they were both thrown into jail. Then the mice came, and dug a hole in the wall. And the dog came through the hole and brought them meat, and the cat brought them bread, so they did not have to hunger in their prison. But the raven flew off and returned with a letter for the judge. The letter had been written by a god, and it said: "I wandered about in the world of men disguised as a beggar woman. And this boy and his mother took me in. The boy treated me like his own grandmother, and did not shrink from washing me when I was dirty. Because of this I saved them out of the great flood by means of which I destroyed the sinful city wherein they dwelt. Do you, O judge, free them, or misfortune shall be your portion!"

So the judge had them brought before him, and asked what they had done, and how they had made their way through the flood. Then they told him everything, and what they said agreed with the god's letter. So the judge punished their accuser, and set them both at liberty.

When the boy had grown up he came to a city of many people, and it was said that the princess intended to take a husband. But in order to find the right man, she had veiled herself, and seated herself in a litter, and she had had the litter, together with many others, carried into the market place. In every litter sat a veiled woman, and the princess was in their midst. And whoever hit upon the right litter, he was to get the princess for his bride. So the youth went there, too, and when he reached the market place, he saw the bees whom he had saved from the great flood, all swarming about a certain litter. Up he stepped to it, and sure enough, the princess was sitting in it. And then their wedding was celebrated, and they lived happily ever afterward.

Note: "The Great Flood" is traditionally narrated and a diluvian legend seems to underlie it. Compare with Grimm's fairytale (No. 73) "The Queen of the Bees."

XI

THE FOX AND THE TIGER

ONCE a fox met a tiger. The latter bared his teeth, stretched out his claws, and was about to devour him. But the fox spoke and said: "My dear sir, you must not think that you are the only king of beasts. Your courage does not compare with my own. Let us walk together, and do you keep behind me. And if men catch sight of me and do not fear me, then you may devour me." The tiger was willing, and so the fox led him along a broad highway. But the travelers, when they saw the tiger in the distance, were all frightened and ran away.

Then the fox said: 'How about it? I went in advance, and the men saw me and had not as yet seen you."

And thereupon the tiger drew in his tail and ran away himself.

The tiger had remarked quite well that the men were afraid of the fox, but he had not noticed that the fox had borrowed the terror he inspired from him.

Note: This universally known fable is traditionally narrated. Animal fables are very rare in China.

XII

THE TIGER'S DECOY

THAT the fox borrowed the terror he inspired from the tiger is more than a simile; but that the tiger has his decoy is something we read about in the story books, and grandfathers talk about a good deal, too. So there must be some truth in it. It is said that when a tiger devours a human being, the latter's spirit cannot free itself, and that the tiger then uses it for a decoy. When he goes out to seek his prey, the spirit of the man he has devoured must go before him, to hide him, so that people cannot see him. And the spirit is apt to change itself into a beautiful girl, or a lump of gold or a bolt of silk. All sorts of deceptions are used to lure folk into the mountain gorges. Then the tiger comes along and devours his victim, and the new spirit must serve as his decoy. The old spirit's time of service is over and it may go. And so it continues, turn by turn. Probably that is why they say of people who are forced to yield themselves up to cunning and powerful men, in order that others may be harmed: "They are the tiger's decoys!"

Note: This tale is traditionally narrated.

XIII

THE FOX AND THE RAVEN

THE fox knows how to flatter, and how to play many cunning tricks. Once upon a time he saw a raven, who alighted on a tree with a piece of meat in his beak. The fox seated himself beneath the tree, looked up at him, and began to praise him.

"Your color," he began, "is pure black. This proves to me that you possess all the wisdom of Laotzse, who knows how to shroud his learning in darkness. The manner in which you manage to feed your mother shows that your filial affection equals that which the Master Dsong had for his parents. Your voice is rough and strong. It proves that you have the courage with which King Hiang once drove his foes to flight by the mere sound of his voice. In truth, you are the king of birds!"

The raven, hearing this, was filled with joy and said: "I thank you! I thank you!"

And before he knew it, the meat fell to earth from his opened beak.

The fox caught it up, devoured it and then said, laughing: "Make note of this, my dear sir: if some one praises you without occasion, he is sure to have a reason for doing so."

Note: Traditionally narrated, it may be taken for granted that this is simply Æsop's fable in Chinese dress. The manner of presentation is characteristically Chinese. For "the wisdom of Laotzse" compare, p. 30, "The Ancient's Book of Wisdom and Life": "Who sees his light, yet dwells in darkness." Master Dsong was King Dsi's most faithful pupil, renowned for his piety. The raven is known in China as "the bird of filial love," for it is said that the young ravens bring forth the food they have eaten from their beaks again, in order to feed the old birds.

XIV

WHY DOG AND CAT ARE ENEMIES

ONCE upon a time there was a man and his wife and they had a ring of gold. It was a lucky ring, and whoever owned it always had enough to live on. But this they did not know, and hence sold the ring for a small sum. But no sooner was the ring gone than they began to grow poorer and poorer, and at last did not know when they would get their next meal. They had a dog and a cat, and these had to go hungry as well. Then the two animals took counsel together as to how they might restore to their owners their former good fortune. At length the dog hit upon an idea.

"They must have the ring back again," he said to the cat.

The cat answered: "The ring has been carefully

locked up in the chest, where no one can get at it."

"You must catch a mouse," said the dog, "and the mouse must gnaw a hole in the chest and fetch out the ring. And if she does not want to, say that you will bite her to death, and you will see that she will do it."

This advice pleased the cat, and she caught a mouse. Then she wanted to go to the house in which stood the chest, and the dog came after. They came to a broad river. And since the cat could not swim, the dog took her on his back and swam across with her. Then the cat carried the mouse to the house in which the chest stood. The mouse gnawed a hole in the chest, and fetched out the ring. The cat put the ring in her mouth and went back to the river, where the dog was waiting for her, and swam across with her. Then they started out together for home, in order to bring the lucky ring to their master and mistress. But the dog could only run along the ground; when there was a house in the way he always had to go around it. The cat, however, quickly climbed over the roof, and so she reached home long before the dog, and brought the ring to her master.

Then her master said to his wife: "What a good creature the cat is! We will always give her enough to eat and care for her as though she were our own child!"

But when the dog came home they beat him and scolded him, because he had not helped to bring home the ring again. And the cat sat by the fireplace, purred and said never a word. Then the dog grew angry at the cat, because she had robbed him of his reward, and when he saw her he chased her and tried to seize her.

And ever since that day cat and dog are enemies.

Note: "Why Dog and Cat are Enemies." This fairy-tale is given in the current popular version.

LEGENDS OF THE GODS

XV

HOW THE FIVE ANCIENTS BECAME MEN

BEFORE the earth was separated from the heavens, all there was was a great ball of watery vapor called chaos. And at that time the spirits of the five elemental powers took shape, and became the five Ancients. The first was called the Yellow Ancient, and he was the ruler of the earth. The second was called the Red Lord, and he was the ruler of the fire. The third was called the Dark Lord, and he was the ruler of the water. The fourth was known as the Wood Prince, and he was the ruler of the wood. The fifth was called the Mother of Metals, and ruled over them. These five Ancients set all their primal spirit into motion, so that water and earth sank down. The heavens floated upward, and the earth grew firm in the depths. Then they allowed the waters to gather into rivers and seas, and hills and plains made their appearance. So the heavens opened and the earth was divided. And there were sun, moon and all the stars, wind, clouds, rain, and dew. The Yellow Ancient set earth's purest power spinning in a circle, and added the effect of fire and water thereto. Then there came forth grasses and trees, birds and beasts, and the tribes of the serpents and insects, fishes and turtles. The Wood Prince and the Mother of Metals combined light and darkness, and thus created the human race as men and women. And thus the world gradually came to be.

At that time there was one who was known as

the True Prince of the Jasper Castle. He had acquired the art of sorcery through the cultivation of magic. The five Ancients begged him to rule as the supreme god. He dwelt above the three and thirty heavens, and the Jasper Castle, of white jade with golden gates, was his. Before him stood the stewards of the eight-and-twenty houses of the moon, and the gods of the thunders and the Great Bear, and in addition a class of baneful gods whose influence was evil and deadly. They all aided the True Prince of the Jasper Castle to rule over the thousand tribes under the heavens, and to deal out life and death, fortune and misfortune. The Lord of the Jasper Castle is now known as the Great God, the White Jade Ruler.

The five Ancients withdrew after they had done their work, and thereafter lived in quiet purity. The Red Lord dwells in the South as the god of fire. The Dark Lord dwells in the North, as the mighty master of the somber polar skies. He lived in a castle of liquid crystal. In later ages he sent Confucius down upon earth as a saint. Hence this saint is known as the Son of Crystal. The Wood Prince dwells in the East. He is honored as the Green Lord, and watches over the coming into being of all creatures. In him lives the power of spring and he is the god of love. The Mother of Metals dwells in the West, by the sea of Jasper, and is also known as the Queen-Mother of the West. She leads the rounds of the fairies, and watches over change and growth. The Yellow Ancient dwells in the middle. He is always going about in the world, in order to save and to help those in any distress. The first time he came to earth he was the Yellow Lord, who taught mankind all sorts of arts. In his later years he fathomed the meaning of the world on the Etherial Mount, and flew up to the radiant sun. Under the rule of the Dschou dynasty he was born again as Li Oerl, and when he was born his hair and beard were white, for which reason he was called Laotsze, "Old Child." He wrote the book of "Meaning and Life" and spread his teachings through the world. He is honored as the head of Taoism. At the beginning of the reign of the Han dynasty, he again appeared as the Old Man of the River, (Ho Schang Gung). He spread the teachings of Tao abroad mightily, so that from that time on Taoism flourished greatly. These doctrines are known to this day as the teachings of the Yellow Ancient. There is also a saying: "First Laotsze was, then the heavens were." And that must mean that Laotsze was that very same Yellow Ancient of primal days.

Note: "How the Five Ancients Became Men." This fairy-tale, the first of the legends of the gods, is given in the version current among the people. In it the five elemental spirits of earth, fire, water, wood and metal are brought into connection with a creation myth. "Prince of the Jasper Castle" or "The White Jade Ruler," Yu Huang Di, is the popular Chinese synonym for "the good lord." The phrase "White Jade" serves merely to express his dignity. All in all, there are 32 other Yu Huangs, among whom he is the highest. He may be compared to Indra, who dwells in a heaven that also comprises 33 halls. The astronomic relationship between the two is very evident.

XVI

THE HERD BOY AND THE WEAVING MAIDEN

THE Herd Boy was the child of poor people. When he was twelve years old, he took service with a farmer to herd his cow. After a few years the cow had grown large and fat, and her hair shone like yellow gold. She must have been a cow of the gods.

One day while he had her out at pasture in the mountains, she suddenly began to speak to the Herd Boy in a human voice, as follows: "This is the Seventh Day. Now the White Jade Ruler has nine daughters, who bathe this day in the Sea of Heaven. The seventh daughter is beautiful and wise beyond all measure. She spins the cloud-silk for the King and Queen of Heaven, and presides over the weaving which maidens do on earth. It is for this reason she is called the Weaving Maiden. And if you go and take away her clothes while she bathes, you may become her husband and gain immortality."

"But she is up in Heaven," said the Herd Boy, "and how can I get there?"

"I will carry you there," answered the yellow cow.

So the Herd Boy climbed on the cow's back. In a moment clouds began to stream out of her hoofs, and she rose into the air. About his ears there was a whistling like the sound of the wind, and they flew along as swiftly as lightning. Suddenly the cow stopped.

"Now we are here," said she.

Then round about him the Herd Boy saw forests of chrysophrase and trees of jade. The grass was of jasper and the flowers of coral. In the midst of all this splendor lay a great, four-square sea, covering some five-hundred acres. Its green waves rose and fell, and fishes with golden scales were swimming about in it. In addition there were countless magic birds who winged above it and sang. Even in the distance the Herd Boy could see the nine maidens in the water. They had all laid down their clothes on the shore.

"Take the red clothes, quickly," said the cow, "and

hide away with them in the forest, and though she ask you for them never so sweetly do not give them back to her until she has promised to become your wife."

Then the Herd Boy hastily got down from the cow's back, seized the red clothes and ran away. At the same moment the nine maidens noticed him and were much frightened.

"O youth, whence do you come, that you dare to take our clothes?" they cried. "Put them down again quickly!"

But the Herd Boy did not let what they said trouble him; but crouched down behind one of the jade trees. Then eight of the maidens hastily came ashore and drew on their clothes.

"Our seventh sister," said they, "whom Heaven has destined to be yours, has come to you. We will leave her alone with you."

The Weaving Maiden was still crouching in the water.

But the Herd Boy stood before her and laughed.

"If you will promise to be my wife," said he, "then I will give you your clothes."

But this did not suit the Weaving Maiden.

"I am a daughter of the Ruler of the Gods," said she, "and may not marry without his command. Give back my clothes to me quickly, or else my father will punish you!"

Then the yellow cow said: "You have been destined for each other by fate, and I will be glad to arrange your marriage, and your father, the Ruler of the Gods, will make no objection. Of that I am sure."

The Weaving Maiden replied: "You are an unreasoning animal! How could you arrange our marriage?"

The cow said: "Do you see that old willow-tree

there on the shore? Just give it a trial and ask it? If the willow tree speaks, then Heaven wishes your union."

And the Weaving Maiden asked the willow.

The willow replied in a human voice:

>"This is the Seventh day,
>The Herd Boy his court to the Weaver doth pay!"

and the Weaving Maiden was satisfied with the verdict. The Herd Boy laid down her clothes, and went on ahead. The Weaving Maiden drew them on and followed him. And thus they became man and wife.

But after seven days she took leave of him.

"The Ruler of Heaven has ordered me to look after my weaving," said she. "If I delay too long I fear that he will punish me. Yet, although we have to part now, we will meet again in spite of it."

When she had said these words she really went away. The Herd Boy ran after her. But when he was quite near she took one of the long needles from her hair and drew a line with it right across the sky, and this line turned into the Silver River. And thus they now stand, separated by the River, and watch for one another.

And since that time they meet once every year, on the eve of the Seventh Day. When that time comes, then all the crows in the world of men come flying and form a bridge over which the Weaving Maiden crosses the Silver River. And on that day you will not see a single crow in the trees, from morning to night, no doubt because of the reason I have mentioned. And besides, a fine rain often falls on the evening of the Seventh Day. Then the women and old grandmothers say to one another: "Those are the tears which the

Herd Boy and the Weaving Maiden shed at parting!"
And for this reason the Seventh Day is a rain festival.

To the west of the Silver River is the constellation of the Weaving Maiden, consisting of three stars. And directly in front of it are three other stars in the form of a triangle. It is said that once the Herd Boy was angry because the Weaving Maiden had not wished to cross the Silver River, and had thrown his yoke at her, which fell down just in front of her feet. East of the Silver River is the Herd Boy's constellation, consisting of six stars. To one side of it are countless little stars which form a constellation pointed at both ends and somewhat broader in the middle. It is said that the Weaving Maiden in turn threw her spindle at the Herd Boy; but that she did not hit him, the spindle falling down to one side of him.

Note: "The Herd Boy and the Weaving Maiden" is retold after an oral source. The Herd Boy is a constellation in Aquila, the Weaving Maiden one in Lyra. The Silver River which separates them is the Milky Way. The Seventh Day of the seventh month is the festival of their reunion. The Ruler of the Heavens has nine daughters in all, who dwell in the nine heavens. The oldest married Li Dsing (comp. Notschka, No. 18); the second is the mother of Yang Oerlang (comp. No. 17); the third is the mother of the planet Jupiter (comp. "Sky O' Dawn," No. 37); and the fourth dwelt with a pious and industrious scholar, by name of Dung Yung, whom she aided to win riches and honor. The seventh is the Spinner, and the ninth had to dwell on earth as a slave because of some transgression of which she had been guilty. Of the fifth, the sixth and the eighth daughters nothing further is known.

XVII

YANG OERLANG

THE second daughter of the Ruler of Heaven once came down upon the earth and secretly became the wife of a mortal man named Yang. And when she returned to Heaven she was blessed with a son. But the Ruler of Heaven was very angry at this desecration of the heavenly halls. He banished her to earth and covered her with the Wu-I hills. Her son, however, Oerlang by name, the nephew of the Ruler of Heaven, was extraordinarily gifted by nature. By the time he was full grown he had learned the magic art of being able to control eight times nine transformations. He could make himself invisible, or could assume the shape of birds and beasts, grasses, flowers, snakes and fishes, as he chose. He also knew how to empty out seas and remove mountains from one place to another. So he went to the Wu-I hills and rescued his mother, whom he took on his back and carried away. They stopped to rest on a flat ledge of rock.

Then the mother said: "I am very thirsty!"

Oerlang climbed down into the valley in order to fetch her water, and some time passed before he returned. When he did his mother was no longer there. He searched eagerly, but on the rock lay only her skin and bones, and a few blood-stains. Now you must know that at that time there were still ten suns in the heavens, glowing and burning like fire. The Daughter of Heaven, it is true, was divine by nature; yet because she had incurred the anger of her father and had been banished to earth, her magic powers had failed her. Then, too, she had been imprisoned so long beneath the hills in the dark that, coming out suddenly into the sunlight, she had been devoured by its blinding radiance.

When Oerlang thought of his mother's sad end, his heart ached. He took two mountains on his shoulders, pursued the suns and crushed them to death between the mountains. And whenever he had crushed another sun-disk, he picked up a fresh mountain. In this way he had already slain nine of the ten suns, and there was but one left. And as Oerlang pursued him relentlessly, he hid himself in his distress beneath the leaves of the portulacca plant. But there was a rainworm close by who betrayed his hiding-place, and kept repeating: "There he is! There he is!"

Oerlang was about to seize him, when a messenger from the Ruler of the Heaven suddenly descended from the skies with a command: "Sky, air and earth need the sunshine. You must allow this one sun to live, so that all created beings may live. Yet, because you rescued your mother, and showed yourself to be a good son, you shall be a god, and be my bodyguard in the Highest Heaven, and shall rule over good and evil in the mortal world, and have power over devils and demons." When Oerlang received this command he ascended to Heaven.

Then the sun-disk came out again from beneath the portulacca leaves, and out of gratitude, since the plant had saved him, he bestowed upon it the gift of a free-blooming nature, and ordained that it never need fear the sunshine. To this very day one may see on the lower side of the portulacca leaves quite delicate little white pearls. They are the sunshine that remained hanging to the leaves when the sun hid under them. But the sun pursues the rainworm, when he ventures forth out of the ground, and dries him up as a punishment for his treachery.

Since that time Yang Oerlang has been honored as a god. He has oblique, sharply marked eyebrows, and holds a double-bladed, three-pointed sword in his hand. Two servants stand beside him, with a falcon and a hound; for Yang Oerlang is a great hunter. The falcon is the falcon of the gods, and the hound is the hound of the gods. When brute creatures gain possession of magic powers or demons oppress men, he subdues them by means of the falcon and hound.

Note: Yang Oerlang is a huntsman, as is indicated by his falcon and hound. His Hound of the Heavens, literally "the divine, biting hound" recalls the hound of Indra. The myth that there were originally ten suns in the skies, of whom nine were shot down by an archer, is also placed in the period of the ruler Yau. In that story the archer is named Hou-I, or I (comp. No. 19). Here, instead of the shooting down of the suns with arrows, we have the Titan motive of destruction with the mountains.

XVIII

NOTSCHA

THE oldest daughter of the Ruler of Heaven had married the great general Li Dsing. Her sons were named Gintscha, Mutscha and Notscha. But when Notscha was given her, she dreamed at night that a Taoist priest came into her chamber and said: "Swiftly receive the Heavenly Son!" And straightway a radiant pearl glowed within her. And she was so frightened at her dream that she awoke. And when Notscha came into the world, it seemed as though a ball of flesh were turning in circles like a wheel, and the whole room was filled with strange fragrances and a crimson light.

Li Dsing was much frightened, and thought it was an apparition. He clove the circling ball with his sword, and out of it leaped a small boy whose whole body glowed with a crimson radiance. But his face was delicately shaped and white as snow. About his right arm he wore a golden armlet and around his thighs was wound a length of crimson silk, whose glittering shine dazzled the eyes. When Li Dsing saw the child he took pity on him and did not slay him, while his wife began to love the boy dearly.

When three days had passed, all his friends came to wish him joy. They were just sitting at the festival meal when a Taoist priest entered and said: "I am the Great One. This boy is the bright Pearl of the Beginning of Things, bestowed upon you as your son. Yet the boy is wild and unruly, and will kill many men. Therefore I will take him as my pupil to gentle his savage ways." Li Dsing bowed his thanks and the Great One disappeared.

When Notscha was seven years old he once ran away from home. He came to the river of nine bends, whose green waters flowed along between two rows of weeping-willows. The day was hot, and Notscha entered the water to cool himself. He unbound his crimson silk cloth and whisked it about in the water to wash it. But while Notscha sat there and whisked about his scarf in the water, it shook the castle of the Dragon-King of the Eastern Sea to its very foundations. So the Dragon-King sent out a Triton, terrible to look upon, who was to find out what was the matter. When the Triton saw the boy he began to scold. But the latter merely looked up and said: "What a strange-looking beast you are, and you can actually talk!" Then the Triton grew enraged, leaped up and struck at Notscha with his ax. But the latter avoided the blow, and threw his golden armlet at him. The armlet struck the Triton on the head and he sank down dead.

Notscha laughed and said: "And there he has gone and made my armlet bloody!" And he once more sat down on a stone, in order to wash his armlet. Then the crystal castle of the dragon began to tremble as though it were about to fall apart. And a watchman also came and reported that the Triton had been slain by a boy. So the Dragon-King sent out his son to capture the boy. And the son seated himself on the water-cleaving beast, and came up with a thunder of great waves of water. Notscha straightened up and said: "That is a big wave!" Suddenly he saw a creature rise out of the waves, on whose back sat an armed man who cried in a loud voice: "Who has slain my Triton?" Notscha answered: "The Triton wanted to slay me so I killed him. What difference does it make?" Then the dragon assailed him with his halberd. But Notscha said: "Tell me who you are before we fight." "I am the son of the Dragon-King," was the reply. "And I am Notscha, the son of General Li Dsing. You must not rouse my anger with your violence, or I will skin you, together with that old mud-fish, your father!" Then the dragon grew wild with rage, and came storming along furiously. But Notscha cast his crimson cloth into the air, so that it flashed like a ball of fire, and cast the dragon-youth from his breast. Then Notscha took his golden armlet and struck him on the forehead with it, so that he had to reveal himself in his true form as a golden dragon, and fall down dead.

Notscha laughed and said: "I have heard tell that dragon-sinews make good cords. I will draw one out and bring it to my father, and he can tie his armor together with it." And with that he drew out the dragon's back sinew and took it home.

In the meantime the Dragon-King, full of fury, had hastened to Notscha's father Li Dsing and demanded that Notscha be delivered up to him. But Li Dsing replied: "You must be mistaken, for my boy is only seven years old and incapable of committing such misdeeds." While they were still quarreling Notscha came running up and cried: "Father, I'm bringing along a dragon's sinew for you, so that you may bind up your armor with it!" Now the dragon broke out into tears and furious scolding. He threatened to report Li Dsing to the Ruler of the Heaven, and took himself off, snorting with rage.

Li Dsing grew very much excited, told his wife what had happened, and both began to weep. Notscha, however, came to them and said: "Why do you weep? I will just go to my master, the Great One, and he will know what is to be done." And no sooner had he said the words than he had disappeared. He came into his master's presence and told him the whole tale. The latter said: "You must get ahead of the dragon, and prevent him from accusing you in Heaven!" Then he did some magic, and Notscha found himself set down by the gate of Heaven, where he waited for the dragon. It was still early in the morning; the gate of Heaven had not yet been opened, nor was the watchman at his post. But the dragon was already climbing up. Notscha, whom his master's magic had rendered invisible, threw the dragon to the ground with his armlet, and began to pitch into him. The dragon scolded and screamed. "There the old worm flounders about," said Notscha, "and does not care how hard he is beaten! I will scratch off some of his scales." And with these words he began to tear open the dragon's festal garments, and rip off some of the scales beneath his left arm, so that the red blood dripped out. Then the dragon could no longer stand the pain and begged for mercy. But first he had to promise Notscha that he would not complain of him, before the latter would let him go. And then the dragon had to turn himself into a little green snake, which Notscha put into his sleeve and took back home with him. But no sooner had he drawn the little snake from his sleeve than it assumed human shape. The dragon then swore that he would punish Li Dsing in a terrible manner, and disappeared in a flash of lightning.

Li Dsing was now angry with his son in earnest. Therefore Notscha's mother sent him to the rear of the house to keep out of his father's sight. Notscha disappeared and went to his master, in order to ask him what he should do when the dragon returned. His master advised him and Notscha went back home. And all the Dragon Kings of the four seas were assembled, and had bound his parents, with cries and tumult, in order to punish them. Notscha ran up and cried with a loud voice: "I will take the punishment for whatever I have done! My parents are blameless! What is the punishment you wish to lay upon me?" "Life for life!" said the dragon. "Very well then, I will destroy myself!" And so he did and the dragons went off satisfied; while Notscha's mother buried him with many tears.

But the spiritual part of Notscha, his soul, fluttered about in the air, and was driven by the wind to the cave of the Great One. He took it in and said to it: 'You must appear to your mother! Forty miles distant from your home rises a green mountain cliff. On this cliff she must build a shrine for you. And after you have enjoyed the incense of human adoration for three years, you shall once more have a human body." Notscha appeared to his mother in a dream, and gave her the whole message, and she awoke in tears. But Li Dsing grew angry when she told him about it. "It serves the accursed boy right that he is dead! It is because you are always thinking of him that he appears to you in dreams. You must pay no attention to him." The woman said no more, but thenceforward he appeared to her daily, as soon as she closed her eyes, and grew more and more urgent in his demand. Finally all that was left for her to do was to erect a temple for Notscha without Li Dsing's knowledge.

And Notscha performed great miracles in his temple. All prayers made in it were granted. And from far away people streamed to it to burn incense in his honor.

Thus half a year passed. Then Li Dsing, on the occasion of a great military drill, once came by the cliff in question, and saw the people crowding thickly about the hill like a swarm of ants. Li Dsing inquired what there were to see upon the hill. "It is a new god, who performs so many miracles that people come from far and near to honor him." "What sort of a god is he?" asked Li Dsing. They did not dare conceal from him who the god was. Then Li Dsing grew angry. He spurred his horse up the hill and, sure enough, over the door of the temple was written: "Notscha's Shrine." And within it was the likeness of Notscha, just as he had appeared while living. Li Dsing said: "While you were alive you brought misfortune to your parents. Now that you are dead you deceive the people. It is disgusting!" With these words he drew forth his whip, beat Notscha's idolatrous likeness to pieces with it, had the temple burned down, and the worshipers mildly reproved. Then he returned home.

Now Notscha had been absent in the spirit upon that day. When he returned he found his temple destroyed; and the spirit of the hill gave him the details. Notscha hurried to his master and related with tears what had befallen him. The latter was roused and said: "It is Li Dsing's fault. After you had given back your body to your parents, you were no further concern of his. Why should he withdraw from you the enjoyment of the incense?" Then the Great One made a body of lotus-plants, gave it the gift of life, and enclosed the soul of Notscha within it. This done he called out in a loud voice: "Arise!" A drawing of breath was heard, and Notscha leaped up once more in the shape of a small boy. He flung himself down before his master and thanked him. The latter bestowed upon him the magic of the fiery lance, and Notscha thenceforward had two whirling wheels beneath his feet: The wheel of the wind and the heel of fire. With these he could rise up and down in the air. The master also gave him a bag of panther-skin in which to keep his armlet and his silken cloth.

Now Notscha had determined to punish Li Dsing. Taking advantage of a moment when he was not watched, he went away, thundering along on his rolling wheels to Li Dsing's dwelling. The latter was unable to withstand him and fled. He was almost exhausted when his second son, Mutscha, the disciple of the holy Pu Hain, came to his aid from the Cave of the White Crane. A violent quarrel took place between the brothers; they began to fight, and Mutscha was overcome; while Notscha once more rushed in pursuit of Li Dsing. At the height of his extremity, however, the holy Wen Dschu of the Hill of the Five Dragons, the master of Gintscha, Li Dsing's oldest son, stepped forth and hid Li Dsing in his cave. Notscha, in a rage, insisted that he be delivered up to him; but Wen Dschu said: "Elsewhere you may indulge your wild nature to your heart's content, but not in this place."

And when Notscha in the excess of his rage turned his fiery lance upon him, Wen Dschu stepped back a pace, shook the seven-petaled lotus from his sleeve, and threw it into the air. A whirlwind arose, clouds and mists obscured the sight, and sand and earth were flung up from the ground. Then the whirlwind collapsed with a great crash. Notscha fainted, and when he regained consciousness found himself bound to a golden column with three thongs of gold, so that he could no longer move. Wen Dschu now called Gintscha to him and ordered him to give his unruly brother a good thrashing. And this he did, while Notscha, obliged to stand it, stood grinding his teeth. In his extremity he saw the Great One floating by, and called out to him: "Save me, O Master!" But the latter did not notice him; instead he entered the cave and thanked Wen Dschu for the severe lesson which he had given Notscha. Finally they called Notscha in to them and ordered him to be reconciled to his father. Then they dismissed them both and seated themselves to play chess. But no sooner was Notscha free than he again fell into a rage, and renewed his pursuit of his father. He had again overtaken Li Dsing when still another saint came forward to defend the latter. This time it was the old Buddha of the Radiance of the Light. When Notscha attempted to battle with him he raised his arm, and a pagoda shaped itself out of red, whirling clouds and closed around Notscha. Then Radiance of Light placed both his hands on the pagoda and a fire arose within it which burned Notscha so that he cried loudly for mercy. Then he had to promise to beg his father's forgiveness and always to obey him in the future. Not till he had promised all this did the Buddha let him out of the pagoda again. And he gave the pagoda to Li Dsing; and taught him a magic saying which would give him the mastery over Notscha. It is for this reason that Li Dsing is called the Pagoda-bearing King of Heaven.

Later on Li Dsing and his three sons, Gintcha, Mutscha and Notscha, aided King Wu of the Dschou dynasty to destroy the tyrant Dschou-Sin.

None could withstand their might. Only once did a sorcerer succeed in wounding Notscha in the left arm. Any other would have died of the wound. But the Great One carried him into his cave, healed his wound and gave him three goblets of the wine of the gods to drink, and three fire-dates to eat. When Notscha had eaten and drunk he suddenly heard a crash at his left side and another arm grew out from it. He could not speak and his eyes stood out from their sockets with horror. But it went on as it had begun: six more arms grew out of his body and two more heads, so that finally he had three heads and eight arms. He called out to his Master: "What does all this mean?" But the latter only laughed and said: "All is as it should be. Thus epuipped you will really be strong!" Then he taught him a magic incantation by means of which he could make his arms and heads visible or invisible as he chose. When the tyrant Dschou-Sin had been destroyed, Li Dsing and his three sons, while still on earth, were taken up into heaven and seated among the gods.

Note: Li Dsing, the Pagoda-bearing King of Heaven, may be traced back to Indra, the Hindoo god of thunder and lightning. The Pagoda might be an erroneous variant of the thunderbolt Vadjra. In such case Notscha would be a personification of the thunder. The Great One (Tai I), is the condition of things before their separation into the active and passive principles. There is a whole geneology of mythical saints and holy men who took part in the battles between King Mu of Dschou and the tyrant Dschou-Sin. These saints are, for the most part, Buddhist-Brahminic figures which have been reshaped. The Dragon-King of the Eastern Sea also occurs in the tale of Sun Wu Kung (No. 73). "Dragon sinew" means the spinal cord, the distinction between nerves and sinews not being carefully observed. "Three spirits and seven souls": man has three spirits usually above his head, and seven animal souls. "Notscha had been absent in the spirit upon that day": the idol is only the seat of the godhead, which the latter leaves or inhabits as he chooses. Therefore the godhead must be summoned when prayers are offered, by means of bells and incense. When the god is not present, his idol is merely a block of wood or stone. Pu Hain, the Buddha of the Lion, is the Indian Samantabharda, one of the four great Buddhisatvas of the Tantra School. Wen Dschu, the Buddha on the Golden-haired Mountain Lion, (Hou), is the Indian Mandjusri. The old Buddha of the Radiance of the Light, Jan Dong Go Fu, is the Indian Dipamkara.

XIX

THE LADY OF THE MOON

IN the days of the Emperor Yau lived a prince by the name of Hou I, who was a mighty hero and a good archer. Once ten suns rose together in the sky, and shone so brightly and burned so fiercely that the people on earth could not endure them. So the Emperor ordered Hou I to shoot at them. And Hou I shot nine of them down from the sky. Beside his bow, Hou I also had a horse which ran so swiftly that even the wind could not catch up with it. He mounted it to go a-hunting, and the horse ran away and could not be stopped. So Hou I came to Kunlun Mountain and met the Queen-Mother of the Jasper Sea. And she gave him the herb of immortality. He took it home with him and hid it in his room. But his wife who was named Tschang O, once ate some of it on the sly when he was not at home, and she immediately floated up to the clouds. When she reached the moon, she ran into the castle there, and has lived there ever since as the Lady of the Moon.

On a night in mid-autumn, an emperor of the Tang dynasty once sat at wine with two sorcerers. And one of them took his bamboo staff and cast it into the air, where it turned into a heavenly bridge, on which the three climbed up to the moon together. There they saw a great castle on which was inscribed: "The Spreading Halls of Crystal Cold." Beside it stood a cassia tree which blossomed and gave forth a fragrance filling all the air. And in the tree sat a man who was chopping off the smaller boughs with an ax. One of the sorcerers said: "That is the man in the moon. The cassia tree grows so luxuriantly that in the course of time it would overshadow all the moon's radiance. Therefore it has to be cut down once in every thousand years." Then they entered the spreading halls. The silver stories of the castle towered one above the other, and its walls and columns were all formed of liquid crystal. In the walls were cages and ponds, where fishes and birds moved as though alive. The whole moon-world seemed made of glass. While they were still looking about them on all sides the Lady of the Moon stepped up to them, clad in a white mantle and a rainbow-colored gown. She smiled and said to the emperor: "You are a prince of the mundane world of dust. Great is your fortune, since you have been able to find your way here!" And she called for her attendants, who came flying up on white birds, and sang and danced beneath the cassia tree. A pure clear music floated through the air. Beside the tree stood a mortar made of white marble, in which a jasper rabbit ground up herbs. That was the dark half of the moon. When the dance had ended, the emperor returned to earth again with the sorcerers. And he had the songs which he had heard on the moon written down and sung to the accompaniment of flutes of jasper in his pear-tree garden.

"BESIDE IT STOOD A CASSIA-TREE."
—Page 54

Note: This fairy-tale is traditional. The archer Hou I (or Count I, the Archer-Prince, comp. Dschuang Dsi), is placed by legend in different epochs. He also occurs in connection with the myths regarding the moon, for one tale recounts how he saved the moon during an eclipse by means of his arrows. The Queen-Mother is Si Wang Mu (comp. with No. 15). The Tang dynasty reigned 618-906 A.D. "The Spreading Halls of Crystal Cold": The goddess of the ice also has her habitation in the moon. The hare in the moon is a favorite figure. He grinds the grains of maturity or the herbs that make the elixir of life. The rain-toad Tschan, who has three legs, is also placed on the moon. According to one version of the story, Tschang O took the shape of this toad.

XX

THE MORNING AND THE EVENING STAR

ONCE upon a time there were two stars, sons of the Golden King of the Heavens. The one was named Tschen and the other Shen. One day they quarreled, and Tschen struck Shen a terrible blow. Thereupon both stars made a vow that they would never again look upon each other. So Tschen only appears in the evening, and Shen only appears in the morning, and not until Tschen has disappeared is Shen again to be seen. And that is why people say: "When two brothers do not live peaceably with one another they are like Tschen and Shen."

Note: Tschen and Shen are Hesperus and Lucifer, the morning and evening stars. The tale is told in its traditional form.

XXI

THE GIRL WITH THE HORSE'S HEAD
OR
THE SILKWORM GODDESS

IN the dim ages of the past there once was an old man who went on a journey. No one remained at home save his only daughter and a white stallion. The daughter fed the horse day by day, but she was lonely and yearned for her father.

So it happened that one day she said in jest to the horse: "If you will bring back my father to me then I will marry you!"

No sooner had the horse heard her say this, than he broke loose and ran away. He ran until he came to the place where her father was. When her father saw the horse, he was pleasantly surprised, caught him and seated himself on his back. And the horse turned back the way he had come, neighing without a pause.

"What can be the matter with the horse?" thought the father. "Something must have surely gone wrong at home!" So he dropped the reins and rode back. And he fed the horse liberally because he had been so intelligent; but the horse ate nothing, and when he saw the girl, he struck out at her with his hoofs and tried to bite her. This surprised the father; he questioned his daughter, and she told him the truth, just as it had occurred.

"You must not say a word about it to any one," spoke her father, "or else people will talk about us."

And he took down his crossbow, shot the horse, and hung up his skin in the yard to dry. Then he went on his travels again.

One day his daughter went out walking with the

daughter of a neighbor. When they entered the yard, she pushed the horse-hide with her foot and said: "What an unreasonable animal you were—wanting to marry a human being! What happened to you served you right!"

But before she had finished her speech, the horse-hide moved, rose up, wrapped itself about the girl and ran off.

Horrified, her companion ran home to her father and told him what had happened. The neighbors looked for the girl everywhere, but she could not be found.

At last, some days afterward, they saw the girl hanging from the branches of a tree, still wrapped in the horse-hide; and gradually she turned into a silkworm and wove a cocoon. And the threads which she spun were strong and thick. Her girl friend then took down the cocoon and let her slip out of it; and then she spun the silk and sold it at a large profit.

But the girl's relatives longed for her greatly. So one day the girl appeared riding in the clouds on her horse, followed by a great company and said: "In heaven I have been assigned to the task of watching over the growing of silkworms. You must yearn for me no longer!" And thereupon they built temples to her in her native land, and every year, at the silkworm season, sacrifices are offered to her and her protection is implored. And the Silkworm Goddess is also known as the girl with the Horse's Head.

Note: This tale is placed in the times of the Emperor Hau, and the legend seems to have originated in Setchuan. The stallion is the sign of the zodiac which rules the springtime, the season when the silkworms are cultivated. Hence she is called the Goddess with the Horse's Head. The legend itself tells a different tale. In addition to this goddess, the spouse of Schen Nung, the "Divine Husbandman," is also worshiped as the goddess of silkworm culture. The

Goddess with the Horse's Head is more of a totemic representation of the silkworm as such; while the wife of Schen Nung is regarded as the protecting goddess of silk culture, and is supposed to have been the first to teach women its details. The spouse of the Yellow Lord is mentioned in the same connection. The popular belief distinguishes three goddesses who protect the silkworm culture in turn. The second is the best of the three, and when it is her year the silk turns out well.

XXII

THE QUEEN OF HEAVEN

THE Queen of Heaven, who is also known as the Holy Mother, was in mortal life a maiden of Fukien, named Lin. She was pure, reverential and pious in her ways and died at the age of seventeen. She shows her power on the seas and for this reason the seamen worship her. When they are unexpectedly attacked by wind and waves, they call on her and she is always ready to hear their pleas.

There are many seamen in Fukien, and every year people are lost at sea. And because of this, most likely, the Queen of Heaven took pity on the distress of her people during her lifetime on earth. And since her thoughts are uninterruptedly turned toward aiding the drowning in their distress, she now appears frequently on the seas.

In every ship that sails a picture of the Queen of Heaven hangs in the cabin, and three paper talismans are also kept on shipboard. On the first she is painted with crown and scepter, on the second as a maiden in ordinary dress, and on the third she is pictured with flowing hair, barefoot, standing with a sword in her hand. When the ship is in danger the first talisman

LEGENDS OF THE GODS

is burnt, and help comes. But if this is of no avail, then the second and finally the third picture is burned. And if no help comes then there is nothing more to be done.

When seamen lose their course among wind and waves and darkling clouds, they pray devoutly to the Queen of Heaven. Then a red lantern appears on the face of the waters. And if they follow the lantern they will win safe out of all danger. The Queen of Heaven may often be seen standing in the skies, dividing the wind with her sword. When she does this the wind departs for the North and South, and the waves grow smooth.

A wooden wand is always kept before her holy picture in the cabin. It often happens that the fish-dragons play in the seas. They are two giant fish who spout up water against one another till the sun in the sky is obscured, and the seas are shrouded in profound darkness. And often, in the distance, one may see a bright opening in the darkness. If the ship holds a course straight for this opening it will win through, and is suddenly floating in calm waters again. Looking back, one may see the two fishes still spouting water, and the ship will have passed directly beneath their jaws. But a storm is always near when the fish dragons swim; therefore it is well to burn paper or wool so that the dragons do not draw the ship down into the depths. Or the Master of the Wand may burn incense before the wand in the cabin. Then he must take the wand and swing it over the water three times, in a circle. If he does so the dragons will draw in their tails and disappear.

When the ashes in the censer fly up into the air without any cause, and are scattered about, it is a sign that great danger is threatening.

Nearly two-hundred years ago an army was fitted out to subdue the island of Formosa. The captain's banner had been dedicated with the blood of a white horse. Suddenly the Queen of Heaven appeared at the tip of the banner-staff. In another moment she had disappeared, but the invasion was successful.

On another occasion, in the days of Kien Lung, the minister Dschou Ling was ordered to install a new king in the Liu-Kiu Islands. When the fleet was sailing by south of Korea, a storm arose, and his ship was driven toward the Black Whirlpool. The water had the color of ink, sun and moon lost their radiance, and the word was passed about that the ship had been caught in the Black Whirlpool, from which no living man had ever returned. The seaman and travelers awaited their end with lamentations. Suddenly an untold number of lights, like red lanterns, appeared on the surface of the water. Then the seamen were overjoyed and prayed in the cabins. "Our lives are saved!" they cried, "the Holy Mother has come to our aid!" And truly, a beautiful maiden with golden earrings appeared. She waved her hand in the air and the winds became still and the waves grew even. And it seemed as though the ship were being drawn along by a mighty hand. It moved plashing through the waves, and suddenly it was beyond the limits of the Black Whirlpool.

Dschou Ling on his return told of this happening, and begged that temples be erected in honor of the Queen of Heaven, and that she be included in the list of the gods. And the emperor granted his prayer.

Since then temples of the Queen of Heaven are to be found in all sea-port towns, and her birthday is celebrated on the eighth day of the fourth month with spectacles and sacrifices.

LEGENDS OF THE GODS

Note: "The Queen of Heaven," whose name is Tian Hau, or more exactly, Tian Fe Niang Niang, is a Taoist goddess of seamen, generally worshiped in all coast towns. Her story is principally made up of local legends of Fukian province, and a variation of the Indian Maritschi (who as Dschunti with the eight arms, is the object of quite a special cult). Tian Hou, since the establishment of the Manchu dynasty, is one of the officially recognized godheads.

XXIII

THE FIRE-GOD

LONG before the time of Fu Hi, Dschu Yung, the Magic Welder, was the ruler of men. He discovered the use of fire, and succeeding generations learned from him to cook their food. Hence his descendents were intrusted with the preservation of fire, while he himself was made the Fire-God. He is a personification of the Red Lord, who showed himself at the beginning of the world as one of the Five Ancients. The Fire-God is worshiped as the Lord of the Holy Southern Mountain. In the skies the Fiery Star, the southern quarter of the heavens and the Red Bird belong to his domain. When there is danger of fire the Fiery Star glows with a peculiar radiance. When countless numbers of fire-crows fly into a house, a fire is sure to break out in it.

In the land of the four rivers there dwelt a man who was very rich. One day he got into his wagon and set out on a long journey. And he met a girl, dressed in red, who begged him to take her with him. He allowed her to get into the wagon, and drove along for half-a-day without even looking in her direction. Then the girl got out again and said in farewell: "You are truly a good and honest man, and for that reason I must tell you the truth. I am the Fire-God. Tomorrow a fire will break out in your house. Hurry home at once to arrange your affairs and save what you can!" Frightened, the man faced his horses about and drove home as fast as he could. All that he possessed in the way of treasures, clothes and jewels, he removed from the house. And, when he was about to lie down to sleep, a fire broke out on the hearth which could not be quenched until the whole building had collapsed in dust and ashes. Yet, thanks to the Fire-God, the man had saved all his movable belongings.

Note: "The Fire-God" (comp. with No. 15). The Holy Southern Mountain is Sung-Schan in Huan. The Fiery Star is Mars. The constellations of the southern quarter of the heavens are grouped by the Chinese as under the name of the "Red Bird." The "land of the four rivers" is Sitchuan, in the western part of present-day China.

XXIV

THE THREE RULING GODS

THERE are three lords: in heaven, and on the earth and in the waters, and they are known as the Three Ruling Gods. They are all brothers, and are descended from the father of the Monk of the Yanktze-Kiang. When the latter was sailing on the river he was cast into the water by a robber. But he did not drown, for a Triton came his way who took him along with him to the dragon-castle. And when the Dragon-King saw him he realized at once that there was something extraordinary about the Monk, and he married him to his daughter.

From their early youth his three sons showed a preference for the hidden wisdom. And together

LEGENDS OF THE GODS

they went to an island in the sea. There they seated themselves and began to meditate. They heard nothing, they saw nothing, they spoke not a word and they did not move. The birds came and nested in their hair; the spiders came and wove webs across their faces; worms and insects came and crawled in and out of their noses and ears. But they paid no attention to any of them.

After they had meditated thus for a number of years, they obtained the hidden wisdom and became gods. And the Lord made them the Three Ruling Gods. The heavens make things, the earth completes things, and the waters create things. The Three Ruling Gods sent out the current of their primal power to aid in ordering all to this end. Therefore they are also known as the primal gods, and temples are erected to them all over the earth.

If you go into a temple you will find the Three Ruling Gods all seated on one pedestal. They wear women's hats upon their heads, and hold scepters in their hands, like kings. But he who sits on the last place, to the right, has glaring eyes and wears a look of rage. If you ask why this is you are told: "These three were brothers and the Lord made them the Ruling Gods. So they talked about the order in which they were to sit. And the youngest said: 'To-morrow morning, before sunrise, we will meet here. Whoever gets here first shall have the seat of honor in the middle; the second one to arrive shall have the second place, and the third the third.' The two older brothers were satisfied. The next morning, very early, the youngest came first, seated himself in the middle place, and became the god of the waters. The middle brother came next, sat down on the left, and became the god of the heavens. Last of all came the oldest brother.

When he saw that his brothers were already sitting in their places, he was disgusted and yet he could not say a word. His face grew red with rage, his eyeballs stood forth from their sockets like bullets, and his veins swelled like bladders. And he seated himself on the right and became god of the earth." The artisans who make the images of the gods noticed this, so they always represent him thus.

Note: "The Three Ruling Gods" is set down as told by the people. It is undoubtedly a version of the Indian Trimurti. The meaning of the terrible appearance of the third godhead, evidently no longer understood by the people, points to Siva, and has given rise to the fairy-tale here told. As regards the Monk of the Yang-tze-Kiang, comp. with No. 68.

XXV

A LEGEND OF CONFUCIUS

WHEN Confucius came to the earth, the Kilin, that strange beast which is the prince of all four-footed animals, and only appears when there is a great man on earth, sought the child and spat out a jade whereon was written: "Son of the Watercrystal you are destined to become an uncrowned king!" And Confucius grew up, studied diligently, learned wisdom and came to be a saint. He did much good on earth, and ever since his death has been reverenced as the greatest of teachers and masters. He had foreknowledge of many things. And even after he had died he gave evidence of this.

Once, when the wicked Emperor Tsin Schi Huang had conquered all the other kingdoms, and was traveling through the entire empire, he came to the homeland of Confucius. And he found his grave. And, finding his grave, he wished to have it opened and see what was in it. All his officials advised him not to do so, but he would not listen to them. So a passage was dug into the grave, and in its main chamber they found a coffin, whose wood appeared to be quite fresh. When struck it sounded like metal. To the left of the coffin was a door, which led into an inner chamber. In this chamber stood a bed, and a table with books and clothing, all as though meant for the use of a living person. Tsin Schi Huang seated himself on the bed and looked down. And there on the floor stood two shoes of red silk, whose tips were adorned with a woven pattern of clouds. A bamboo staff leaned against the wall. The Emperor, in jest, put on the shoes, took the staff and left the grave. But as he did so a tablet suddenly appeared before his eyes on which stood the following lines:

> O'er kingdoms six Tsin Schi Huang his army led,
> To ope my grave and find my humble bed;
> He steals my shoes and takes my staff away
> To reach Shakiu—and his last earthly day!

Tsin Schi Huang was much alarmed, and had the grave closed again. But when he reached Schakiu he fell ill of a hasty fever of which he died.

Note: The Kilin is an okapi-like legendary beast of the most perfected kindness, prince of all the four-footed animals. The "Watercrystal" is the dark Lord of the North, whose element is water and wisdom, for which last reason Confucius is termed his son. Tsin Schi Huang (B.C. 200) is the burner of books and reorganizer of China famed in history. Schakiu (Sandhill) was a city in the western part of the China of that day.

XXVI

THE GOD OF WAR

THE God of War, Guan Di, was really named Guan Yu. At the time when the rebellion of the Yellow Turbans was raging throughout the empire, he, together with two others whom he met by the wayside, and who were inspired with the same love of country which possessed him, made a pact of friendship. One of the two was Liu Be, afterward emperor, the other was named Dschang Fe. The three met in a peach-orchard and swore to be brothers one to the other, although they were of different families. They sacrificed a white steed and vowed to be true to each other to the death.

Guan Yu was faithful, honest, upright and brave beyond all measure. He loved to read Confucius's "Annals of Lu," which tell of the rise and fall of empires. He aided his friend Liu Be to subdue the Yellow Turbans and to conquer the land of the four rivers. The horse he rode was known as the Red Hare, and could run a thousand miles in a day. Guan Yu had a knife shaped like a half-moon which was called the Green Dragon. His eyebrows were beautiful like those of the silk-butterflies, and his eyes were long-slitted like the eyes of the Phenix. His face was scarlet-red in color, and his beard so long that it hung down over his stomach. Once, when he appeared before the emperor, the latter called him Duke Fairbeard, and presented him with a silken pocket in which to place his beard. He wore a garment of green brocade. Whenever he went into battle he showed invincible bravery. Whether he were opposed by a thousand armies or by ten thousand horsemen—he attacked them as though they were merely air.

Once the evil Tsau Tsau had incited the enemies of his master, the Emperor, to take the city by treachery. When Guan Yu heard of it he hastened up with an army to relieve the town. But he fell into an ambush, and, together with his son, was brought a captive to the capital of the enemy's land. The prince of that country would have been glad to have had him go over to his side; but Guan Yu swore that he would not yield to death himself. Thereupon father and son were slain. When he was dead, his horse Red Hare ceased to eat and died. A faithful captain of his, by name of Dschou Dsang, who was black-visaged and wore a great knife, had just invested a fortress when the news of the sad end of the duke reached him. And he, as well as other faithful followers would not survive their master, and perished.

At the time a monk, who was an old compatriot and acquaintance of Duke Guan was living in the Hills of the Jade Fountains. He used to walk at night in the moonlight.

Suddenly he heard a loud voice cry down out of the air: "I want my head back again!"

The monk looked up and saw Duke Guan, sword in hand, seated on his horse, just as he appeared while living. And at his right and left hand, shadowy figures in the clouds, stood his son Gaun Ping and his captain, Dschou Dsang.

The monk folded his hands and said: "While you lived you were upright and faithful, and in death you have become a wise god; and yet you do not understand fate! If you insist on having your head back again, to whom shall the many thousands of your enemies who lost their lives through you appeal, in order to have life restored to them?"

When he heard this the Duke Guan bowed and disappeared. Since that time he has been without interruption spiritually active. Whenever a new dynasty is founded, his holy form may be seen. For this reason temples and sacrifices have been instituted for him, and he has been made one of the gods of the empire. Like Confucius, he received the great sacrifice of oxen, sheep and pigs. His rank increases with the passing of centuries. First he was worshiped as Prince Guan, later as King Guan, and then as the great god who conquers the demons. The last dynasty, finally, worships him as the great, divine Helper of the Heavens. He is also called the God of War, and is a strong deliverer in all need, when men are plagued by devils and foxes. Together with Confucius, the Master of Peace, he is often worshiped as the Master of War.

Note: The Chinese God of War is a historical personality from the epoch of the three empires, which later joined the Han dynasty, about 250 A.D. Liu Be founded the "Little Han dynasty" in Setchuan, with the aid of Guan Yu and Dschang Fe. Guan Yu or Guan Di, i. e., "God Yuan," has become one of the most popular figures in Chinese legend in the course of time, God of War and deliverer in one and the same person. The talk of the monk with the God Guan Di in the clouds is based on the Buddhist law of Karma. Because Guan Di—even though his motives might be good—had slain other men, he must endure like treatment at their hands, even while he is a god.

TALES OF SAINTS AND MAGICIANS

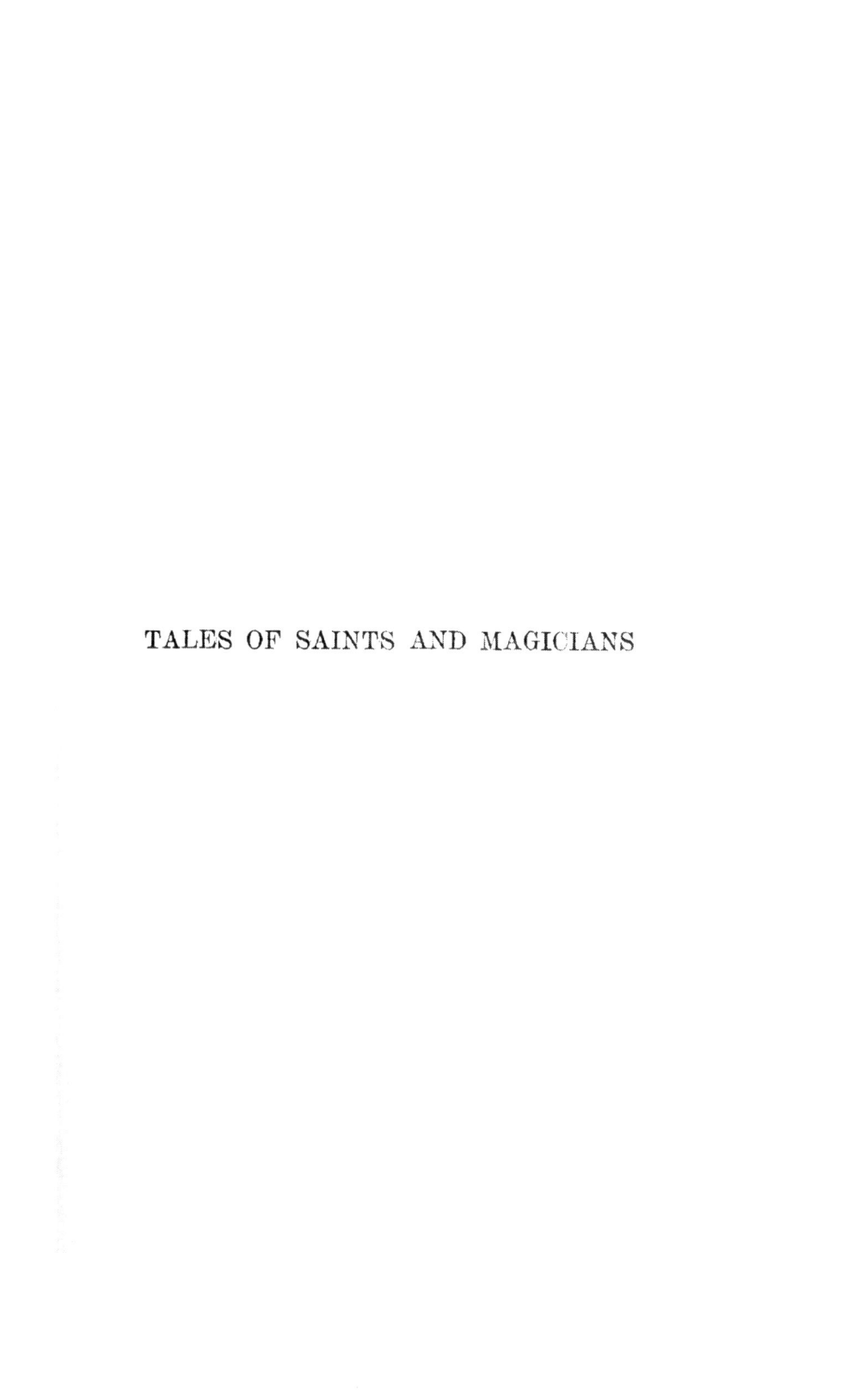

XXVII

THE HALOS OF THE SAINTS

THE true gods all have halos around their heads. When the lesser gods and demons see these halos, they hide and dare not move. The Master of the Heavens on the Dragon-Tiger Mountain meets the gods at all times. One day the God of War came down to the mountain while the mandarin of the neighboring district was visiting the Master of the Heavens. The latter advised the mandarin to withdraw and hide himself in an inner chamber. Then he went out to receive the God of War. But the mandarin peeped through a slit in the door, and he saw the red face and green garment of the God of War as he stood there, terrible and awe-inspiring. Suddenly a red halo flashed up above his head, whose beams penetrated into the inner chamber so that the mandarin grew blind in one eye. After a time the God of War went away again, and the Master of the Heavens accompanied him. Suddenly Guan Di said, with alarm: "Confucius is coming! The halo he wears illumines the whole world. I cannot endure its radiance even a thousand miles away, so I must hurry and get out of the way!" And with that he stepped into a cloud and disappeared. The Master of the Heavens then told the mandarin what had happened, and added: "Fortunately you did not see the God of War face to face! Whoever does not possess the greatest virtue and the greatest wisdom, would be melted by the red glow of his halo." So saying he gave him a pill of the elixir of life to eat, and his blind eye gradually regained its sight.

It is also said that scholars wear a red halo around their heads which devils, foxes and ghosts fear when they see it.

There was once a scholar who had a fox for a friend. The fox came to see him at night, and went walking with him in the villages. They could enter the houses, and see all that was going on, without people being any the wiser. But when at a distance the fox saw a red halo hanging above a house he would not enter it. The scholar asked him why not.

"Those are all celebrated scholars," answered the fox. "The greater the halo, the more extensive is their knowledge. I dread them and do not dare enter their houses."

Then the man said: "But I am a scholar, too! Have I no halo which makes you fear me, instead of going walking with me?"

"There is only a black mist about your head," answered the fox. "I have never yet seen it surrounded by a halo."

The scholar was mortified and began to scold him; but the fox disappeared with a horse-laugh.

Note: This tale is told as traditionally handed down. The Master of the Heavens, Tian Schi, who dwells on the Lung Hu Schan, is the so-called Taoist pope.

XXVIII

LAOTSZE

LAOTSZE is really older than heaven and earth put together. He is the Yellow Lord or Ancient, who created this world together with the other four. At various times he has appeared on earth, under various names. His most celebrated incarnation, however, is that of Laotsze, "The Old Child," which name he was given because he made his appearance on earth with white hair.

He acquired all sorts of magic powers by means of which he extended his life-span. Once he hired a servant to do his bidding. He agreed to give him a hundred pieces of copper daily; yet he did not pay him, and finally he owed him seven million, two hundred thousand pieces of copper. Then he mounted a black steer and rode to the West. He wanted to take his servant along. But when they reached the Han-Gu pass, the servant refused to go further, and insisted on being paid. Yet Laotsze gave him nothing.

When they came to the house of the guardian of the pass, red clouds appeared in the sky. The guardian understood this sign and knew that a holy man was drawing near. So he went out to meet him and took him into his house. He questioned him with regard to hidden knowledge, but Laotsze only stuck out his tongue at him and would not say a word. Nevertheless, the guardian of the pass treated him with the greatest respect in his home. Laotsze's servant told the servant of the guardian that his master owed him a great deal of money, and begged the latter to put in a good word for him. When the guardian's servant heard how large a sum it was, he was tempted to win so wealthy a man for a son-in-law, and he married him to his daughter. Finally the guardian heard of the matter and came to Laotsze together with the servant. Then Laotsze said to his servant: "You rascally servant. You really should have been dead long ago. I hired you, and since I was poor and could give you no money, I gave you a life-giving talisman to eat. That is how you still happen to be alive. I said to you: 'If you will follow me into the West, the land of Blessed Repose, I will pay you your wages in yellow gold. But you did not wish to do this.'" And with that he patted his servant's neck. Thereupon the latter opened his mouth, and spat out the life-giving talisman. The magic signs written on it with cinnabar, quite fresh and well-preserved, might still be seen. But the servant suddenly collapsed and turned into a heap of dry bones. Then the guardian of the pass cast himself to earth and pleaded for him. He promised to pay the servant for Laotsze and begged the latter to restore him to life. So Laotsze placed the talisman among the bones and at once the servant came to life again. The guardian of the pass paid him his wages and dismissed him. Then he adored Laotsze as his master, and the latter taught him the art of eternal life, and left him his teachings, in five thousand words, which the guardian wrote down. The book which thus came into being is the Tao Teh King, "The Book of the Way and Life." Laotsze then disappeared from the eyes of men. The guardian of the pass however, followed his teachings, and was given a place among the immortals.

Note: The Taoists like to assert that Laotsze's journey to the West was undertaken before the birth of Buddha, who, according to many, is only a reincarnation of Laotsze. The guardian of the

SAINTS AND MAGICIANS

Han-Gu pass is mentioned by the name of Guan Yin Hi, in the Lia Dsi and the Dschuang Dsi.

XXIX

THE ANCIENT MAN

ONCE upon a time there was a man named Huang An. He must have been well over eighty and yet he looked like a youth. He lived on cinnabar and wore no clothing. Even in winter he went about without garments. He sat on a tortoise three feet long. Once he was asked: "About how old might this tortoise be?" He answered: "When Fu Hi first invented fish-nets and eel-pots he caught this tortoise and gave it to me. And since then I have worn its shield quite flat sitting on it. The creature dreads the radiance of the sun and moon, so it only sticks its head out of its shell once in two thousand years. Since I have had the beast, it has already stuck its head out five times." With these words he took his tortoise on his back and went off. And the legend arose that this man was ten thousand years old.

Note: Cinnabar is frequently used in the preparation of the elixir of life (comp. No. 31). Fu Hi is "the life-breeding breath." Tortoises live to a great age.

XXX

THE EIGHT IMMORTALS

THERE is a legend which declares that Eight Immortals dwell in the heavens. The first is named Dschung Li Kuan. He lived in the time of the Han dynasty, and discovered the wonderful magic of golden cinnabar, the philosopher's stone. He could melt quicksilver and burn lead and turn them into yellow gold and white silver. And he could fly through the air in his human form. He is the chief of the Eight Immortals.

The second is named Dschang Go. In primal times he gained hidden knowledge. It is said that he was really a white bat, who turned into a man. In the first days of the Tang dynasty an ancient with a white beard and a bamboo drum on his back, was seen riding backward on a black ass in the town of Tschang An. He beat the drum and sang, and called himself old Dschang Go. Another legend says that he always had a white mule with him which could cover a thousand miles in a single day. When he had reached his destination he would fold up the animal and put it in his trunk. When he needed it again, he would sprinkle water on it with his mouth, and the beast would regain its first shape.

The third is named Lu Yuan or Lu Dung Bin (The Mountain Guest). His real name was Li, and he belonged to the ruling Tang dynasty. But when the Empress Wu seized the throne and destroyed the Li family to almost the last man, he fled with his wife into the heart of the mountains. They changed their names to Lu, and, since they lived in hiding in the caverns in

SAINTS AND MAGICIANS

the rocks, he called himself the Mountain Guest or the Guest of the Rocks. He lived on air and ate no bread. Yet he was fond of flowers. And in the course of time he acquired the hidden wisdom.

In Lo Yang, the capital city, the peonies bloomed with special luxuriance. And there dwelt a flower fairy, who changed herself into a lovely maiden with whom Guest of the Rocks, when he came to Lo Yang, was wont to converse. Suddenly along came the Yellow Dragon, who had taken the form of a handsome youth. He mocked the flower fairy. Guest of the Rocks grew furious and cast his flying sword at him, cutting off his head. From that time onward he fell back again into the world of mundane pleasure and death. He sank down into the dust of the diurnal, and was no longer able to wing his way to the upper regions. Later he met Dschung Li Kuan, who delivered him, and then he was taken up in the ranks of the Immortals.

Willowelf was his disciple. This was an old willow-tree which had drawn into itself the most ethereal powers of the sunrays and the moonbeams, and had thus been able to assume the shape of a human being. His face is blue and he has red hair. Guest of the Rocks received him as a disciple. Emperors and kings of future times honor Guest of the Rocks as the ancestor and master of the pure sun. The people call him Grandfather Lu. He is very wise and powerful. And therefore the people still stream into Grandfather Lu's temples to obtain oracles and pray for good luck. If you want to know whether you will be successful or not in an undertaking, go to the temple, light incense and bow your head to earth. On the altar is a bamboo goblet, in which are some dozens of little lottery sticks. You must shake them while kneeling, until one of the sticks flies out. On the lottery-stick is inscribed a number. This number must then be looked up in the Book of Oracles, where it is accompanied by a four-line stanza. It is said that fortune and misfortune, strange to think, occur to one just as foretold by the oracle.

The fourth Immortal is Tsau Guo Gui (Tsau the Uncle of the State). He was the younger brother of the Empress Tsau, who for a time ruled the land. For this reason he was called the Uncle of the State. From his earliest youth he had been a lover of the hidden wisdom. Riches and honors were no more to him than dust. It was Dschung Li Kuan who aided him to become immortal.

The fifth is called Lan Tsai Ho. Nothing is known of his true name, his time nor his family. He was often seen in the market-place, clad in a torn blue robe and wearing only a single shoe, beating a block of wood and singing the nothingness of life.

The sixth Immortal is known as Li Tia Guai (Li with the iron crutch). He lost his parents in early youth and was brought up in his older brother's home. His sister-in-law treated him badly and never gave him enough to eat. Because of this he fled into the hills, and there learned the hidden wisdom.

Once he returned in order to see his brother, and said to his sister-in-law: "Give me something to eat!" She answered: "There is no kindling wood on hand!" He replied: "You need only to prepare the rice. I can use my leg for kindling wood, only you must not say that the fire might injure me, and if you do not no harm will be done."

His sister-in-law wished to see his art, so she poured the rice into the pot. Li stretched one of his legs out under it and lit it. The flames leaped high and the leg burned like coal.

When the rice was nearly boiled his sister-in-law said: "Won't your leg be injured?"

And Li replied angrily: "Did I not warn you not to say anything! Then no harm would have been done. Now one of my legs is lamed." With these words he took an iron poker and fashioned it into a crutch for himself. Then he hung a bottle-gourd on his back, and went into the hills to gather medicinal herbs. And that is why he is known as Li with the Iron Crutch.

It is also told of him that he often was in the habit of ascending into the heavens in the spirit to visit his master Laotsze. Before he left he would order a disciple to watch his body and soul within it, so that the latter did not escape. Should seven days have gone by without his spirit returning, then he would allow his soul to leave the empty tenement. Unfortunately, after six days had passed, the disciple was called to the death-bed of his mother, and when the master's spirit returned on the evening of the seventh day, the life had gone out of its body. Since there was no place for his spirit in his own body, in his despair he seized upon the first handy body from which the vital essence had not yet dispersed. It was the body of a neighbor, a lame cripple, who had just died, so that from that time on the master appeared in his form.

The seventh Immortal is called Hang Siang Dsi. He was the nephew of the famous Confucian scholar Han Yu, of the Tang dynasty. From his earliest youth he cultivated the arts of the deathless gods, left his home and became a Taoist. Grandfather Lu awakened him and raised him to the heavenly world.

Once he saved his uncle's life. The latter had been driven from court, because he had objected when the emperor sent for a bone of Buddha with great pomp. When he reached the Blue Pass in his flight, a deep snow-fall had made the road impassable. His horse had floundered in a snow-drift, and he himself was well-nigh frozen. Then Hang Siang Dsi suddenly appeared, helped him and his horse out of the drift, and brought them safely to the nearest inn along the Blue Pass. Han Yu sang a verse, in which the lines occurred:

> Tsin Ling Hill 'mid clouds doth lie,
> And home is far, beyond my sight!
> Round the Blue Pass snow towers high,
> And who will lead the horse aright?

Suddenly it occured to him that several years before, Hang Siang Dsi had come to his house to congratulate him on his birthday. Before he had left, he had written these words on a slip of paper, and his uncle had read them, without grasping their meaning. And now he was unconsciously singing the very lines of that song that his nephew had written. So he said to Hang Siang Dsi, with a sigh: "You must be one of the Immortals," since you were able thus to foretell the future!"

And thrice Hang Siang Dsi sought to deliver his wife from the bonds of earth. For when he left his home to seek the hidden wisdom, she sat all day long yearning for his presence. Hang Siang Dsi wished to release her into immortality, but he feared she was not capable of translation. So he appeared to her in various forms, in order to try her, once as a beggar, another time as a wandering monk. But his wife did not grasp her opportunities. At last he took the shape of a lame Taoist, who sat on a mat, beat a block of wood and read sutras before the house.

His wife said: "My husband is not at home. I can give you nothing."

The Taoist answered: "I do not want your gold and silver, I want you. Sit down beside me on the mat, and we will fly up into the air and you shall find your husband again!"

Hereupon the woman grew angry and struck at him with a cudgel.

Then Hang Siang Dsi changed himself into his true form, stepped on a shining cloud and was carried aloft. His wife looked after him and wept loudly; but he had disappeared and was not seen again.

The eighth Immortal is a girl and was called Ho Sian Gu. She was a peasant's daughter, and though her step-mother treated her harshly she remained respectful and industrious. She loved to give alms, though her step-mother tried to prevent her. Yet she was never angry, even when her step-mother beat her. She had sworn not to marry, and at last her step-mother did not know what to do with her. One day, while she was cooking rice, Grandfather Du came and delivered her. She was still holding the rice-spoon in her hand as she ascended into the air. In the heavens she was appointed to sweep up the fallen flowers at the Southern Gate of Heaven.

Note: The legends of the Eight Immortals, regarded as one group, do not go back further than the Manchu dynasty, though individual ones among them were known before. Some of the Immortals, like Han Siang Dsi, are historic personages, others purely mythical. In the present day they play an important part in art and in the art-crafts. Their emblems also occur frequently: Dschung Li Kuan is represented with a fan. Dschang Go has a bamboo drum with two drum-sticks (and his donkey). Lo Dung

Bin has a sword and a flower-basket on his back. Tsau Go Giu has two small boards, (Yin Yang Ban), which he can throw into the air. Li Tia Guai has the bottle-gourd, out of which emerges a bat, the emblem of good fortune. Tsai Ho, who is also pictured as a woman, has a flute. Han Siang Dsi has a flower-basket and a dibble. Ho Sian Gu has a spoon, usually formed in the shape of a lotus-flower.

XXXI

THE EIGHT IMMORTALS

ONCE upon a time there was a poor man, who at last had no roof to shelter him and not a bite to eat. So, weary and worn, he lay down beside a little temple of the field-god that stood by the roadside and fell asleep. And he dreamed that the old, white-bearded field-god came out of his little shrine and said to him: "I know of a means to help you! To-morrow the Eight Immortals will pass along this road. Cast yourself down before them and plead to them!"

When the man awoke he seated himself beneath the great tree beside the field-god's little temple, and waited all day long for his dream to come true. At last, when the sun had nearly sunk, eight figures came down the road, which the begger clearly recognized as those of the Eight Immortals. Seven of them were hurrying as fast as they could, but one among them, who had a lame leg, limped along after the rest. Before him—it was Li Tia Guai—the man cast himself to earth. But the lame Immortal did not want to bother with him, and told him to go away. Yet the poor man would not give over pleading with him, begging that he might go with them and be one of the Immortals, too. That would be impossible, said the cripple. Yet, as the poor man did not cease his prayers and would not leave him, he at last said: "Very well, then, take hold of my coat!" This the man did and off they went in flying haste over paths and fields, on and on, and even further on. Suddenly they stood together high up on the tower of Ponglai-schan, the ghost mountain by the Eastern Sea. And, lo, there stood the rest of the Immortals as well! But they were very discontented with the companion whom Li Tia Guai had brought along. Yet since the poor man pleaded so earnestly, they too allowed themselves to be moved, and said to him: "Very well! We will now leap down into the sea. If you follow us you may also become an Immortal!" And one after another the seven leaped down into the sea. But when it came to the man's turn he was frightened, and would not dare the leap. Then the cripple said to him: "If you are afraid, then you cannot become an Immortal!"

"But what shall I do now?" wailed the man, "I am far from my home and have no money!" The cripple broke off a fragment of the battlement of the tower, and thrust it into the man's hand; then he also leaped from the tower and disappeared into the sea like his seven companions.

When the man examined the stone in his hand more closely, he saw that it was the purest silver. It provided him with traveling money during the many weeks it took him to reach his home. But by that time the silver was completely used up, and he found himself just as poor as he had been before.

Note: Little field-god temples, Tu Di Miau, are miniature stone chapels which stand before every village. As regards the field-god, see No. 63.

XXXII

THE TWO SCHOLARS

ONCE upon a time there were two scholars. One was named Liu Tschen and the other Yuan Dschau. Both were young and handsome. One spring day they went together into the hills of Tian Tai to gather curative herbs. There they came to a little valley where peach-trees blossomed luxuriantly on either side. In the middle of the valley was a cave, where two maidens stood under the blossoming trees, one of them clad in red garments, the other in green. And they were beautiful beyond all telling. They beckoned to the scholars with their hands.

"And have you come?" they asked. "We have been waiting for you overlong!"

Then they led them into the cave and served them with tea and wine.

"I have been destined for the lord Liu," said the maiden in the red gown; "and my sister is for the lord Yuan!"

And so they were married. Every day the two scholars gazed at the flowers or played chess so that they forgot the mundane world completely. They only noticed that at times the peach-blossoms on the trees before the cave opened, and at others that they fell from the boughs. And, at times, unexpectedly, they felt cold or warm, and had to change the clothing they were wearing. And they marveled within themselves that it should be so.

Then, one day, they were suddenly overcome by homesickness. Both maidens were already aware of it.

"When our lords have once been seized with homesickness, then we may hold them no longer," said they.

On the following day they prepared a farewell banquet, gave the scholars magic wine to take along with them and said:

"We will see one another again. Now go your way!"

And the scholars bade them farewell with tears.

When they reached home the gates and doors had long since vanished, and the people of the village were all strangers to them. They crowded about the scholars and asked who they might be.

"We are Liu Tschen and Dschau. Only a few days ago we went into the hills to pick herbs!"

With that a servant came hastening up and looked at them. At last he fell at Liu Tschen's feet with great joy and cried: "Yes, you are really my master! Since you went away, and we had no news of any kind regarding you some seventy years or more have passed."

Thereupon he drew the scholar Liu through a high gateway, ornamented with bosses and a ring in a lion's mouth, as is the custom in the dwellings of those of high estate.

And when he entered the hall, an old lady with white hair and bent back, leaning on a cane, came forward and asked: "What man is this?"

"Our master has returned again," replied the servant. And then, turning to Liu he added: "That is the mistress. She is nearly a hundred years old, but fortunately is still strong and in good health."

Tears of joy and sadness filled the old lady's eyes.

"Since you went away among the immortals, I had thought that we should never see each other again in this life," said she. "What great good fortune that you should have returned after all!"

And before she had ended the whole family, men

and women, came streaming up and welcomed him in a great throng outside the hall.

And his wife pointed out this one and that and said: "That is so and so, and this is so and so!"

At the time the scholar had disappeared there had been only a tiny boy in his home, but a few years old. And he was now an old man of eighty. He had served the empire in a high office, and had already retired to enjoy his old age in the ancestral gardens. There were three grand-children, all celebrated ministers; there were more than ten great-grand-children, of whom five had already passed their examinations for the doctorate; there were some twenty great-great-grand-children, of whom the oldest had just returned home after having passed his induction examinations for the magistracy with honor. And the little ones, who were carried in their parents' arms, were not to be counted. The grand-children, who were away, busy with their duties, all asked for leave and returned home when they heard that their ancestor had returned. And the girl grand-children, who had married into other families, also came. This filled Liu with joy, and he had a family banquet prepared in the hall, and all his descendants, with their wives and husbands sat about him in a circle. He himself and his wife, a white-haired, wrinkled old lady, sat in their midst at the upper end. The scholar himself still looked like a youth of twenty years, so that all the young people in the circle looked around and laughed.

Then the scholar said: "I have a means of driving away old age!"

And he drew out his magic wine and gave his wife some of it to drink. And when she had taken three glasses, her white hair gradually turned black again, her wrinkles disappeared, and she sat beside her husband, a handsome young woman. Then his son and

SAINTS AND MAGICIANS

the older grand-children came up and all asked for a drink of the wine. And whichever of them drank only so much as a drop of it was turned from an old man into a youth. The tale was bruited abroad and came to the emperor's ears. The emperor wanted to call Liu to his court, but he declined with many thanks. Yet he sent the emperor some of his magic wine as a gift. This pleased the emperor greatly, and he gave Liu a tablet of honor, with the inscription:

"The Common Home of Five Generations"

Besides this he sent him three signs which he had written with his own imperial brush signifying:

"Joy in longevity"

As to the other of the two scholars, Yuan Dschau, he was not so fortunate. When he came home he found that his wife and child had long since died, and his grand-children and great-grand-children were mostly useless people. So he did not remain long, but returned to the hills. Yet Liu Tschen remained for some years with his family, then taking his wife with him, went again to the Tai Hills and was seen no more.

Note: This tale is placed in the reign of the Emperor Ming Di (A. D. 58-75). Its motive is that of the legend of the Seven Sleepers, and is often found in Chinese fairy tales.

XXXIII

THE MISERLY FARMER

ONCE upon a time there was a farmer who had carted pears to market. Since they were very sweet and fragrant, he hoped to get a good price for them. A bonze with a torn cap and tattered robe stepped up to his cart and asked for one. The farmer repulsed him, but the bonze did not go. Then the farmer grew angry and began to call him names. The bonze said: "You have pears by the hundred in your cart. I only ask for one. Surely that does you no great injury. Why suddenly grow so angry about it?"

The bystanders told the farmer that he ought to give the bonze one of the smaller pears and let him go. But the farmer would not and did not. An artisan saw the whole affair from his shop, and since the noise annoyed him, he took some money, bought a pear and gave it to the bonze.

The bonze thanked him and said: "One like myself, who has given up the world, must not be miserly. I have beautiful pears myself, and I invite you all to eat them with me." Then some one asked: "If you have pears then why do you not eat your own?" He answered: "I first must have a seed to plant."

And with that he began to eat the pear with gusto. When he had finished, he held the pit in his hand, took his pick-ax from his shoulder; and dug a hole a couple of inches deep. Into this he thrust the pit, and covered it with earth. Then he asked the folk in the market place for water, with which to water it. A pair of curiosity seekers brought him hot water from

SAINTS AND MAGICIANS

the hostlery in the street, and with it the bonze watered the pit. Thousands of eyes were turned on the spot. And the pit could already be seen to sprout. The sprout grew and in a moment it had turned into a tree. Branches and leaves burgeoned out from it. It began to blossom and soon the fruit had ripened: large, fragrant pears, which hung in thick clusters from the boughs. The bonze climbed into the tree and handed down the pears to the bystanders. In a moment all the pears had been eaten up. Then the bonze took his pick-ax and cut down the tree. Crash, crash! so it went for a while, and the tree was felled. Then he took the tree on his shoulder and walked away at an easy gait.

When the bonze had begun to make his magic, the farmer, too, had mingled with the crowd. With neck out-stretched and staring eyes he had stood there and had entirely forgotten the business he hoped to do with his pears. When the bonze had gone off he turned around to look after his cart. His pears had all disappeared. Then he realized that the pears the bonze had divided had been his own. He looked more closely, and the axle of his cart had disappeared. It was plainly evident that it had been chopped off quite recently. The farmer fell into a rage and hastened after the bonze as fast as ever he could. And when he turned the corner, there lay the missing piece from the axle by the city wall. And then he realized that the pear-tree which the bonze had chopped down must have been his axle. The bonze, however, was nowhere to be found. And the whole crowd in the market burst out into loud laughter.

Note: The axle in China is really a handle, for the little Chinese carts are one-wheel push-carts with two handles or shafts.

XXXIV

SKY O'DAWN

ONCE upon a time there was a man who took a child to a woman in a certain village, and told her to take care of him. Then he disappeared. And because the dawn was just breaking in the sky when the woman took the child into her home, she called him Sky O'Dawn. When the child was three years old, he would often look up to the heavens and talk with the stars. One day he ran away and many months passed before he came home again. The woman gave him a whipping. But he ran away again, and did not return for a year. His foster-mother was frightened, and asked: "Where have you been all year long?" The boy answered: "I only made a quick trip to the Purple Sea. There the water stained my clothes red. So I went to the spring at which the sun turns in, and washed them. I went away in the morning and I came back at noon. Why do you speak about my having been gone a year?"

Then the woman asked: "And where did you pass on your way?"

The boy answered: "When I had washed my clothes, I rested for a while in the City of the Dead and fell asleep. And the King-Father of the East gave me red chestnuts and rosy dawn-juice to eat, and my hunger was stilled. Then I went to the dark skies and drank the yellow dew, and my thirst was quenched. And I met a black tiger and wanted to ride home on his back. But I whipped him too hard, and he bit me in the leg. And so I came back to tell you about it."

Once more the boy ran away from home, thousands

"AND I CROSSED THE WATER ON THE SHOE."
—Page 91

of miles, until he came to the swamp where dwelt the Primal Mist. There he met an old man with yellow eyebrows and asked him how old he might be. The old man said: "I have given up the habit of eating, and live on air. The pupils of my eyes have gradually acquired a green glow, which enables me to see all hidden things. Whenever a thousand years have passed I turn around my bones and wash the marrow. And every two thousand years I scrape my skin to get rid of the hair. I have already washed my bones thrice and scraped my skin five times."

Afterward Sky O'Dawn served the Emperor Wu of the Han dynasty. The Emperor, who was fond of the magic arts, was much attached to him. One day he said to him: "I wish that the empress might not grow old. Can you prevent it?"

Sky O'Dawn answered: "I know of only one means to keep from growing old."

The Emperor asked what herbs one had to eat. Sky O'Dawn replied: "In the North-East grow the mushrooms of life. There is a three-legged crow in the sun who always wants to get down and eat them. But the Sun-God holds his eyes shut and does not let him get away. If human beings eat them they become immortal, when animals eat them they grow stupified."

"And how do you know this?" asked the Emperor.

"When I was a boy I once fell into a deep well, from which I could not get out for many decades. And down there was an immortal who led me to this herb. But one has to pass through a red river whose water is so light that not even a feather can swim on it. Everything that touches its surface sinks to the depths. But the man pulled off one of his shoes and gave it to me. And I crossed the water on the shoe, picked the herb and ate it. Those who dwell in that place weave mats of pearls and precious stones. They led me to a spot before which hung a curtain of delicate, colored skin. And they gave me a pillow carved of black jade, on which were graven sun and moon, clouds and thunder. They covered me with a dainty coverlet spun of the hair of a hundred gnats. A cover of that kind is very cool and refreshing in summer. I felt of it with my hands, and it seemed to be formed of water; but when I looked at it more closely, it was pure light."

Once the Emperor called together all his magicians in order to talk with them about the fields of the blessed spirits. Sky O'Dawn was there, too, and said: "Once I was wandering about the North Pole and I came to the Fire-Mirror Mountain. There neither sun nor moon shines. But there is a dragon who holds a fiery mirror in his jaws in order to light up the darkness. On the mountain is a park, and in the park is a lake. By the lake grows the glimmer-stalk grass, which shines like a lamp of gold. If you pluck it and use it for a candle, you can see all things visible, and the shapes of the spirits as well. It even illuminates the interior of a human being."

Once Sky O'Dawn went to the East, into the country of the fortunate clouds. And he brought back with him from that land a steed of the gods, nine feet high. The Emperor asked him how he had come to find it.

So he told him: "The Queen-Mother of the West had him harnessed to her wagon when she went to visit the King-Father of the East. The steed was staked out in the field of the mushrooms of life. But he trampled down several hundred of them. This made the King-Father angry, and he drove the steed away to the heavenly river. There I found him and rode him home. I rode three times around the sun, because I had fallen asleep on the steed's back. And then, before I knew it, I was here. This steed can catch up with the sun's shadow. When I found him he was quite thin and as sad as an aged donkey. So I mowed the grass of the country of the fortunate clouds, which grows once every two-thousand years on the Mountain of the Nine Springs and fed it to the horse; and that made him lively again."

The Emperor asked what sort of a place the country of the fortunate clouds might be. Sky O'Dawn answered: "There is a great swamp there. The people prophesy fortune and misfortune by the air and the clouds. If good fortune is to befall a house, clouds of five colors form in the rooms, which alight on the grass and trees and turn into a colored dew. This dew tastes as sweet as cider."

The Emperor asked whether he could obtain any of this dew. Sky O'Dawn replied: "My steed could take me to the place where it falls four times in the course of a single day!"

And sure enough he came back by evening, and brought along dew of every color in a crystal flask. The Emperor drank it and his hair grew black again. He gave it to his highest officials to drink, and the old grew young again and the sick became well.

Once, when a comet appeared in the heavens, Sky O'Dawn gave the Emperor the astrologer's wand. The Emperor pointed it at the comet and the comet was quenched.

Sky O'Dawn was an excellent whistler. And whenever he whistled in full tones, long drawn out, the motes in the sunbeams danced to his music.

Once he said to a friend: "There is not a soul on earth who knows who I am with the exception of the astrologer!"

When Sky O'Dawn had died, the Emperor called

the astrologer to him and asked: "Did you know Sky O'Dawn?"

He replied: "No!"

The Emperor said: "What do you know?"

The astrologer answered: "I know how to gaze on the stars."

"Are all the stars in their places?" asked the Emperor.

"Yes, but for eighteen years I have not seen the Star of the Great Year. Now it is visible once more."

Then the Emperor looked up towards the skies and sighed: "For eighteen years Sky O'Dawn kept me company, and I did not know that he was the Star of the Great Year!"

Note: The mother of Sky O'Dawn, (Dung Fang So) who makes so mysterious an appearance on earth, according to one tradition, is the third daughter of the Lord of the Heavens. (Comp. Note to No. 16). Dung Fang So is an incarnation of the Wood Star or Star of the Great Year (Jupiter). The King-Father of the East, one of the Five Ancients, is the representative of wood (comp. No. 15). Red chestnuts, like fire-dates, are fruits of the gods, and bestow immortality. Sky O'Dawn was an excellent whistler. Whistling is a famous means of magic among the Taoists. The Emperor Wu of the Han dynasty, was a prince who is reputed to have devoted much attention to the magic arts. He reigned from 140 to 86 B. C. The three-legged crow in the sun is the counterpart of the three-legged ram-toad in the moon. The Red River recalls the Weak River by the Castle of the Queen-Mother of the West.

XXXV

KING MU OF DSCHOU

IN the days of King Mu of Dschou a magician came out of the uttermost West, who could walk through water and fire, and pass through metal and stone. He could make mountains and rivers change place, shift about cities and castles, rise into emptiness without falling, strike against solid matter without finding it an obstruction; and he knew a thousand transformations in all their inexhaustible variety. And he could not only change the shape of things but he could change men's thoughts. The King honored him like a god, and served him as he would a master. He resigned his own apartments that the magician might be lodged in them, had beasts of sacrifice brought to offer him, and selected sweet singers to give him pleasure. But the rooms in the King's palace were too humble—the magician could not dwell in them; and the King's singers were not musical enough to be allowed to be near him. So King Mu had a new palace built for him. The work of bricklayers and carpenters, of painters and stainers left nothing to be desired with regard to skill. The King's treasury was empty when the tower had reached its full height. It was a thousand fathoms high, and rose above the top of the mountain before the capital. The King selected maidens, the loveliest and most dainty, gave them fragrant essences, had their eyebrows curved in lines of beauty, and adorned their hair and ears with jewels. He garbed them in fine cloth, and with white silks fluttering about them, and had their faces painted white and their eyebrows stained black. He had them put on armlets of precious stones and mix sweet-smelling herbs. They filled the palace and sang the songs of the ancient kings in order to please the magician. Every month the most costly garments were brought him, and every morning the most delicate food. The magician allowed them to do so, and since he had no choice, made the best of it.

Not long afterward the magician invited the King to go traveling with him. The King grasped the magician's sleeve, and thus they flew up through the air to the middle of the skies. When they stopped they found they had reached the palace of the magician. It was built of gold and silver, and adorned with pearls and precious stones. It towered high over the clouds and rain; and none could say whereon it rested. To the eye it had the appearance of heaped-up clouds. All that it offered the senses was different from the things of the world of men. It seemed to the King as though he were bodily present in the midst of the purple depths of the city of the air, of the divine harmony of the spheres, where the Great God dwells. The King looked down, and his castles and pleasure-houses appeared to him like hills of earth and heaps of straw. And there the King remained for some decades and thought no more of his kingdom.

Then the magician again invited the King to go traveling with him once more. And in the place to which they came there was to be seen neither sun nor moon above, nor rivers or sea below. The King's dazzled eyes could not see the radiant shapes which showed themselves; the King's dulled ears could not hear the sounds which played about them. It seemed as though his body were dissolving in confusion; his thoughts began to stray, and consciousness threatened to leave him. So he begged the magician to return. The magi-

SAINTS AND MAGICIANS

cian put his spell upon him, and it seemed to the King as though he were falling into empty space.

When he regained consciousness, he was sitting at the same place where he had been sitting when the magician had asked him to travel with him for the first time. The servants waiting on him were the same, and when he looked down, his goblet was not yet empty, and his food had not yet grown cold.

The King asked what had happened. And the servants answered, "The King sat for a space in silence." Whereupon the King was quite bereft of reason, and it was three months before he regained his right mind. Then he questioned the magician. The magician said: "I was traveling with you in the spirit, O King! What need was there for the body to go along? And the place in which we stayed at that time was no less real than your own castle and your own gardens. But you are used only to permanent conditions, therefore visions which dissolve so suddenly appear strange to you."

The King was content with the explanation. He gave no further thought to the business of government and took no more interest in his servants, but resolved to travel afar. So he had the eight famous steeds harnessed, and accompanied by a few faithful retainers, drove a thousand miles away. There he came to the country of the great hunters. The great hunters brought the King the blood of the white brant to drink, and washed his feet in the milk of mares and cows. When the King and his followers had quenched their thirst, they drove on and camped for the night on the slope of the Kunlun Mountain, south of the Red River. The next day they climbed to the peak of Kunlun Mountain and gazed at the castle of the Lord of the Yellow

Earth. Then they traveled on to the Queen-Mother of the West. Before they got there they had to pass the Weak River. This is a river whose waters will bear neither floats nor ships. All that attempts to float over it sinks into its depths. When the King reached the shore, fish and turtles, crabs and salamanders came swimming up and formed a bridge, so that he could drive across with the wagon.

It is said of the Queen-Mother of the West that she goes about with hair unkempt, with a bird's beak and tiger's teeth, and that she is skilled in playing the flute. Yet this is not her true figure, but that of a spirit who serves her, and rules over the Western sky. The Queen-Mother entertained King Mu in her castle by the Springs of Jade. And she gave him rock-marrow to drink and fed him with the fruit of the jade-trees. Then she sang him a song and taught him a magic formula by means of which one could obtain long life. The Queen-Mother of the West gathers the immortals around her, and gives them to eat of the peaches of long life; and then they come to her with wagons with purple canopies, drawn by flying dragons. Ordinary mortals sink in the Weak River when they try to cross. But she was kindly disposed to King Wu.

When he took leave of her, he also went on to the spot where the sun turns in after running three thousand miles a day. Then he returned again to his kingdom.

When King Wu was a hundred years old, the Queen-Mother of the West drew near his palace and led him away with her into the clouds.

And from that day on he was seen no more.

Note: King Mu of Dschou reigned from 1001 to 946 B.C. With his name are associated the stories of the marvelous travels into the land of the far West, and especially to the Queen-Mother (who is identified by some with Juno). The peaches of immortality suggest the apples of the Hesperides. (Comp. with the story of "The Ape Sun Wu Kung".)

XXXVI

THE KING OF HUAI NAN

THE King of Huai Nan was a learned man of the Han dynasty. Since he was of the blood royal the emperor had given him a kingdom in fee. He cultivated the society of scholars, could interpret signs and foretell the future. Together with his scholars he had compiled the book which bears his name.

One day eight aged men came to see him. They all had white beards and white hair. The gate-keeper announced them to the King. The King wished to try them, so he sent back the gate-keeper to put difficulties in the way of their entrance. The latter said to them: "Our King is striving to learn the art of immortal life. You gentlemen are old and feeble. How can you be of aid to him? It is unnecessary for you to pay him a visit."

The eight old men smiled and said: "Oh, and are we too old to suit you? Well, then we will make ourselves young!" And before they had finished speaking they had turned themselves into boys of fourteen and fifteen, with hair-knots as black as silk and faces like peach-blossoms. The gate-keeper was frightened, and at once informed the King of what had happened. When the King heard it, he did not even take time to slip into his shoes, but hurried out barefoot to receive them. He led them into his palace, had rugs of brocade spread for them, and beds of ivory set up, fragrant herbs burned and tables of gold and precious stones set in front of them. Then he bowed before them as pupils do before a teacher, and told them how glad he was that they had come.

The eight boys changed into old men again and said: "Do you wish to go to school to us, O King? Each one of us is master of a particular art. One of us can call up wind and rain, cause clouds and mists to gather, rivers to flow and mountains to heave themselves up, if he wills it so. The second can cause high mountains to split asunder and check great streams in their course. He can tame tigers and panthers and soothe serpents and dragons. Spirits and gods do his bidding. The third can send out doubles, transform himself into other shapes, make himself invisible, cause whole armies to disappear, and turn day into night. The fourth can walk through the air and clouds, can stroll on the surface of the waves, pass through walls and rocks and cover a thousand miles in a single breath. The fifth can enter fire without burning, and water without drowning. The winter frost cannot chill him, nor the summer heat burn him. The sixth can create and transform living creatuers if he feel inclined. He can form birds and beasts, grasses and trees. He can transplace houses and castles. The seventh can bake lime so that it turns to gold, and cook lead so that it turns to silver; he can mingle water and stone so that the bubbles effervesce and turn into pearls. The eighth can ride on dragons and cranes to the eight poles of the world, converse with the immortals, and stand in the presence of the Great Pure One."

The King kept them beside him from morning to night, entertained them and had them show him what they could do. And, true enough, they could do everything just as they had said. And now the King began to distil the elixir of life with their aid. He had finished, but not yet imbibed it when a misfortune overtook his family. His son had been playing with a courtier and the latter had heedlessly wounded him. Fearing that the prince might punish him, he joined other discontented persons and excited a revolt. And the emperor, when he heard of it, sent one of his captains to judge between the King and the rebels.

The eight aged men spoke: "It is now time to go. This misfortune has been sent you from heaven, O King! Had it not befallen you, you would not have been able to resolve to leave the splendors and glories of this world!"

They led him on to a mountain. There they offered sacrifices to heaven, and buried gold in the earth. Then they ascended into the skies in bright daylight. The footprints of the eight aged men and of the king were imprinted in the rock of the mountain, and may be seen there to this very day. Before they had left the castle, however, they had set what was left of the elixir of life out in the courtyard. Hens and hounds picked and licked it up, and all flew up into the skies. In Huai Nan to this very day the crowing of cocks and the barking of hounds may be heard up in the skies. and it is said that these are the creatures who followed the King at the time.

One of the King's servants, however, followed him to an island in the sea, whence he sent him back. He told that the King himself had not yet ascended to the skies, but had only become immortal and was wandering about the world. When the emperor heard of the matter he regretted greatly that he had sent soldiers into the King's land and thus driven him out. He called in magicians to aid him, in hope of meeting the eight old men himself. Yet, for all that he spent great sums, he was not successful. The magicians only cheated him.

Note: The King of Huai Nan was named Liu An. He belonged to the Han dynasty. He dabbled largely in magic, and drew to his court many magicians whose labors are collected in the philosophical work which bears his name. Liu An lived at the time of the Emperor Wu (see No. 34). The latter having no heirs, Liu An entered into a conspiracy which, however, was discovered. As a consequence he killed himself, 122 B. C. Our fairy-tale presents these events in their legendary transformation.

XXXVII

OLD DSCHANG

ONCE upon a time there was a man who went by the name of Old Dschang. He lived in the country, near Yangdschou, as a gardener. His neighbor, named Sir We, held an official position in Yangdschou. Sir We had decided that it was time for his daughter to marry, so he sent for a match-maker and commissioned her to find a suitable husband. Old Dschang heard this, and was pleased. He prepared food and drink, entertained the match-maker, and told her to recommend him as a husband. But the old match-maker went off scolding.

The next day he invited her to dinner again and gave her money. Then the old match-maker said: "You do not know what you wish! Why should a gentleman's beautiful daughter condescend to marry a poor old gardener like yourself? Even though you had money to burn, your white hair would not match her black locks. Such a marriage is out of the question!"

But Old Dschang did not cease to entreat her:

SAINTS AND MAGICIANS 103

"Make an attempt, just one attempt, to mention me! If they will not listen to you, then I must resign myself to my fate!"

The old match-maker had taken his money, so she could not well refuse, and though she feared being scolded, she mentioned him to Sir We. He grew angry and wanted to throw her out of the house.

"I knew you would not thank me," said she, "but the old man urged it so that I could not refuse to mention his intention."

"Tell the old man that if this very day he brings me two white jade-stones, and four hundred ounces of yellow gold, then I will give him my daughter's hand in marriage."

But he only wished to mock the old man's folly, for he knew that the latter could not give him anything of the kind. The match-maker went to Old Dschang and delivered the message. And he made no objection; but at once brought the exact quantity of gold and jewels to Sir We's house. The latter was very much frightened and when his wife heard of it, she began to weep and wail loudly. But the girl encouraged her mother: "My father has given his word now and cannot break it. I will know how to bear my fate."

So Sir We's daughter was married to Old Dschang. But even after the wedding the latter did not give up his work as a gardener. He spaded the field and sold vegetables as usual, and his wife had to fetch water and build the kitchen fire herself. But she did her work without false shame and, though her relatives reproached her, she continued to do so.

Once an aristocratic relative visited Sir We and said: "If you had really been poor, were there not enough young gentlemen in the neighborhood for your daughter? Why did you have to marry her to such a wrinkled old gardener? Now that you have thrown her away, so to speak, it would be better if both of them left this part of the country."

Then Sir We prepared a banquet and invited his daughter and Old Dschang to visit him. When they had had sufficient to eat and drink he allowed them to get an inkling of what was in his mind.

Said Old Dschang: "I have only remained here because I thought you would long for your daughter. But since you are tired of us, I will be glad to go. I have a little country house back in the hills, and we will set out for it early to-morrow morning."

The following morning, at break of dawn, Old Dschang came with his wife to say farewell. Sir We said: "Should we long to see you at some later time, my son can make inquiries." Old Dschang placed his wife on a donkey and gave her a straw hat to wear. He himself took his staff and walked after.

A few years passed without any news from either of them. Then Sir We and his wife felt quite a longing to see their daughter and sent their son to make inquiries. When the latter got back in the hills he met a plow-boy who was plowing with two yellow steers. He asked him: "Where is Old Dschang's country house?" The plow-boy left the plow in the harrow, bowed and answered: "You have been a long time coming, sir! The village is not far from here: I will show you the way."

They crossed a hill. At the foot of the hill flowed a brook, and when they had crossed the brook they had to climb another hill. Gradually the landscape changed. From the top of the hill could be seen a valley, level in the middle, surrounded by abrupt crags and shaded by green trees, among which houses and towers peeped forth. This was the country house of

SAINTS AND MAGICIANS

Old Dschang. Before the village flowed a deep brook full of clear, blue water. They passed over a stone bridge and reached the gate. Here flowers and trees grew in luxurious profusion, and peacocks and cranes flew about. From the distance could be heard the sound of flutes and of stringed instruments. Crystal-clear tones rose to the clouds. A messenger in a purple robe received the guest at the gate and led him into a hall of surpassing splendor. Strange fragrances filled the air, and there was a ringing of little bells of pearl. Two maid-servants came forth to greet him, followed by two rows of beautiful girls in a long processional. After them a man in a flowing turban, clad in scarlet silk, with red slippers, came floating along. The guest saluted him. He was serious and dignified, and at the same time seemed youthfully fresh. At first We's son did not recognize him, but when he looked more closely, why it was Old Dschang! The latter said with a smile: "I am pleased that the long road to travel has not prevented your coming. Your sister is just combing her hair. She will welcome you in a moment." Then he had him sit down and drink tea.

After a short time a maid-servant came and led him to the inner rooms, to his sister. The beams of her room were of sandalwood, the doors of tortoise-shell and the windows inlaid with blue jade; her curtains were formed of strings of pearls and the steps leading into the room of green nephrite. His sister was magnificently gowned, and far more beautiful than before. She asked him carelessly how he was getting along, and what her parents were doing; but was not very cordial. After a splendid meal she had an apartment prepared for him.

"My sister wishes to make an excursion to the Mountain of the Fairies," said Old Dschang to him.

"We will be back about sunset, and you can rest until we return."

Then many-colored clouds rose in the courtyard, and dulcet music sounded on the air. Old Dschang mounted a dragon, while his wife and sister rode on phenixes and their attendants on cranes. So they rose into the air and disappeared in an easterly direction. They did not return until after sunset.

Old Dschang and his wife then said to him: "This is an abode of the blessed. You cannot remain here overlong. To-morrow we will escort you back."

On the following day, when taking leave, Old Dschang gave him eighty ounces of gold and an old straw hat. "Should you need money," said he, "you can go to Yangdschou and inquire in the northern suburb for old Wang's drug-shop. There you can collect ten million pieces of copper. This hat is the order for them." Then he ordered his plow-boy to take him home again.

Quite a few of the folks at home, to whom he described his adventures, thought that Old Dschang must be a holy man, while others regarded the whole thing a magic vision.

After five or six years Sir We's money came to an end. So his son took the straw hat to Yangdschou and there asked for old Wang. The latter just happened to be standing in his drug-shop, mixing herbs. When the son explained his errand he said: "The money is ready. But is your hat genuine?" And he took the hat and examined it. A young girl came from an inner room and said: "I wove the hat for Old Dschang myself. There must be a red thread in it." And sure enough, there was. Then old Wang gave young We the ten million pieces of copper, and the latter now believed that Old Dschang was really a saint. So he once more went over the hills to look for him. He asked the forest-keepers, but they could tell him naught. Sadly he retraced his steps and decided to inquire of old Wang, but he had also disappeared.

When several years had passed he once more came to Yangdschou, and was walking in the meadow before the city gate. There he met Old Dschang's plow-boy. The latter cried out: "How are you? How are you?" and drew out ten pounds of gold, which he gave to him, saying: "My mistress told me to give you this. My master is this very moment drinking tea with old Wang in the inn." Young We followed the plow-boy, intending to greet his brother-in-law. But when he reached the inn there was no one in sight. And when he turned around the plow-boy had disappeared as well. And since that time no one ever heard from Old Dschang again.

Note: The match-maker, according to Chinese custom—and the custom of other oriental peoples—is an absolutely necessary mediator between the two families. There are old women who make their living at this profession.

XXXVIII

THE KINDLY MAGICIAN

ONCE upon a time there was a man named Du Dsi Tschun. In his youth he was a spendthrift and paid no heed to his property. He was given to drink and idling. When he had run through all his money, his relatives cast him out. One winter day he was walking barefoot about the city, with an empty stomach and torn clothes. Evening came on and still he had not found any food. Without end or aim he wandered about the market place. He was hungry, and the cold seemed well nigh unendurable. So he turned his eyes upward and began to lament aloud.

Suddenly an ancient man stood before him, leaning on a staff, who said: "What do you lack since you complain so?"

"I am dying of hunger," replied Du Dsi Tschun, "and not a soul will take pity on me!"

The ancient man said: "How much money would you need in order to live in all comfort?"

"If I had fifty thousand pieces of copper it would answer my purpose," replied Du Dsi Tschun.

The ancient said: "That would not answer."

"Well, then, a million!"

"That is still too little!"

"Well, then, three million!"

The ancient man said: "That is well spoken!" He fetched a thousand pieces of copper out of his sleeve and said: "That is for this evening. Expect me tomorrow by noon, at the Persian Bazaar!"

At the time set Du Dsi Tschun went there, and, sure enough, there was the ancient, who gave him three million pieces of copper. Then he disappeared, without giving his name.

When Du Dsi Tschun held the money in his hand, his love for prodigality once more awoke. He rode pampered steeds, clothed himself in the finest furs, went back to his wine, and led such an extravagant life that the money gradually came to an end. Instead of wearing brocade he had to wear cotton, and instead of riding horseback he went to the dogs. Finally he was again running about barefoot and in rags as before, and did not know how to satisfy his hunger. Once more he stood in the market-place and sighed. But the ancient was already there, took him by the hand and said: "Are you back already to where you were? That is strange! However, I will aid you once more!"

But Du Dsi Tschun was ashamed and did not want to accept his help. Yet the ancient insisted, and led him along to the Persian Bazaar. This time he gave him ten million pieces of copper, and Du Dsi Tschun thanked him with shame in his heart.

With money in hand, he tried to give time to adding to it, and saving in order to gain great wealth. But, as is always the case, it is hard to overcome ingrown faults. Gradually he began to fling his money away again, and gave free rein to all his desires. And once more his purse grew empty. In a couple of years he was as poor as ever he had been.

Then he met the ancient the third time, but was so ashamed of himself that he hid his face when he passed him.

The ancient seized his arm and said: "Where are you going? I will help you once more. I will give you thirty million. But if then you do not improve you are past all aid!"

Full of gratitude, Du Dsi Tschun bowed before him and said: "In the days of my poverty my wealthy relatives did not seek me out. You alone have thrice aided me. The money you give me to-day shall not be squandered, that I swear; but I will devote it to good works in order to repay your great kindness. And when I have done this I will follow you, if needs be through fire and through water."

The ancient replied: "That is right! When you have ordered these things ask for me in the temple of Laotsze beneath the two mulberry trees!"

Du Dsi Tschun took the money and went to Yang-dschou. There he bought a hundred acres of the best land, and built a lofty house with many hundreds of rooms on the highway. And there he allowed widows and orphans to live. Then he bought a burial-place for his ancestors, and supported his needy relations. Countless people were indebted to him for their livelihood.

When all was finished, he went to inquire after the ancient in the temple of Laotsze. The ancient was sitting in the shade of the mulberry trees blowing the flute. He took Du Dsi Tschun along with him to the cloudy peaks of the holy mountains of the West. When they had gone some forty miles into the mountains, he saw a dwelling, fair and clean. It was surrounded by many-colored clouds, and peacocks and cranes were flying about it. Within the house was a herb-oven nine feet high. The fire burned with a purple flame, and its glow leaped along the walls. Nine fairies stood at the oven, and a green dragon and a white tiger crouched beside it. Evening came. The ancient was no longer clad like an ordinary man; but wore a yellow cap and wide, flowing garments. He took three pellets of the White Stone, put them into a flagon of wine, and gave them to Du Dsi Tschun to drink. He spread out a tiger-skin against the western wall of the inner chamber, and bade Du Dsi Tschun sit down on it, with his face turned toward the East. Then he said to him: "Now beware of speaking a single word—no matter what happens to you, whether You encounter powerful gods or terrible demons, wild beasts or ogres, or all the tortures of the nether world, or even if you see your own relatives suffer—for all these things are only deceitful images! They cannot harm you. Think only of what I have said, and let your soul be at rest!" And when he had said this the ancient disappeared.

Then Du Dsi Tschun saw only a large stone jug

SAINTS AND MAGICIANS

full of clear water standing before him. Fairies, dragon and tiger had all vanished. Suddenly he heard a tremendous crash, which made heaven and earth tremble. A man towering more than ten feet in height appeared. He called himself the great captain, and he and his horse were covered with golden armor. He was surrounded by more than a hundred soldiers, who drew their bows and swung their swords, and halted in the courtyard.

The giant called out harshly: "Who are you? Get out of my way!"

Du Dsi Tschun did not move. And he returned no answer to his questions.

Then the giant flew into a passion and cried with a thundering voice: "Chop off his head!"

But Du Dsi Tschun remained unmoved, so the giant went off raging.

Then a furious tiger and a poisonous serpent came up roaring and hissing. They made as though to bite him and leaped over him. But Du Dsi Tschun remained unperturbed in spirit, and after a time they dissolved and vanished.

Suddenly a great rain began to fall in streams. It thundered and lightninged incessantly, so that his ears rang and his eyes were blinded. It seemed as though the house would fall. The water rose to a flood in a few moments' time, and streamed up to the place where he was sitting. But Du Dsi Tschun remained motionless and paid no attention to it. And after a time the water receded.

Then came a great demon with the head of an ox. He set up a kettle in the middle of the courtyard, in which bubbled boiling oil. He caught Du Dsi Tschun by the neck with an iron fork and said: "If you will tell me who you are I will let you go!"

Du Dsi Tschun shut his eyes and kept silent. Then

the demon picked him up with the fork and flung him into the kettle. He withstood the pain, and the boiling oil did not harm him. Finally the demon dragged him out again, and drew him down the steps of the house before a man with red hair and a blue face, who looked like the prince of the nether world. The latter cried: "Drag in his wife!"

After a time Du Dsi Tschun's wife was brought on in chains. Her hair was torn and she wept bitterly.

The demon pointed to Du Dsi Tschun and said: "If you will speak your name we will let her go!"

But he answered not a word.

Then the prince of evil had the woman tormented in all sorts of ways. And she pleaded with Du Dsi Tschun: "I have been your wife now for ten years. Will you not speak one little word to save me? I can endure no more!" And the tears ran in streams from her eyes. She screamed and scolded. Yet he spoke not a word.

Thereupon the prince of evil shouted: "Chop her into bits!" And there, before his eyes, it seemed as though she were really being chopped to pieces. But Du Dsi Tschun did not move.

"The scoundrel's measure is full!" cried the prince of evil. "He shall dwell no longer among the living! Off with his head!" And so they killed him, and it seemed to him that his soul fled his body. The ox-headed demon dragged him down into the nether regions, where he tasted all the tortures in turn. But Du Dsi Tschun remembered the words of the ancient. And the tortures, too, seemed bearable. So he did not scream and said not a word.

Now he was once more dragged before the prince of evil. The latter said: "As punishment for his obstinacy this man shall come to earth again in the shape of a woman!"

The demon dragged him to the wheel of life and he returned to earth in the shape of a girl. He was often ill, had to take medicine continually, and was pricked and burned with hot needles. Yet he never uttered a sound. Gradually he grew into a beautiful maiden. But since he never spoke, he was known as the dumb maid. A scholar finally took him for his bride, and they lived in peace and good fellowship. And a son came to them who, in the course of two years was already beyond measure wise and intelligent. One day the father was carrying the son on his arm. He spoke jestingly to his wife and said: "When I look at you it seems to me that you are not really dumb. Won't you say one little word to me? How delightful it would be if you were to become my speaking rose!"

The woman remained silent. No matter how he might coax and try to make her smile, she would return no answer.

Then his features changed: "If you will not speak to me, it is a sign that you scorn me; and in that case your son is nothing to me, either!" And with that he seized the boy and flung him against the wall.

But since Du Dsi Tschun loved this little boy so dearly, he forgot the ancient's warning, and cried out: "Oh, oh!"

And before the cry had died away Du Dsi Tschun awoke as though from a dream and found himself seated in his former place. The ancient was there as well. It must have been about the fifth hour of the night. Purple flames rose wildly from the oven, and flared up to the sky. The whole house caught fire and burned like a torch.

" You have deceived me!" cried the ancient. Then he seized him by the hair and thrust him into the jug of water. And in a minute the fire went out. The ancient spoke: "You overcame joy and rage, grief and fear, hate and desire, it is true; but love you had not driven from your soul. Had you not cried out when the child was flung against the wall, then my elixir would have taken shape and you would have attained immortality. But in the last moment you failed me. Now it is too late. Now I can begin brewing my elixir of life once more from the beginning, and you will remain a mere mortal man!"

Du Dsi Tschun saw that the oven had burst, and that instead of the philosopher's stone it held only a lump of iron. The ancient man cast aside his garments and chopped it up with a magic knife. Du Dsi Tschun took leave of him and returned to Yangdschou, where he lived in great affluence. In his old age he regretted that he had not completed his task. He once more went to the mountain to look for the ancient. But the ancient had vanished without leaving a trace.

Note: The "pieces of copper" are the ancient Chinese copper coins, with a hole in the middle, usually hung on strings to the number of 500 or 1000. Money had a greater purchasing value in ancient China, however, than in the China of to-day. The "Persian Bazaar": During the reign of the Tang dynasty China maintained an active intercourse with the West, traces of which are at present being investigated in Central Asia. At that time Persian bazaars were no novelty in the city of Si-An-Fu, then the capital. "Herboven": a tripod kettle used for brewing the elixir of life, with which the fairies, dragon and tiger (both the last-mentioned star-incarnations) are connected. In order to prepare the elixir the master must have absolute endurance. It is for this reason that he had placed Du Dsi Tschun in his debt by means of kindness. The yellow cap which the master wears is connected with the teachings of the Yellow Ancient (comp. w. No. 15). The "prince of the nether world," Yan Wang, or Yan Lo Wang, is the Indian god Yama. There are in all ten princes of the nether world, of whom the fifth is the highest and most feared. "Obstinacy," literally; his real offense is reticence, or the keeping secret of a thing. This quality belongs to the Yin, the dark or feminine principle, and determines Du Dsi Tschun's reappearance on earth as a woman. "Purple flames rose wildly from the oven": Though Du Dsi Tschun had overcome his other emotions, so that fear and terror did not affect him, love, and love in its highest form, mother-love, still remained in him. This love created the flames which threatened to destroy the building. The highest point in Taoism—as in Buddhism—is, however, the absolute negation of all feeling.

NATURE AND ANIMAL TALES

XXXIX

THE FLOWER-ELVES

ONCE upon a time there was a scholar who lived retired from the world in order to gain hidden wisdom. He lived alone and in a secret place. And all about the little house in which he dwelt he had planted every kind of flower, and bamboos and other trees. There it lay, quite concealed in its thick grove of flowers. With him he had only a boy servant, who dwelt in a separate hut, and who carried out his orders. He was not allowed to appear before his master unless summoned. The scholar loved his flowers as he did himself. Never did he set his foot beyond the boundaries of his garden.

It chanced that once there came a lovely spring evening. Flowers and trees stood in full bloom, a fresh breeze was blowing, the moon shone clearly. And the scholar sat over his goblet and was grateful for the gift of life.

Suddenly he saw a maiden in dark garments come tripping up in the moonlight. She made a deep courtesy, greeted him and said: "I am your neighbor. We are a company of young maids who are on our way to visit the eighteen aunts. We should like to rest in this court for awhile, and therefore ask your permission to do so."

The scholar saw that this was something quite out of the common, and gladly gave his consent. The maiden thanked him and went away.

In a short time she brought back a whole crowd of maids carrying flowers and willow branches. All greeted the scholar. They were charming, with delicate features, and slender, graceful figures. When they moved their sleeves, a delightful fragrance was exhaled. There is no fragrance known to the human world which could be compared with it.

The scholar invited them to sit down for a time in his room. Then he asked them: "Whom have I really the honor of entertaining? Have you come from the castle of the Lady in the Moon, or the Jade Spring of the Queen-Mother of the West?"

"How could we claim such high descent?" said a maiden in a green gown, with a smile. "My name is Salix." Then she presented another, clad in white, and said: "This is Mistress Prunophora"; then one in rose, "and this is Persica;" and finally one in a dark-red gown, "and this is Punica." We are all sisters and we want to visit the eighteen zephyr-aunts to-day. The moon shines so beautifully this evening and it is so charming here in the garden. We are most grateful to you for taking pity on us."

"Yes, yes," said the scholar.

Then the sober-clad servant suddenly announced: "The zephyr-aunts have already arrived!"

At once the girls rose and went to the door to meet them.

"We were just about to visit you, aunts," they said, smiling. "This gentleman here had just invited us to sit for a moment. What a pleasant coincidence that you aunts have come here, too. This is such a lovely night that we must drink a goblet of nectar in honor of you aunts!"

Thereon they ordered the servant to bring what was needed.

NATURE AND ANIMAL TALES

"May one sit down here?" asked the aunts.

"The master of the house is most kind," replied the maids, "and the spot is quiet and hidden."

And then they presented the aunts to the scholar. He spoke a few kindly words to the eighteen aunts. They had a somewhat irresponsible and airy manner. Their words fairly gushed out, and in their neighborhood one felt a frosty chill.

Meanwhile the servants had already brought in table and chairs. The eighteen aunts sat at the upper end of the board, the maids followed, and the scholar sat down with them at the lowest place. Soon the entire table was covered with the most delicious foods and most magnificent fruits, and the goblets were filled with a fragrant nectar. They were delights such as the world of men does not know! The moon shone brightly and the flowers exhaled intoxicating odors. After they had partaken of food and drink the maids rose, danced and sung. Sweetly the sound of their singing echoed through the falling gloam, and their dance was like that of butterflies fluttering about the flowers. The scholar was so overpowered with delight that he no longer knew whether he were in heaven or on earth.

When the dance had ended, the girls sat down again at the table, and drank the health of the aunts in flowing nectar. The scholar, too, was remembered with a toast, to which he replied with well-turned phrases.

But the eighteen aunts were somewhat irresponsible in their ways. One of them, raising her goblet, by accident poured some nectar on Punica's dress. Punica, who was young and fiery, and very neat, stood up angrily when she saw the spot on her red dress.

"You are really very careless," said she, in her anger. "My other sisters may be afraid of you, but I am not!"

Then the aunts grew angry as well and said: "How dare this young chit insult us in such a manner!"

And with that they gathered up their garments and rose.

All the maids then crowded about them and said: "Punica is so young and inexperienced! You must not bear her any ill-will! To-morrow she shall go to you switch in hand, and receive her punishment!"

But the eighteen aunts would not listen to them and went off. Thereupon the maids also said farewell, scattered among the flower-beds and disappeared. The scholar sat for a long time lost in dreamy yearning.

On the following evening the maids all came back again.

"We all live in your garden," they told him. "Every year we are tormented by naughty winds, and therefore we have always asked the eighteen aunts to protect us. But yesterday Punica insulted them, and now we fear they will help us no more. But we know that you have always been well disposed toward us, for which we are heartily grateful. And now we have a great favor to ask, that every New Year's day you make a small scarlet flag, paint the sun, moon and five planets on it, and set it up in the eastern part of the garden. Then we sisters will be left in peace and will be protected from all evil. But since New Year's day has passed for this year, we beg that you will set up the flag on the twenty-first of this month. For the East Wind is coming and the flag will protect us against him!"

The scholar readily promised to do as they wished, and the maids all said with a single voice: "We thank you for your great kindness and will repay it!" Then they departed and a sweet fragrance filled the entire garden.

The scholar, however, made a red flag as described,

NATURE AND ANIMAL TALES

and when early in the morning of the day in question the East Wind really did begin to blow, he quickly set it up in the garden.

Suddenly a wild storm broke out, one that caused the forests to bend, and broke the trees. The flowers in the garden alone did not move.

Then the scholar noticed that Salix was the willow; Prunophora the plum; Persica the peach, and the saucy Punica the Pomegranate, whose powerful blossoms the wind cannot tear. The eighteen zephyr-aunts, however, were the spirits of the winds.

In the evening the flower-elves all came and brought the scholar radiant flowers as a gift of thanks.

"You have saved us," they said, "and we have nothing else we can give you. If you eat these flowers you will live long and avoid old age. And if you, in turn, will protect us every year, then we sisters, too, will live long."

The scholar did as they told him and ate the flowers. And his figure changed and he grew young again like a youth of twenty. And in the course of time he attained the hidden wisdom and was placed among the Immortals.

Note. Salix: the names of the "Flower Elves" are given in the Chinese as family names, whose sound suggests the flower-names without exactly using them. In the translation the play on words is indicated by the Latin names. "Zephyr-aunts": In Chinese the name given the aunt is "Fong," which in another stylization means "wind."

XL

THE SPIRIT OF THE WU-LIAN MOUNTAIN

TO the west of the gulf of Kisutschou is the Wu-Lian Mountain, where there are many spirits. Once upon a time a scholar who lived there was sitting up late at night, reading. And, as he stepped out before the house, a storm rose up suddenly, and a monster stretched out his claws and seized him by the hair. And he lifted him up in the air and carried him away. They passed by the tower which looks out to sea, a Buddhist temple in the hills. And in the distance, in the clouds, the scholar saw the figure of a god in golden armor. The figure looked exactly like the image of Weto which was in the tower. In its right hand it held an iron mace, while its left pointed toward the monster, and it looked at it with anger. Then the monster let the scholar fall, right on top of the tower, and disappeared. No doubt the saint in the tower had come to the scholar's aid, because his whole family worshiped Buddha dutifully.

When the sun rose the priest came and saw the scholar on his tower. He piled up hay and straw on the ground; so that he could jump down without hurting himself. Then he took the scholar home, yet there where the monster had seized his hair, the hair remained stiff and unyielding. It did not improve until half a year had gone by.

Note: This legend comes from Dschungschong, west of the gulf of Kiautschou. "The tower which looks out to sea," a celebrated tower which gives a view of the ocean. At present the people give this name to the Tsingtau Signal Station. Weto (Sanscrit, Veda), a legendary Boddhisatva, leader of the hosts of the four kings of heaven. His picture, with drawn sword, may be found at the entrance of every Buddhist temple. In China, he is often represented with a mace (symbolizing a thunderbolt) instead of a sword. When this is the case he has probably been confused with Vaisramana.

XLI

THE KING OF THE ANTS

ONCE upon a time there was a scholar, who wandered away from his home and went to Emmet village. There stood a house which was said to be haunted. Yet it was beautifully situated and surrounded by a lovely garden. So the scholar hired it. One evening he was sitting over his books, when several hundred knights suddenly came galloping into the room. They were quite tiny, and their horses were about the size of flies. They had hunting falcons and dogs about as large as gnats and fleas.

They came to his bed in the corner of the room, and there they held a great hunt, with bows and arrows: one could see it all quite plainly. They caught a tremendous quantity of birds and game, and all this game was no larger than little grains of rice.

When the hunt was over, in came a long procession with banners and standards. They wore swords at their side and bore spears in their hands, and came to a halt in the north-west corner of the room. They were followed by several hundred servingmen. These brought with them curtains and covers, tents and tent-poles, pots and kettles, cups and plates, tables and chairs. And after them some hundreds of other servants carried in all sorts of fine dishes, the best that land and water had to offer. And several hundred more ran to and fro without stopping, in order to guard the roads and carry messages.

The scholar gradually accustomed himself to the sight. Although the men were so very small he could distinguish everything quite clearly.

Before long, a bright colored banner appeared. Behind it rode a personage wearing a scarlet hat and garments of purple. He was surrounded by an escort of several thousands. Before him went runners with whips and rods to clear the way.

Then a man wearing an iron helmet and with a golden ax in his hand cried out in a loud voice: "His Highness is graciously pleased to look at the fish in the Purple Lake!" Whereupon the one who wore the scarlet hat got down from his horse, and, followed by a retinue of several hundred men, approached the saucer which the scholar used for his writing-ink. Tents were put up on the edge of the saucer and a banquet was prepared. A great number of guests sat down to the table. Musicians and dancers stood ready. There was a bright confusion of mingled garments of purple and scarlet, crimson and green. Pipes and flutes, fiddles and cymbals sounded, and the dancers moved in the dance. The music was very faint, and yet its melodies could be clearly distinguished. All that was said, too, the table-talk and orders, questions and calls, could be quite distinctly heard.

After three courses, he who wore the scarlet hat said: "Quick! Make ready the nets and lines for fishing!"

And at once nets were thrown out into the saucer which held the water in which the scholar dipped his brush. And they caught hundreds of thousands of fishes. The one with the scarlet hat contented himself with casting a line in the shallow waters of the saucer, and caught a baker's dozen of red carp.

Then he ordered the head cook to cook the fish, and the most varied dishes were prepared with them. The odor of roasting fat and spices filled the whole room.

And then the wearer of the scarlet hat in his arrogance, decided to amuse himself at the scholar's expense. So he pointed to him and said: "I know nothing at all about the writings and customs of the saints and wise men, and still I am a king who is highly honored! Yonder scholar spends his whole life toiling over his books and yet he remains poor and gets nowhere. If he could make up his mind to serve me faithfully as one of my officials, I might allow him to partake of our meal."

This angered the scholar, and he took his book and struck at them. And they all scattered, wriggling and crawling out of the door. He followed them and dug up the earth in the place where they had disappeared. And there he found an ants' nest as large as a barrel, in which countless green ants were wriggling around. So he built a large fire and smoked them out.

Note: This charming tale is taken from the Tang Dai Tsung Schu.

XLII

THE LITTLE HUNTING DOG

ONCE upon a time, in the city of Shansi, there lived a scholar who found the company of others too noisy for him. So he made his home in a Buddhist temple. Yet he suffered because there were always so many gnats and fleas in his room that he could not sleep at night.

Once he was resting on his bed after dinner, when suddenly two little knights with plumes in their helmets rode into the room. They might have been two inches high, and rode horses about the size of grasshoppers. On their gauntleted hands they held hunting falcons as large as flies. They rode about the room with great rapidity. The scholar had no more than set eyes on them when a third entered, clad like the others, but carrying a bow and arrows and leading a little hunting dog the size of an ant with him. After him came a great throng of footmen and horsemen, several hundred in all. And they had hunting falcons and hunting dogs by the hundred, too. Then the fleas and gnats began to rise in the air; but were all slain by the falcons. And the hunting dogs climbed on the bed, and sniffed along the walls trailing the fleas, and ate them up. They followed the trace of whatever hid in the cracks, and nosed it out, so that in a short space of time they had killed nearly all the vermin.

The scholar pretended to be asleep and watched them. And the falcons settled down on him, and the dogs crawled along his body. Shortly after came a man clad in yellow, wearing a king's crown, who climbed on an empty couch and seated himself there. And at once all the horsemen rode up, descended from their horses and brought him all the birds and game. They then gathered beside him in a great throng, and conversed with him in a strange tongue.

Not long after the king got into a small chariot and his bodyguards saddled their horses with the greatest rapidity. Then they galloped out with great cries of homage, till it looked as though some one were scattering beans and a heavy cloud of dust rose behind them.

They had nearly all of them disappeared, while the scholar's eyes were still fixed on them full of terror and astonishment, and he could not imagine whence they had come. He slipped on his shoes and looked; but they had vanished without a trace. Then he returned and looked all about his room; but there was nothing to be seen. Only, on a brick against the wall, they had forgotten a little hunting dog. The scholar quickly caught it and found it quite tame. He put it in his paint-box and examined it closely. It had a very smooth, fine coat, and wore a little collar around its neck. He tried to feed it a few bread-crumbs, but the little dog only sniffed at them and let them lie. Then it leaped into the bed and hunted up some nits and gnats in the folds of the linen, which it devoured. Then it returned and lay down. When the night had passed the scholar feared it might have run away; but there it lay, curled up as before. Whenever the scholar went to bed, the dog climbed into it and bit to death any vermin it could find. Not a fly or gnat dared alight while it was around. The scholar loved it like a jewel of price.

But once he took a nap in the daytime, and the little dog crawled into bed beside him. The scholar woke and turned around, supporting himself on his side. As he did so he felt something, and feared it might be his little dog. He quickly rose and looked, but it was already dead—pressed flat, as though cut out of paper!

But at any rate none of the vermin had survived it.

Note: This tale is taken from the Liau Dschai ("Strange Stories") of P'u Sung Lang (b. 1622). It is a parallel of the preceding one and shows how the same material returns in a different working-out.

XLIII

THE DRAGON AFTER HIS WINTER SLEEP

ONCE there was a scholar who was reading in the upper story of his house. It was a rainy, cloudy day and the weather was gloomy. Suddenly he saw a little thing which shone like a fire-fly. It crawled upon the table, and wherever it went it left traces of burns, curved like the tracks of a rainworm. Gradually it wound itself about the scholar's book and the book, too, grew black. Then it occurred to him that it might be a dragon. So he carried it out of doors on the book. There he stood for quite some time; but it sat uncurled, without moving in the least.

Then the scholar said: "It shall not be said of me that I was lacking in respect." With these words he carried back the book and once more laid it on the table. Then he put on his robes of ceremony, made a deep bow and escorted the dragon out on it again.

No sooner had he left the door, than he noticed that the dragon raised his head and stretched himself. Then he flew up from the book with a hissing sound, like a radiant streak. Once more he turned around toward the scholar, and his head had already grown to the size of a barrel, while his body must have been a full fathom in length. He gave one more snaky twist, and then there was a terrible crash of thunder and the dragon went sailing through the air.

The scholar then returned and looked to see which way the little creature had come. And he could follow his tracks hither and thither, to his chest of books.

Note: This tale is also from the "Strange Stories." The dragon, head of all scaled creatures and insects, hibernates during the winter according to the Chinese belief. At the time he is quite small. When the first spring storm comes he flies up to the clouds on the lightning. Here the dragon's nature as an atmospheric apparition is expressed.

XLIV

THE SPIRITS OF THE YELLOW RIVER

THE spirits of the Yellow River are called Dai Wang—Great King. For many hundreds of years past the river inspectors had continued to report that all sorts of monsters show themselves in the waves of the stream, at times in the shape of dragons, at others in that of cattle and horses, and whenever such a creature makes an appearance a great flood follows. Hence temples are built along the river banks. The higher spirits of the river are honored as kings, the lower ones as captains, and hardly a day goes by without their being honored with sacrifices or theatrical performances. Whenever, after a dam has been broken, the leak is closed again, the emperor sends officials with sacrifices and ten great bars of Tibetan incense. This incense is burned in a great sacrificial censer in the temple court, and the river inspectors and their subordinates all go to the temple to thank the gods for their aid. These river gods, it is said, are good and faithful servants of former rulers, who died in consequence of their toil in keeping the dams unbroken. After they died their spirits became river-kings; in their physical bodies, however, they appear as lizards, snakes and frogs.

The mightiest of all the river-kings is the Golden Dragon-King. He frequently appears in the shape of a small golden snake with a square head, low forehead and four red dots over his eyes. He can make himself large or small at will, and cause the waters to rise and fall. He appears and vanishes unexpectedly, and lives in the mouths of the Yellow River and the Imperial Canal. But in addition to the Golden Dragon-King there are dozens of river-kings and captains, each of whom has his own place. The sailors of the Yellow River all have exact lists in which the lives and deeds of the river-spirits are described in detail.

The river-spirits love to see theatrical performances. Opposite every temple is a stage. In the hall stands the little spirit-table of the river-king, and on the altar in front of it a small bowl of golden lacquer filled with clean sand. When a little snake appears in it, the river-king has arrived. Then the priests strike the gong and beat the drum and read from the holy books. The official is at once informed and he sends for a company of actors. Before they begin to perform the actors go up to the temple, kneel, and beg the king to let them know which play they are to give. And the river-god picks one out and points to it with his head; or else he writes signs in the sand with his tail. The actors then at once begin to perform the desired play.

The river-god cares naught for the fortunes or misfortunes of human beings. He appears suddenly and disappears in the same way, as best suits him.

Between the outer and the inner dam of the Yellow River are a number of settlements. Now it often happens that the yellow water moves to the very edge of the inner walls. Rising perpendicularly, like a wall, it gradually advances. When people see it coming they hastily burn incense, bow in prayer before the waters, and promise the river-god a theatrical performance. Then the water retires and the word goes round: "The river-god has asked for a play again!"

In a village in that section there once dwelt a wealthy man. He built a stone wall, twenty feet high, around the village, to keep away the water. He did not believe in the spirits of the river, but trusted in his strong wall and was quite unconcerned.

One evening the yellow water suddenly rose and towered in a straight line before the village. The rich man had them shoot cannon at it. Then the water grew stormy, and surrounded the wall to such a height that it reached the openings in the battlements. The water foamed and hissed, and seemed about to pour over the wall. Then every one in the village was very much frightened. They dragged up the rich man and he had to kneel and beg for pardon. They promised the river-god a theatrical performance, but in vain; but when they promised to build him a temple in the middle of the village and give regular performances, the water sank more and more and gradually returned to its bed. And the village fields suffered no damage, for the earth, fertilized by the yellow slime, yielded a double crop.

Once a scholar was crossing the fields with a friend in order to visit a relative. On their way they passed a temple of the river-god where a new play was just being performed. The friend asked the scholar to go in with him and look on. When they entered the temple court they saw two great snakes upon the front pillars, who had wound themselves about the colums, and were thrusting out their heads as though watching the performance. In the hall of the temple stood the altar with the bowl of sand. In it lay a small snake with a golden body, a green head and red dots above his eyes. His neck was thrust up and his glittering little eyes never left the stage. The friend bowed and the scholar followed his example.

Softly he said to his friend: "What are the three river-gods called?"

"The one in the temple," was the reply, "is the Golden Dragon-King. The two on the columns are two captains. They do not dare to sit in the temple together with the king."

This surprised the scholar, and in his heart he thought: "Such a tiny snake! How can it possess a god's power? It would have to show me its might before I would worship it."

He had not yet expressed these secret thoughts before the little snake suddenly stretched forth his head from the bowl, above the altar. Before the altar burned two enormous candles. They weighed more than ten pounds and were as thick as small trees. Their flame burned like the flare of a torch. The snake now thrust his head into the middle of the candle-flame. The flame must have been at least an inch broad, and was burning red. Suddenly its radiance turned blue, and was split into two tongues. The candle was so enormous and its fire so hot that even copper and iron would have melted in it; but it did not harm the snake.

Then the snake crawled into the censer. The censer was made of iron, and was so large one could not clasp it with both arms. Its cover showed a dragon design in open-work. The snake crawled in and out of the holes in this cover, and wound his way through all of them, so that he looked like an embroidery in threads of gold. Finally all the openings of the cover, large and small, were filled by the snake. In order to do so, he must have made himself several dozen feet long. Then he stretched out his head at the top of the censer and once more watched the play.

Thereupon the scholar was frightened, he bowed twice, and prayed: "Great King, you have taken this trouble on my account! I honor you from my heart!"

No sooner had he spoken these words than, in a moment, the little snake was back in his bowl, and just as small as he had been before.

In Dsiningdschou they were celebrating the river god's birthday in his temple. They were giving him a theatrical performance for a birthday present. The spectators crowded around as thick as a wall, when who should pass but a simple peasant from the country, who said in a loud voice: "Why, that is nothing but a tiny worm! It is a great piece of folly to honor it like a king!"

Before ever he had finished speaking the snake flew out of the temple. He grew and grew, and wound himself three times around the stage. He became as thick around as a small pail, and his head seemed like that of a dragon. His eyes sparkled like golden lamps, and he spat out red flame with his tongue. When he coiled and uncoiled the whole stage trembled and it seemed as though it would break down. The actors stopped their music and fell down on the stage in prayer. The whole multitude was seized with terror and bowed to the ground. Then some of the old men came along, cast the peasant on the ground, and gave him a good thrashing. So he had to cast himself on his knees before the snake and worship him. Then all heard a noise as though a great many firecrackers were being shot off. This lasted for some time, and then the snake disappeared.

East of Shantung lies the city of Dongschou. There rises an observation-tower with a great temple. At its feet lies the water-city, with a sea-gate at the North, through which the flood-tide rises up to the city. A camp of the boundary guard is established at this gate.

Once upon a time there was an officer who had been transferred to this camp as captain. He had formerly belonged to the land forces, and had not yet been long at his new post. He gave some friends of his a banquet, and before the pavilion in which they feasted lay a great stone shaped somewhat like a table. Suddenly a little snake was seen crawling on this stone. It was spotted with green, and had red dots on its square head. The soldiers were about to kill the little creature, when the captain went out to look into the matter. When he had looked he laughed and said: "You must not harm him! He is the river-king of Dsiningdschou. When I was stationed in Dsiningdschou he sometimes visited me, and then I always gave sacrifices and performances in his honor. Now he has come here expressly in order to wish his old friend luck, and to see him once more."

There was a band in camp; the bandsmen could dance and play like a real theatrical troupe. The captain quickly had them begin a performance, had another banquet with wine and delicate foods prepared, and invited the river-god to sit down to the table.

Gradually evening came and yet the river-god made no move to go.

So the captain stepped up to him with a bow and said: "Here we are far removed from the Yellow River, and these people have never yet heard your name spoken. Your visit has been a great honor for me. But the women and fools who have crowded together chattering outside, are afraid of hearing about you. Now you have visited your old friend, and I am sure you wish to get back home again."

With these words he had a litter brought up; cymbals were beaten and fire-works set off, and finally a salute of nine guns was fired to escort him on his way. Then the little snake crawled into the litter, and the

NATURE AND ANIMAL TALES

captain followed after. In this order they reached the port, and just when it was about time to say farewell, the snake was already swimming in the water. He had grown much larger, nodded to the captain with his head, and disappeared.

Then there were doubts and questionings: "But the river-god lives a thousand miles away from here, how does he get to this place?"

Said the captain: "He is so powerful that he can get to any place, and besides, from where he dwells a waterway leads to the sea. To come down that way and swim to sea is something he can do in a moment's time!"

Note: "The Spirits of the Yellow River." The place of the old river-god Ho Be (Count of the Stream), also mentioned in No. 62, has to-day been taken by the Dai Wang in the popular belief. These spirits are thought to have placed many hindrances in the way of the erection of the railroad bridge across the Yellow River. The "spirit-tablet": images of the gods were first introduced in China by the Buddhists. The old custom, which Confucianism and ancestor-worship still follow, holds that the seat of the gods is a small wooden tablet on which the name of the god to be honored is written. Theatrical performances as religious services are as general in China as they were in ancient Greece. Dsiningdschou is a district capital on the Imperial Canal, near the Yellow River.

XLV

THE DRAGON-PRINCESS

IN the Sea of Dungting there is a hill, and in that hill there is a hole, and this hole is so deep that it has no bottom.

Once a fisherman was passing there who slipped and fell into the hole. He came to a country full of winding ways which led over hill and dale for several miles. Finally he reached a dragon-castle lying in a great plain. There grew a green slime which reached to his knees. He went to the gate of the castle. It was guarded by a dragon who spouted water which dispersed in a fine mist. Within the gate lay a small hornless dragon who raised his head, showed his claws, and would not let him in.

The fisherman spent several days in the cave, satisfying his hunger with the green slime, which he found edible and which tasted like rice-mush. At last he found a way out again. He told the district mandarin what had happened to him, and the latter reported the matter to the emperor. The emperor sent for a wise man and questioned him concerning it.

The wise man said: "There are four paths in this cave. One path leads to the south-west shore of the Sea of Dungting, the second path leads to a valley in the land of the four rivers, the third path ends in a cave on the mountain of Lo-Fu and the fourth in an island of the Eastern Sea. In this cave dwells the seventh daughter of the Dragon-King of the Eastern Sea, who guards his pearls and his treasure. It happened once in the ancient days, that a fisherboy dived into the water and brought up a pearl from beneath the chin of a black dragon. The dragon was asleep, which was the reason the fisherboy brought the pearl to the surface without being harmed. The treasure which the daughter of the Dragon-King has in charge is made up of thousands and millions of such jewels. Several thousands of small dragons watch over them in her service. Dragons have the peculiarity of fighting shy of wax. But they are fond of beautiful jadestones, and of kung-tsing, the hollowgreen wood, and like to eat swallows. If one were to send a messenger with a letter, it would be possible to obtain precious pearls."

The emperor was greatly pleased, and announced

"A FISHERBOY DIVED INTO THE WATER AND BROUGHT UP A PEARL FROM BENEATH THE CHIN OF A BLACK DRAGON."

a large reward for the man who was competent to go to the dragon-castle as his messenger.

The first man to come forward was named So Pi-Lo. But the wise man said: "A great-great-great-great-grandfather of yours once slew more than a hundred of the dragons of the Eastern Sea, and was finally himself slain by the dragons. The dragons are the enemies of your family and you cannot go."

Then came a man from Canton, Lo-Dsi-Tschun, with his two brothers, who said that his ancestors had been related to the Dragon-King. Hence they were well liked by the dragons and well known to them. They begged to be entrusted with the message.

The wise man asked: "And have you still in your possession the stone which compels the dragons to do your will?"

"Yes," said they, "we have brought it along with us."

The wise man had them show him the stone; then he spoke: "This stone is only obeyed by the dragons who make clouds and send down the rain. It will not do for the dragons who guard the pearls of the sea-king." Then he questioned them further: "Have you the dragon-brain vapor?"

When they admitted that they had not, the wise man said: "How then will you compel the dragons to yield their treasure?"

And the emperor said: "What shall we do?"

The wise man replied: "On the Western Ocean sail foreign merchants who deal in dragon-brain vapor. Some one must go to them and seek it from them. I also know a holy man who is an adept in the art of taming dragons, and who has prepared ten pounds of the dragon-stone. Some one should be sent for that as well."

The emperor sent out his messengers. They met one of the holy man's disciples and obtained two fragments of dragon-stone from him.

Said the wise man: "That is what we want!"

Several more months went by, and at last a pill of dragon-brain vapor had also been secured. The emperor felt much pleased and had his jewelers carve two little boxes of the finest jade. These were polished with the ashes of the Wutung-tree. And he had an essence prepared of the very best hollowgreen wood, pasted with sea-fish lime, and hardened in the fire. Of this two vases were made. Then the bodies and the clothing of the messengers were rubbed with treewax, and they were given five hundred roasted swallows to take along with them.

They went into the cave. When they reached the dragon-castle, the little dragon who guarded the gate smelled the tree-wax, so he crouched down and did them no harm. They gave him a hundred roasted swallows as a bribe to announce them to the daughter of the Dragon-King. They were admitted to her presence and offered her the jade caskets, the vases and the four hundred roasted swallows as gifts. The dragon's daughter received them graciously, and they unfolded the emperor's letter.

In the castle there was a dragon who was over a thousand years old. He could turn himself into a human being, and could interpret the language of human beings. Through him the dragon's daughter learned that the emperor was sending her the gifts, and she returned them with a gift of three great pearls, seven smaller pearls and a whole bushel of ordinary pearls. The messengers took leave, rode off with their pearls on a dragon's back, and in a moment they had reached the banks of the Yangtze-kiang.

They made their way to Nanking, the imperial capital, and there handed over their treasure of gems.

The emperor was much pleased and showed them to the wise man. He said: "Of the three great pearls one is a divine wishing-pearl of the third class, and two are black dragon-pearls of medium quality. Of the seven smaller pearls two are serpent-pearls, and five are mussel-pearls. The remaining pearls are in part sea-crane pearls, in part snail and oyster-pearls. They do not approach the great pearls in value, and yet few will be found to equal them on earth."

The emperor also showed them to all his servants. They, however, thought the wise man's words all talk, and did not believe what he said.

Then the wise man said: "The radiance of wishing-pearls of the first class is visible for forty miles, that of the second class for twenty miles, and that of the third for ten miles. As far as their radiance carries, neither wind nor rain, thunder nor lightning, water, fire nor weapons may reach. The pearls of the black dragon are nine-colored and glow by night. Within the circle of their light the poison of serpents and worms is powerless. The serpent-pearls are seven-colored, the mussel-pearls five-colored. Both shine by night. Those most free from spots are the best. They grow within the mussel, and increase and decrease in size as the moon waxes and wanes."

Some one asked how the serpent- and sea-crane pearls could be told apart, and the wise man answered: "The animals themselves recognize them."

Then the emperor selected a serpent-pearl and a sea-crane pearl, put them together with a whole bushel of ordinary pearls, and poured the lot out in the courtyard. Then a large yellow serpent and a black crane were fetched and placed among the pearls. At once the crane took up a sea-crane pearl in his bill and began to dance and sing and flutter around. But the serpent snatched at the serpent-pearl, and wound himself about it in many coils. And when the people saw this they acknowledged the truth of the wise man's words. As regards the radiance of the larger and smaller pearls it turned out, too, just as the wise man had said.

In the dragon-castle the messengers had enjoyed dainty fare, which tasted like flowers, herbs, ointment and sugar. They had brought a remnant of it with them to the capital; yet exposed to the air it had become as hard as stone. The emperor commanded that these fragments be preserved in the treasury. Then he bestowed high rank and titles on the three brothers, and made each one of them a present of a thousand rolls of fine silk stuff. He also had investigated why it was that the fisherman, when he chanced upon the cave, had not been destroyed by the dragons. And it turned out that his fishing clothes had been soaked in oil and tree-wax. The dragons had dreaded the odor.

Note: As regards the Dragon-King of the Eastern Sea, see Nos. 18 and 75. The pearl under the dragon's chin comes from Dschuang Dsi. With regard to So Pi-Lo and Lo Dsi-Tschun, see No. 45.

XLVI

HELP IN NEED

SOME twenty miles east of Gingdschou lies the Lake of the Maidens. It is several miles square and surrounded on all sides by thick green thickets and tall forests. Its waters are clear and dark-blue. Often all kinds of wondrous creatures show themselves in the lake. The people of the vicinity have erected a temple there for the Dragon Princess. And in times of drought all make pilgrimage there to offer up prayers.

West of Gingdschou, two hundred miles away, is another lake, whose god is named Tschauna, and who performs many miracles. During the time of the Tang dynasty there lived in Gingdschou a mandarin by name of Dschou Bau. While he was in office it chanced that in the fifth month clouds suddenly arose in the sky, piling themselves up like mountains, among which wriggled dragons and serpents; they rolled up and down between the two seas. Tempest and rain, thunder and lightning arose so that houses fell to pieces, trees were torn up by the roots, and much damage was done the crops. Dschou Bau took the blame upon himself, and prayed to the heavens that his people might be pardoned.

On the fifth day of the sixth month he sat in his hall of audience and gave judgment; and suddenly he felt quite weary and sleepy. He took off his hat and laid down on the cushions. No sooner had he closed his eyes than he saw a warrior in helmet and armor, with a halberd in his hand, standing on the steps leading to the hall, who announced: "A lady is waiting outside who wishes to enter!" Dschou Bau asked him: "Who are you?" The answer was: "I am your door-keeper. In the invisible world I already have been performing his duty for many years." Meanwhile two figures clad in green came up the steps, knelt before him and said: "Our mistress has come to visit you!" Dschou Bau rose. He beheld lovely clouds, from which fell a fine rain, and strange fragrances enchanted him. Suddenly he saw a lady clad in a simple gown, but of surpassing beauty, float down from on high, with a retinue of many female servants. These were all neat and clean in appearance, and waited upon the lady as though she were a princess. When the latter entered the hall she raised her arms in greeting. Dschou Bau came forward to meet her and invited her to be seated. From all sides bright-colored clouds came floating in, and the court-yard was filled with a purple ether. Dschou Bau had wine and food brought and entertained them all in the most splendid way. But the goddess sat staring straight before her with wrinkled brows, and seemed to feel very sad. Then she rose and said with a blush: "I have been living in this neighborhood for many years. A wrong which has been done me, permits me to pass the bounds of what is fitting, and encourages me to ask a favor of you. Yet I do not know whether you wish to save me!"

"May I hear what it is all about," answered Dschou Bau. "If I can help you, I will be glad to place myself at your disposal."

The goddess said: "For hundreds of years my family has been living in the depth of the Eastern Sea. But we were unfortunate in that our treasures excited the jealousy of men. The ancestor of Pi-Lo nearly destroyed our entire clan by fire. My ancestors had to fly and hide themselves. And not long ago, our enemy Pi-Lo himself wanted to deliver an imperial letter in the cave of the Sea of Dungting. Under the pretext of begging for pearls and treasures, he wished to enter the dragon-castle and destroy our family. Fortunately a wise man saw through his treacherous purpose, and Lo-Dsi-Tschun and his brothers were sent in his stead. Yet my people did not feel safe from future attacks. For this reason they withdrew to the distant West. My father has done much good to mankind and hence is highly honored there. I am his ninth daughter. When I was sixteen I was wedded to the youngest son of the Rock-Dragon. But my good husband had a fiery temper, which often caused him to offend against the laws of courtesy, and in less than a year's time the punishment of heaven was his portion. I was left alone and returned to the home of my parents. My father wished me to marry again; but I had promised to remain true to the memory of my husband, and made a vow not to comply with my father's wish. My parents grew angry, and I was obliged to retire to this place in view of their anger. That was three years ago. Who could imagine that the contemptible dragon Tschauna, who was seeking a wife for his youngest brother, would try to force the wedding-gift upon me? I refused to accept it; but Tschauna knew how to gain his point with my father, and was determined to carry out his intention. My father, regardless of my wishes, promised me to him. And then the dragon Tschauna appeared with his youngest brother and wanted to carry me off by sheer force of arms. I encountered him with fifty faithful followers, and we fought on the meadow before the city. We were defeated, and I am more than ever afraid that Tschauna will attempt to drag me off. So I have plucked up courage to beg you to lend me your mercenaries so that I may beat off my foes and remain as I am. If you will help me I will be grateful to you till the end of my days."

Dschou Bau answered: "You come from a noble family. Have you no kinsfolk who will hasten to help you in your need, that you are compelled to turn to a mortal man?"

"It is true that my kinsfolk are far-famed and numerous. If I were to send out letters and they came to my aid, they would rub out that scaly scoundrel Tschauna as one might rub garlic. But my deceased husband offended the high heavens and he has not yet been pardoned. And my parents' will, too, is opposed to mine, so that I dare not call upon my kinsfolk for help.

You will understand my need." Then Dschou Bau promised to help her, and the princess thanked him and departed.

When he awoke, he sighed long thinking over his strange experience. And the following day he sent off fifteen hundred soldiers to stand guard by the Lake of the Maidens.

On the seventh day of the sixth month Dschou Bau rose early. Darkness still lay before the windows, yet it seemed to him as though he could glimpse a man before the curtain. He asked who it might be. The man said: "I am the princess's adviser. Yesterday you were kind enough to send soldiers to aid us in our distress. But they were all living men, and such cannot fight against invisible spirits. You will have to send us soldiers of yours who have died, if you wish to aid us."

Dschou Bau reflected for a time, and then it occurred to him that of course such must be the case. So he had his field-secretary examine the roster to see how many of his soldiers had fallen in battle. And the latter counted up to some two thousand foot-soldiers and five-hundred horsemen. Dschou Bau appointed his deceased officer Mong Yuan as their leader, and wrote his commands on a paper which he burned, in order thus to place them at the princess's disposal. The living soldiers he recalled. When they were being reviewed in the courtyard after their return, a soldier suddenly fell unconscious. It was not until early the following morning that he came to his senses again. He was questioned and replied: "I saw a man clad in red who approached me and said: 'Our princess is grateful for the aid your master has so kindly given her. Yet she still has a request to make and has asked me to call you.' I followed him to the temple. The princess bade me come forward and said to me: 'I thank your master from my heart for sending me the ghost soldiers, but Mong Yuan, their leader is incapable. Yesterday the robbers came with three thousand men, and Mong Yuan was beaten by them. When you return and again see your master, say that I earnestly beg him to send me a good general. Perhaps that will save me in my need.' Then she had me led back again and I regained consciousness."

When Dschou Bau had heard these words, which seemed to fit strangely well with what he had dreamed, he thought he would try to see if this were really the case. Therefore he chose his victorious general Dschong Tschong-Fu to take the place of Mong Yaun. That evening he burned incense, offered wine and handed over to the princess this captain's soul.

On the twenty-sixth of the month news came from the general's camp that he had suddenly died at midnight on the thirteenth. Dschou Bau was frightened, and sent a man to bring him a report. The latter informed him that the general's heart had hardly ceased to beat, and that, in spite of the hot summer weather, his body was free from any trace of decay. So the order was given not to bury him.

Then one night an icy, spectral wind arose, which whirled up sand and stones, broke trees and tore down houses. The standing corn in the fields was blown down. The storm lasted all day. Finally, the crash of a terrific thunderbolt was heard, and then the skies cleared and the clouds scattered. That very hour the dead general began to breathe painfully on his couch, and when his attendants came to him, he had returned to life again.

They questioned him and he told them: "First I saw a man in a purple gown riding a black horse, who came up with a great retinue. He dismounted before the door. In his hand he held a decree of appointment which he gave me, saying: 'Our princess begs you most respectfully to become her general. I hope that you will not refuse.' Then he brought forth gifts and heaped them up before the steps. Jade-stones, brocades, and silken garments, saddles, horses, helmets and suits of mail—he heaped them all up in the courtyard. I wished to decline, but this he would not allow, and urged me to enter his chariot with him. We drove a hundred miles and met a train of three-hundred armored horsemen who had ridden out to escort me. They led me to a great city, and before the city a tent had been erected in which played a band of musicians. A high official welcomed me. When I entered the city the onlookers were crowded together like walls. Servants ran to and fro bearing orders. We passed through more than a dozen gates before we reached the princess. There I was requested to dismount and change my clothes in order to enter the presence of the princess, for she wished to receive me as her guest. But I thought this too great an honor and greeted her below, on the steps. She, however, invited me to seat myself near her in the hall. She sat upright in all her incomparable beauty, surrounded by female attendants adorned with the richest jewels. These plucked lute-strings and played flutes. A throng of servitors stood about in golden girdles with purple tassels, ready to carry out her commands. Countless crowds were assembled before the palace. Five or six visitors sat in a circle about the princess, and a general led me to my place. The princess said to me: 'I have begged you to come here in order to entrust the command of my army to you. If you will break the power of my foe I will reward you richly.' I promised to obey her.

Then wine was brought in, and the banquet was served to the sound of music. While we were at table a messenger entered: 'The robber Tschauna has invaded our land with ten thousand footmen and horsemen, and is approaching our city by various roads. His way is marked by columns of fire and smoke!' The guests all grew pale with terror when they heard the news. And the princess said: 'This is the foe because of whom I have sought your aid. Save me in my hour of need!' Then she gave me two chargers, a suit of golden armor, and the insignia of a commander-in-chief, and bowed to me. I thanked her and went, called together the captains, had the army mustered and rode out before the city. At several decisive points I placed troops in ambush. The enemy was already approaching in great force, careless and unconcerned, intoxicated by his former victories. I sent out my most untrustworthy soldiers in advance, who allowed themselves to be beaten in order to lure him on. Light-armed men then went out against him, and retreated in skirmish order. And thus he fell into my ambush. Drums and kettledrums sounded together, the ring closed around them on all sides and the robber army suffered a grievous defeat. The dead lay about like hemp-stalks, but little Tschauna succeeded in breaking through the circle. I sent out the light horsemen after him, and they seized him before the tent of the enemy's commanding general. Hastily I sent word to the princess, and she reviewed the prisoners before the palace. All the people, high and low, streamed together, to acclaim her. Little Tschauna was about to be executed in the market place when a messenger came spurring up with a command from the princess's father to pardon him. The princess did not dare to disobey. So he was dismissed to his home after he had sworn to give up all thought of realizing his traitorous plans. I was loaded wth benefits as a reward for my victory. I was invested with an estate with three thousand peasants, and was given a palace, horses and wagons, all sorts of jewels, men-servants and women-servants, gardens and forests, banners and suits of mail. And my subordinate officers, too, were duly rewarded. On the following day a banquet was held, and the princess herself filled a goblet, sent it to me by one of her attendants, and said: 'Widowed early in life, I opposed the wishes of my stern father and fled to this spot. Here the infamous Tschauna harassed me and wellnigh put me to shame. Had not your master's great kindness and your own courage come to my assistance, hard would have been my lot!' Then she began to thank me and her tears of emotion flowed like a stream. I bowed and begged her to grant me leave of absence, so that I might look after my family. I was given a month's leave and the following day she dismissed me with a splendid retinue. Before the city a pavilion had been erected in which I drank the stirrup-cup. Then I rode away and when I arrived before our own gate a thunder-peal crashed and I awoke."

Thereupon the general wrote an account of what had happened to Dschou Bau, in which he conveyed the princess's thanks. Then he paid no further heed to worldly matters, but set his house in order and turned it over to his wife and son. When a month had passed, he died without any sign of illness.

That same day one of his officers was out walking. Suddenly he saw a heavy cloud of dust rising along the highway, while flags and banners darkened the sun. A thousand knights were escorting a man who sat his horse proudly and like a hero. And when the officer looked at his face, it was the general Dschong Tschong-**Fu**. Hastily he stepped to the edge of the road, in

NATURE AND ANIMAL TALES

order to allow the cavalcade to pass, and watched it ride by. The horsemen took the way to the Lake of the Maidens, where they disappeared.

Note: The expression: "Dschou Bau took the blame upon himself" is explained by the fact that the territorial mandarin is responsible for his district, just as the emperor is for the whole empire. Since extraordinary natural phenomena are the punishment of heaven, their occurrence supposed the guilt of man. This train of thought is in accord with the idea, as in this case, that differences occurring among the spirits of the air lead to misfortune, since where virtue is in the ascendant in the mortal world, the spirits are prevented from giving way to such demonstrations. "Drums and kettledrums sounded together": the kettledrums sounded the attack, and the drums the retreat. The simultaneous sounding of both signals was intended to throw the enemy's army into disorder.

XLVII

THE DISOWNED PRINCESS

AT the time that the Tang dynasty was reigning there lived a man named Liu I, who had failed to pass his examinations for the doctorate. So he traveled home again. He had gone six or seven miles when a bird flew up in a field, and his horse shied and ran ten miles before he could stop him. There he saw a woman who was herding sheep on a hillside. He looked at her and she was lovely to look upon, yet her face bore traces of hidden grief. Astonished, he asked her what was the matter.

The woman began to sob and said: "Fortune has forsaken me, and I am in need and ashamed. Since you are kind enough to ask I will tell you all. I am the youngest daughter of the Dragon-King of the Sea of

Dungting, and was married to the second son of the Dragon-King of Ging Dschou. Yet my husband ill-treated and disowned me. I complained to my step-parents, but they loved their son blindly and did nothing. And when I grew insistent they both became angry, and I was sent out here to herd sheep." When she had done, the woman burst into tears and lost all control of herself. Then she continued: "The Sea of Dungting is far from here; yet I know that you will have to pass it on your homeward journey. I should like to give you a letter to my father, but I do not know whether you would take it."

Liu I answered: "Your words have moved my heart. Would that I had wings and could fly away with you. I will be glad to deliver the letter to your father. Yet the Sea of Dungting is long and broad, and how am I to find him?"

"On the southern shore of the Sea stands an orange-tree," answered the woman, "which people call the tree of sacrifice. When you get there you must loosen your girdle and strike the tree with it three times in succession. Then some one will appear whom you must follow. When you see my father, tell him in what need you found me, and that I long greatly for his help."

Then she fetched out a letter from her breast and gave it to Liu I. She bowed to him, looked toward the east and sighed, and, unexpectedly, the sudden tears rolled from the eyes of Liu I as well. He took the letter and thrust it in his bag.

Then he asked her: "I cannot understand why you have to herd sheep. Do the gods slaughter cattle like men?"

"These are not ordinary sheep," answered the woman; "these are rain-sheep."

"But what are rain-sheep?"

"They are the thunder-rams," replied the woman.

And when he looked more closely he noticed that these sheep walked around in proud, savage fashion, quite different from ordinary sheep.

Liu I added: "But if I deliver the letter for you, and you succeed in getting back to the Sea of Dungting in safety, then you must not use me like a stranger."

The woman answered: "How could I use you as a stranger? You shall be my dearest friend."

And with these words they parted.

In course of a month Liu I reached the Sea of Dungting, asked for the orange-tree and, sure enough, found it. He loosened his girdle, and struck the tree with it three times. At once a warrior emerged from the waves of the sea, and asked: "Whence come you, honored guest?"

Liu I said: "I have come on an important mission and want to see the King."

The warrior made a gesture in the direction of the water, and the waves turned into a solid street along which he led Liu I. The dragon-castle rose before them with its thousand gates, and magic flowers and rare grasses bloomed in luxurious profusion. The warrior bade him wait at the side of a great hall.

Liu I asked: "What is this place called?"

"It is the Hall of the Spirits," was the reply.

Liu I looked about him: all the jewels known to earth were there in abundance. The columns were of white quartz, inlaid with green jade; the seats were made of coral, the curtains of mountain crystal as clear as water, the windows of burnished glass, adorned with rich lattice-work. The beams of the ceiling, ornamented with amber, rose in wide arches. An exotic fragrance filled the hall, whose outlines were lost in darkness.

Liu I had waited for the king a long time. To all

his questions the warrior replied: "Our master is pleased at this moment to talk with the priest of the sun up on the coral-tower about the sacred book of the fire. He will, no doubt, soon be through."

Liu I went on to ask: "Why is he interested in the sacred book of the fire?"

The reply was: "Our master is a dragon. The dragons are powerful through the power of water. They can cover hill and dale with a single wave. The priest is a human being. Human beings are powerful through fire. They can burn the greatest palaces by means of a torch. Fire and water fight each other, being different in their nature. For that reason our master is now talking with the priest, in order to find a way in which fire and water may complete each other."

Before they had quite finished there appeared a man in a purple robe, bearing a scepter of jade in his hand.

The warrior said: "This is my master!"

Liu I bowed before him.

The king asked: "Are you not a living human being? What has brought you here?"

Liu I gave his name and explained: "I have been to the capital and there failed to pass my examination. When I was passing by the Ging Dschou River, I saw your daughter, whom you love, herding sheep in the wilderness. The winds tousled her hair, and the rain drenched her. I could not bear to see her trouble and spoke to her. She complained that her husband had cast her out and wept bitterly. Then she gave me a letter for you. And that is why I have come to visit you, O King!"

With these words he fetched out his letter and handed it to the king. When the latter had read it, he hid his face in his sleeve and said with a sigh: "It is my own fault. I picked out a worthless husband for her. Instead of securing her happiness I have brought her to shame in a distant land. You are a stranger and yet you have been willing to help her in her distress, for which I am very grateful to you." Then he once more began to sob, and all those about him shed tears. Thereupon the monarch gave the letter to a servant who took it into the interior of the palace; and soon the sound of loud lamentations rose from the inner rooms.

The king was alarmed and turned to an official: "Go and tell them within not to weep so loudly! I am afraid that Tsian Tang may hear them."

"Who is Tsian Tang?" asked Liu I.

"He is my beloved brother," answered the king. "Formerly he was the ruler of the Tsian-Tang River, but now he has been deposed."

Liu I asked: "Why should the matter be kept from him?"

"He is so wild and uncontrollable," was the reply, "that I fear he would cause great damage. The deluge which covered the earth for nine long years in the time of the Emperor Yau was the work of his anger. Because he fell out with one of the kings of heaven, he caused a great deluge that rose and covered the tops of five high mountains. Then the king of heaven grew angry with him, and gave him to me to guard. I had to chain him to a column in my palace."

Before he had finished speaking a tremendous turmoil arose, which split the skies and made the earth tremble, so that the whole palace began to rock, and smoke and clouds rose hissing and puffing. A red dragon, a thousand feet long, with flashing eyes, blood-red tongue, scarlet scales and a fiery beard came surging up. He was dragging along through the air the column to which he had been bound, together with its chain. Thunders and lightnings roared and darted around his body; sleet and snow, rain and hail-stones whirled about him in confusion. There was a crash of thunder, and he flew up to the skies and disappeared.

Liu I fell to earth in terror. The king helped him up with his own hand and said: "Do not be afraid! That is my brother, who is hastening to Ging Dschou in his rage. We will soon have good news!"

Then he had food and drink brought in for his guest. When the goblet had thrice made the rounds, a gentle breeze began to murmur and a fine rain fell. A youth clad in a purple gown and wearing a lofty hat entered. A sword hung at his side. His appearance was manly and heroic. Behind him walked a girl radiantly beautiful, wearing a robe of misty fragrance. And when Liu I looked at her, lo, it was the dragon-princess whom he had met on his way! A throng of maidens in rosy garments received her, laughing and giggling, and led her into the interior of the palace. The king, however, presented Liu I to the youth and said: "This is Tsian Tang, my brother!"

Tsian Tang thanked him for having brought the message. Then he turned to his brother and said: "I have fought against the accursed dragons and have utterly defeated them!"

"How many did you slay?"

"Six hundred thousand."

"Were any fields damaged?"

"The fields were damaged for eight hundred miles around."

"And where is the heartless husband?"

"I ate him alive!"

Then the king was alarmed and said: "What the fickle boy did was not to be endured, it is true. But

"TSIAN TANG BROUGHT OUT A PLATTER OF RED AMBER
ON WHICH LAY A CARBUNCLE."
—Page 157

still you were a little too rough with him; in future you must not do anything of the sort again." And Tsian Tang promised not to.

That evening Liu I was feasted at the castle. Music and dancing lent charm to the banquet. A thousand warriors with banners and spears in their hands stood at attention. Trombones and trumpets resounded, and drums and kettledrums thundered and rattled as the warriors danced a war-dance. The music expressed how Tsian Tang had broken through the ranks of the enemy, and the hair of the guest who listened to it rose on his head in terror. Then, again, there was heard the music of strings, flutes and little golden bells. A thousand maidens in crimson and green silk danced around. The return of the princess was also told in tones. The music sounded like a song of sadness and plaining, and all who heard it were moved to tears. The King of the Sea of Dungting was filled with joy. He raised his goblet and drank to the health of his guest, and all sorrow departed from them. Both rulers thanked Liu I in verses, and Liu I answered them in a rimed toast. The crowd of courtiers in the palace-hall applauded. Then the King of the Sea of Dungting drew forth a blue cloud-casket in which was the horn of a rhinoceros, which divides the water. Tsian Tang brought out a platter of red amber on which lay a carbuncle. These they presented to their guest, and the other inmates of the palace also heaped up embroideries, brocades and pearls by his side. Surrounded by shimmer and light Liu I sat there, smiling, and bowed his thanks to all sides. When the banquet was ended he slept in the Palace of Frozen Radiance.

On the following day another banquet was held. Tsian Tang, who was not quite himself, sat carelessly on his seat and said: "The Princess of the Dungting

Sea is handsome and delicately fashioned. She has had the misfortune to be disowned by her husband, and to-day her marriage is annulled. I should like to find another husband for her. If you were agreeable it would be to your advantage. But if you were not willing to marry her, you may go your way, and should we ever meet again we will not know each other."

Liu I was angered by the careless way in which Tsian Tang spoke to him. The blood rose to his head and he replied: "I served as a messenger, because I felt sorry for the princess, but not in order to gain an advantage for myself. To kill a husband and carry off a wife is something an honest man does not do. And since I am only an ordinary man, I prefer to die rather than do as you say."

Tsian Tang rose, apologized and said: "My words were over-hasty. I hope you will not take them ill!" And the King of the Dungting Sea also spoke kindly to him, and censured Tsian Tang because of his rude speech. So there was no more said about marriage.

On the following day Liu I took his leave, and the Queen of the Dungting Sea gave a farewell banquet in his honor.

With tears the queen said to Liu I: "My daughter owes you a great debt of gratitude, and we have not had an opportunity to make it up to you. Now you are going away and we see you go with heavy hearts!"

Then she ordered the princess to thank Liu I.

The princess stood there, blushing, bowed to him and said: "We will probably never see each other again!" Then tears choked her voice.

It is true that Liu I had resisted the stormy urging of her uncle, but when he saw the princess standing before him in all the charm of her loveliness, he felt sad at heart; yet he controlled himself and went his way.

The treasures which he took with him were incalculable. The king and his brother themselves escorted him as far as the river.

When, on his return home, he sold no more than a hundredth part of what he had received, his fortune already ran into the millions, and he was wealthier than all his neighbors. He decided to take a wife, and heard of a widow who lived in the North with her daughter. Her father had become a Taoist in his later years and had vanished in the clouds without ever returning. The mother lived in poverty with the daughter; yet since the girl was beautiful beyond measure she was seeking a distinguished husband for her.

Liu I was content to take her, and the day of the wedding was set. And when he saw his bride unveiled on the evening of her wedding day, she looked just like the dragon-princess. He asked her about it, but she merely smiled and said nothing.

After a time heaven sent them a son. Then she told her husband: "To-day I will confess to you that I am truly the Princess of Dungting Sea. When you had rejected my uncle's proposal and gone away, I fell ill of longing, and was near death. My parents wanted to send for you, but they feared you might take exception to my family. And so it was that I married you disguised as a human maiden. I had not ventured to tell you until now, but since heaven has sent us a son, I hope that you will love his mother as well."

Then Liu I awoke as though from a deep sleep, and from that time on both were very fond of each other.

One day his wife said: "If you wish to stay with me eternally, then we cannot continue to dwell in the world of men. We dragons live ten thousand years, and you shall share our longevity. Come back with me to the Sea of Dungting!"

Ten years passed and no one knew where Liu I, who had disappeared, might be. Then, by accident, a relative went sailing across the Sea of Dungting. Suddenly a blue mountain rose up out of the water.

The seamen cried in alarm: "There is no mountain on this spot! It must be a water-demon!"

While they were still pointing to it and talking, the mountain drew near the ship, and a gaily-colored boat slid from its summit into the water. A man sat in the middle, and fairies stood at either side of him. The man was Liu I. He beckoned to his cousin, and the latter drew up his garments and stepped into the boat with him. But when he had entered the boat it turned into a mountain. On the mountain stood a splendid castle, and in the castle stood Liu I, surrounded with radiance, and with the music of stringed instruments floating about him.

They greeted each other, and Liu I said to his cousin: "We have been parted no more than a moment, and your hair is already gray!"

His cousin answered: "You are a god and blessed: I have only a mortal body. Thus fate has decreed."

Then Liu I gave him fifty pills and said: "Each pill will extend your life for the space of a year. When you have lived the tale of these years, come to me and dwell no longer in the earthly world of dust, where there is nothing but toil and trouble."

Then he took him back across the sea and disappeared.

His cousin, however, retired from the world, and fifty years later, and when he had taken all the pills, he disappeared and was never seen again.

Note: The outcast princess is represented as "herding sheep." In Chinese the word sheep is often used as an image for clouds. (Sheep and goats are designated by the same word in Chinese.) Tsian

NATURE AND ANIMAL TALES

Tang is the name of a place used for the name of the god of that place. The deluge is the flood which the great Yu regulated as minister of the Emperor Yau. It is here represented in an exaggerated sense, as a deluge.

XLVIII

FOX-FIRE

ONCE upon a time there was a strong young farmer who came home late one evening from market. His way led him past the gardens of a wealthy gentleman, in which stood a number of tall buildings. Suddenly he saw something shining floating in the air inside the gardens, something which glowed like a ball of crystal. He was astonished, and climbed the wall around the gardens, but there was not a human being in sight; all he saw was, at a distance, something which appeared to be a dog, looking up at the moon. And whenever it blew its breath out a ball of fire came out of its mouth, and rose to the moon. And whenever it drew its breath in the ball sank down again, and it caught it in its jaws. And so it went on without a stop. Then the farmer realized that it was a fox, who was preparing the elixir of life. He hid in the grass and waited until the ball of fire came down again, at about the heighth of his own head. Then he stepped hastily from his hiding-place, took it away and at once swallowed it. And he could feel it glow as it passed down his throat into his stomach. When the fox saw what had happened he grew angry. He looked furiously at the farmer, but feared his strength. For this reason he did not dare attack him, but went angrily on his way.

From that time on the farmer-boy could make himself invisible, was able to see ghosts and devils, and had intercourse with the spirit-world. In cases of sickness, when people lay unconscious, he could call back their souls, and if some one had committed a sin he could plead for them. He earned much money owing to these gifts.

When he reached his fiftieth year, he withdrew from all things and would no longer exercise his arts. One summer evening he was sitting in his courtyard, enjoying the cool air. While there he drank a number of goblets of wine, and by midnight had fallen fast asleep. Suddenly he awoke, feeling ill. It seemed as though some one were patting him on the back, and before he knew it, the ball of fire had leaped out from his throat. At once a hand reached for it and a voice said: "For thirty long years you kept my treasure from me, and from a poor farmer-lad you have grown to be a wealthy man. Now you have enough, and I would like to have my fire-ball back again!"

Then the man knew what had happened, but the fox was gone.

Note: The thought underlying the story is the belief that the fox prepares the elixir of life out of his own breath, which he allows to rise to the moon. If a thief can rob him of the elixir he gains supernatural powers.

GHOST STORIES

XLIX

THE TALKING SILVER FOXES

THE silver foxes resemble other foxes, but are yellow, fire-red or white in color. They know how to influence human beings, too. There is a kind of silver fox which can learn to speak like a man in a year's time. These foxes are called "Talking Foxes."

South-west of the bay of Kaiutschou there is a mountain by the edge of the sea, shaped like a tower, and hence known as Tower Mountain. On the mountain there is an old temple with the image of a goddess, who is known as the Old Mother of Tower Mountain. When children fall ill in the surrounding villages, the magicians often give orders that paper figures of them be burned at her altar, or little lime images of them be placed around it. And for this reason the altar and its surroundings are covered with hundreds of figures of children made in lime. Paper flowers, shoes and clothing are also brought to the Old Mother, and lie in a confusion of colors. The pilgrimage festivals take place on the third day of the third month, and the ninth day of the ninth month, and then there are theatrical performances, and the holy writings are read. And there is also an annual fair. The girls and women of the neighborhood burn incense and pray to the goddess. Parents who have no children go there and pick out one of the little children made of lime, and tie a red thread around its neck, or even secretly break off a small bit of its body, dissolve it in water and drink it. Then they pray quietly that a child may be sent them.

Behind the temple is a great cave where, in former times, some talking foxes used to live. They would even come out and seat themselves on the point of a steep rock by the wayside. When a wanderer came by they would begin to talk to him in this fashion: "Wait a bit, neighbor; first smoke a pipe!" The traveler would look around in astonishment, to see where the voice came from, and would become very much frightened. If he did not happen to be exceptionally brave, he would begin to perspire with terror, and run away. Then the fox would laugh: "Hi hi!"

Once a farmer was plowing on the side of the mountain. When he looked up he saw a man with a straw hat, wearing a mantle of woven grass and carrying a pick across his shoulder coming along the way.

"Neighbor Wang," said he, "first smoke a pipeful and take a little rest! Then I will help you plow."

Then he called out "Hu!" the way farmers do when they talk to their cattle.

The farmer looked at him more closely and saw then that he was a talking fox. He waited for a favorable opportunity, and when it came gave him a lusty blow with his ox-whip. He struck home, for the fox screamed, leaped into the air and ran away. His straw hat, his mantle of woven grass and the rest he left lying on the ground. Then the farmer saw that the straw hat was just woven out of potato-leaves; he had cut it in two with his whip. The mantle was made of oak-leaves, tied together with little blades of grass. And the pick was only the stem of a kau-ling plant, to which a bit of brick had been fastened.

Not long after, a woman in a neighboring village became possessed. A picture of the head priest of the

Taoists was hung up in her room, but the evil spirit did not depart. Since there were none who could exorcise devils in the neighborhood, and the trouble she gave was unendurable, the woman's relatives decided to send to the temple of the God of War and beg for aid.

But when the fox heard of it he said: "I am not afraid of your Taoist high-priest nor of your God of War; the only person I fear is your neighbor Wang in the Eastern village, who once struck me cruelly with his whip."

This suited the people to a T. They sent to the Eastern village, and found out who Wang was. And Wang took his ox-whip and entered the house of the possessed woman.

Then he said in a deep voice: "Where are you? Where are you? I have been on your trail for a long time. And now, at last, I have caught you!"

With that he snapped his whip.

The fox hissed and spat and flew out of the window.

They had been telling stories about the talking fox of Tower Mountain for more than a hundred years when one fine day, a skilful archer came to that part of the country who saw a creature like a fox, with a fiery-red pelt, whose back was striped with gray. It was lying under a tree. The archer aimed and shot off its hind foot.

At once it said in a human voice: "I brought myself into this danger because of my love for sleep; but none may escape their fate! If you capture me you will get at the most no more than five thousand pieces of copper for my pelt. Why not let me go instead? I will reward you richly, so that all your poverty will come to an end."

But the archer would not listen to him. He killed

him, skinned him and sold his pelt; and, sure enough, he received five thousand pieces of copper for it.

From that time on the fox-spirit ceased to show itself.

Note: The silver fox is known in Chinese as "Pi," the same word also being used for "panthers," since this legendary beast partakes of the nature of both animals. "The Old Mother" is really the mother-goddess of the Taischan. But in other localities she is chiefly honored as a child-giving goddess. "A picture of the head priest of the Taoists": Talismans painted by the head priest of the Taoists or the Taoist pope, the so-called "Master of the Heavens," (Tian Schi) have special virtues against all kinds of sorcery and enchantment. The war god Guan Di also is appealed to as a savior in all sorts of emergencies.

L

THE CONSTABLE

IN a city in the neighborhood of Kaiutschou there once lived a constable by the name of Dung. One day when he returned from a hunt after thieves the twilight had already begun to fall. So before he waded through the stream that flowed through the city he sat down on the bank, lit a pipe and took off his shoes. When he looked up, he suddenly saw a man in a red hat dressed as a constable crouching beside him.

Astonished, he inquired: "Who are you? Your clothes indicate that you are a member of our profession, but I have never yet seen you among the men of our local force. Tell me, pray, whence you come?"

The other answered: "I am weary, having come a long journey, and would like to enjoy a pipeful of tobacco in your company. I am sure you will not object to that."

Dung handed him a pipe and tobacco.

But the other constable said: "I do not need them. Just you keep on smoking. It is enough for me to enjoy the odor."

So they chatted awhile together, and together waded through the stream. And gradually they became quite confidential and the stranger said: "I will be quite frank with you. I am the head constable of the Nether World, and am subject to the Lord of the Great Mountain. You yourself are a constable of reputation here in the upper world. And, because of my skill, I have standing in the world below. Since we are so well suited to each other, I should like to enter into a bond of brotherhood with you."

Dung was agreeable and asked: "But what really brings you here?"

Said the other: "In your district there lives a certain Wang, who was formerly superintendent of the granaries, and at that time caused the death of an officer. This man has now accused him in the Nether World. The King of the Nether World cannot come to a decision in the case, and therefore has asked the Lord of the Great Mountain to settle it. The Lord of the Great Mountain has ordered that Wang's property and life be shortened. First his property is to be sequestered here in the upper world, and then his soul is to be dragged to the nether one. I have been sent out by the Judge of the Dead to fetch him. Yet the established custom is, when some one is sent for, that the constable has first to report to the god of the city. The god of the city then issues a summons, and sends one of his own spirit constables to seize the soul and deliver it over to me. Only then may I take it away with me."

Dung asked him further particulars; but the other

merely said: "Later on you will see it all for yourself."

When they reached the city Dung invited his colleague to stay at his home, and entertained him with wine and food. But the other only talked and touched neither the goblet nor the chop-sticks.

Said Dung: "In my haste I could not find any better meal for you. I am afraid it is not good enough."

But his guest replied: "O no, I am already surfeited and satisfied! We spirits feed only on odors; in which respect we differ from men."

It was late at night before he set out to visit the temple of the city god.

No sooner did morning dawn that he reappeared to take farewell and said: "Now all is in order: I am off! In two years' time you will go to Yaianfu, the city near the Great Mountain, and there we will meet again."

Dung began to feel ill at ease. A few days later, in fact, came the news that Wang had died. The district mandarin journeyed to the dead man's natal village in order to express his sympathy. Among his followers was Dung. The inn-keeper there was a tenant of Wang's.

Dung asked him: "Did anything out of the ordinary happen when Sir Wang died?"

"It was all very strange," answered the inn-keeper, "and my mother who had been very busy in his house, came home and fell into a violent fever. She was unconscious for a day and a night, and could hardly breathe. She came to on the very day when the news of Sir Wang's death was made public, and said: 'I have been to the Nether World and I met him there. He had chains about his neck and several devils were

dragging him along. I asked him what he had done, but he said: "I have no time to tell you now. When you return ask my wife and she will tell you all!"'
And yesterday my mother went there and asked her. And Wang's wife told her with tears: 'My master was an official, but for a long time he did not make any head-way. He was superintendent of the granaries in Nanking, and in the same city was a high officer, with whom my master became very intimate. He always came to visit at our house and he and my master would talk and drink together. One day my master said to him: "We administrative mandarins have a large salary and a good income besides. You are an officer, and have even reached the second step in rank, yet your salary is so small that you cannot possibly make it do. Have you any other income aside from it?" The officer replied: "We are such good friends that I know I can speak openly to you. We officers are compelled to find some additional sources of revenue in order that our pockets may not be altogether empty. When we pay our men we make a small percentage of gains on the exchange; and we also carry more soldiers on our rosters than there actually are present. If we had to live on our salaries we would die of hunger!"

"'When my husband heard him say this he could not rid himself of the idea that by disclosing these criminal proceedings the State would be indebted to him, and that it would surely aid his plans for advancement. On the other hand, he reflected that it would not be right to abuse his friend's confidence. With these ideas in his mind he retired to his inner rooms. In the courtyard stood a round pavilion. Lost in heavy thought, he crossed his hands behind his back, and for a long time walked round and round the pavilion. Finally he said with a sigh: "Charity begins at home; I will sacrifice my friend!" Then he drew up his report, in which the officer was indicted. An imperial order was issued, the matter was investigated, and the officer was condemned to death. My husband, however, was at once increased in rank, and from that time on advanced rapidly. And with the exception of myself no one ever knew anything of the matter.' When my mother told them of her encounter with Wang in the Nether World, the whole family burst into loud weeping. Four tents full of Buddhist and Taoist priests were sent for, who fasted and read masses for thirty-five days in order that Wang might be delivered. Whole mountains of paper money, silk and straw figures were burned, and the ceremonies have not as yet come to an end."

When Dung heard this he was very much frightened.

Two years later he received an order to journey to Taianfu in order to arrest some robbers there. He thought to himself: "My friend, the spirit, must be very powerful indeed, to have known about this trip so far in advance. I must inquire for him. Perhaps I will see him again."

When he reached Taianfu he sought out an inn.

The inn-keeper received him with the words: "Are you Master Dung, and have you come from the bay of Kaiutschou?"

"I am the man," answered Dung, alarmed, "how do you happen to know me?"

The inn-keeper replied: "The constable of the temple of the Great Mountain appeared to me last night and said: 'To-morrow a man by the name of Dung who is a good friend of mine is coming from the bay of Kaiutschou!' And then he described your appearance and your clothes to me exactly, and told me to make careful note of them, and when you came to treat you with the greatest consideration, and to take no pay from you, since he would repay me lavishly. So when I saw you coming everything was exactly as my dreams had foretold, and I knew you at once. I have already prepared a quiet room for you, and beg that you will condescend to make yourself at ease.''

Joyfully Dung followed him, and the inn-keeper waited on him with the greatest consideration, and saw that he had great plenty to eat and to drink.

At midnight the spirit arrived. Without having opened the door, he stood by Dung's bedside, gave him his hand, and asked how things had gone with him since he had last seen him.

Dung answered all his questions and thanked him into the bargain for appearing to the inn-keeper in a dream.

He continued to live for some days at the inn. During the day he went walking on the Great Mountain and at night his friend came to visit him and talked with him, and at the same time asked him what had happened to Sir Wang.

"His sentence has already been spoken," answered the other. "This man pretended to be conscientious, and traitorously brought about the death of his friend. Of all sins there is no greater sin than this. As a punishment he will be sent forth again into the world as an animal." Then he added: "When you reach home you must take constant care of your health. Fate has allowed you seventy-eight years of mortal life When your time is up I will come to fetch you myself. Then I will see that you obtain a place as constable in the Nether World, where we can always be together."

When he had said this, he disappeared.

Note: "The Constable" is a tale of modern origin. The Lord of the Great Mountain (Taischan) is even greater than Yan Wang, the God of Death. His Temple of the Easterly Holy Mountain (Dung Yuo Miau), is to be found in every district capital. These temples play an important part in the care of the dead before interment.

LI

THE DANGEROUS REWARD

ONCE upon a time a man named Hu-Wu-Bau, who lived near the Great Mountain, went walking there one day. And there, under a tree, he met a messenger in a red robe who called out to him: "The Lord of the Great Mountain would like to see you!" The man was much frightened, but dared offer no objection. The messenger bade him shut his eyes, and when he was allowed to open them again after a short time, he found himself standing before a lofty palace. He entered it to see the god. The latter had a meal prepared for him and said: "I only sent for you to-day because I had heard you intended traveling to the West. And in that case I should like to give you a letter to take to my daughter."

"But where is your daughter?" asked the man.

"She is married to the river-god," was the reply. "All you need to do is to take along the letter lying there. When you reach the middle of the Yellow River, beat against the side of the ship and call out: 'Green-coat!' Then some one will appear and take the letter from you."

And with these words he handed Hu-Wu-Bau the letter, and he was taken back again to the upper world.

When he came to the Yellow River on his journey, he did what the Lord of the Great Mountain had told him, and cried: "Greencoat!" And sure enough, a girl in green garments rose from the water, took him by the hand and told him to close his eyes. Then she led him into the palace of the river-god and he delivered the letter. The river-god entertained him splendidly, and thanked him as best he knew how. At parting he said: "I am grateful that you have made this long journey to see me. I have nothing to give you, however, save this pair of green silk shoes. While you are wearing them you can keep on walking as long as you like and never grow weary. And they will give you the second sight, so that you will be able to see the spirits and gods."

The man thanked him for the gift and returned to his ship. He continued on his journey to the West, and after a year had passed, came back again. When he reached the Great Mountain, he thought it would be fit and proper to report to the god. So he once more knocked against the tree and gave his name. In a moment the red-clad messenger appeared and led him to the Lord of the Mountain. So he reported that he had delivered the letter to the river-god, and how all things were there, and the Lord of the Mountain thanked him. During the meal which the god had prepared for him, he withdrew for a few moments to a quiet spot. Suddenly he saw his deceased father, bound and loaded with chains, who together with several hundred other criminals, was doing menial labor.

Moved to tears, he asked: "O my father, why are you here?"

His father replied: "During my life on earth I happened to tread on bread, hence I was condemned to hard labor at this spot. I have passed two years in this manner, yet their bitterness has been unspeakable. Since you are acquainted with the Lord of the Mountain, you might plead for me, and beg him to excuse me from this task and make me the field-god in our village."

His son promised to do so, and went back and pleaded with the Lord of the Mountain as he had agreed. The latter seemed inclined to listen to his prayer, yet said warningly: "The quick and the dead tread different paths. It is not well for the dead and the living to abide near one another permanently."

The man returned home. Yet, in about a year's time nearly all his children had died. In the terror of his heart he turned to the Lord of the Great Mountain. He beat on the tree; the red-coat came and led him into the palace. There he told of his misfortune and begged the god to protect him. The Lord of the Mountain smiled: "Did I not tell you in the start that the quick and the dead tread different paths, and that it is not well if they abide near each other permanently? Now you see what has happened!" Yet he sent his messenger to fetch the man's father. The father came and the god spake to him as follows: "I forgave you your offense and sent you back to your home as a field-god. It was your duty to bring happiness to your family. Instead, nearly all of your grand-children have died off. Why is this?"

And the father said: "I had been away from home so long that I was overjoyed to return. Besides I had meat and drink in overflowing measure. So I thought of my little grand-children and called them to me."

Then the Lord of the Great Mountain appointed another field-god for that village, and also gave the father another place. And from that time no further misfortune happened to the family of Hu-Wu-Bau.

Note: The Lord of the Great Mountain was originally Huang Fe-Hu, a faithful servant of the tyrant Dschou-Sin. Because of an insult offered him, he joined King Wu, and when the latter overcame the tyrant, was made Lord of the Mountain, and overlord of the ten princes of the nether world.

LII

RETRIBUTION

ONCE upon a time there was a boy named Ma, whose father taught him himself, at home. The window of the upper story looked out on the rear upon a terrace belonging to old Wang, who had a garden of chrysanthemums there. One day Ma rose early, and stood leaning against the window, watching the day dawn. And out came old Wang from his terrace and watered his chrysanthemums. When he had just finished and was going in again, along came a water-carrier, bearing two pails on his shoulders, who seemed to want to help him. But the old man grew annoyed and motioned him off. Yet the water-carrier insisted on mounting the terrace. So they pulled each other about on the terrace-edge. It had been raining, the terrace was slippery, its border high and narrow, and when the old man thrust back the water-carrier with his hand, the latter lost his balance, slipped and tumbled down the slope. Then the old man hastened down to pick him up; but the two pails had fallen on his chest and he lay there with feet outstretched. The old man was extremely frightened. Without uttering a sound, he took hold of the water-carrier's feet, and dragged him through the back door to the bank of the stream which flowed by the garden. Then he fetched the pails and set them down beside the corpse. After that he went home, locked the door and went to bed again.

Little Ma, in spite of his youth, thought it would be

better to say nothing about an affair of this kind, in which a human life was involved. He shut the window and withdrew. The sun rose higher, and soon he heard a clamor without: "A dead man is lying on the riverbank!" The constable gave notice, and in the afternoon the judge came up to the beating of gongs, and the inspector of the dead knelt down and uncovered the corpse; yet the body showed no wound. So it was said: "He slipped and fell to his death!" The judge questioned the neighbors, but the neighbors all insisted that they knew nothing of the matter. Thereupon the judge had the body placed in a coffin, sealed it with his seal, and ordered that the relatives of the deceased be found. And then he went his way.

Nine years passed by, and young Ma had reached the age of twenty-one and become a baccalaureate. His father had died, and the family was poor. So it came about that in the same room in which he had formerly studied his lessons, he now gathered a few pupils about him, to instruct them.

The time for examinations drew near. Ma had risen early, in order to work. He opened the window and there, in the distant alley, he saw a man with two pails gradually drawing nearer. When he looked more closely, it was the water-carrier. Greatly frightened, he thought that he had returned to repay old Wang. Yet he passed the old man's door without entering it. Then he went a few steps further to the house of the Lis; and there went in. The Lis were wealthy people, and since they were near neighbors the Mas and they were on a visiting footing. The matter seemed very questionable to Ma, and he got up and followed the water-carrier.

At the door of Li's house he met an old servant who was just coming out and who said: "Heaven is about to send a child to our mistress! I must go buy incense to burn to the gods in order to show our gratitude!"

Ma asked: "Did not a man with two pails of water on his shoulder just go in?"

The servant said there had not, but before he had finished speaking a maid came from the house and said: "You need not go to buy incense, for I have found some. And, through the favor of heaven, the child has already come to us." Then Ma began to realize that the water-carrier had returned to be born again into the life of earth, and not to exact retribution. He wondered, though, for what merit of his the former water-carrier happened to be re-born into so wealthy a family. So he kept the matter in mind, and from time to time inquired as to the child's well-being.

Seven more years went by, and the boy gradually grew up. He did not show much taste for learning, but he loved to keep birds. Old Wang was still strong and healthy. And though he was by this time more than eighty years old, his love for his chrysanthemums had only increased with age.

One day Ma once more rose early, and stood leaning against his window. And he saw old Wang come out upon his terrace and begin to water his chrysanthemums. Little Li sat in the upper story of his house flying his pigeons. Suddenly some of the pigeons flew down on the railing of the flower-garden. The boy was afraid they might fly off and called them, but the pigeons did not move. The boy did not know what to do: he picked up stones and threw them at the birds. By mistake one of them struck old Wang. The old man started, slipped, and fell down over the terrace. Time passed and he did not rise. He lay there with his feet outstretched. The boy was very much frightened.

Without uttering a sound he softly closed his window and went away. The sun gradually rose higher, and the old man's sons and grandsons all came out to look for him. They found him and said: "He slipped and fell to his death!" And they buried him as was the custom.

Note: This little tale, from the "Sin Tsi Hia," is a literary masterpiece because of the exactness with which the punishment follows upon the act, long after the latter has been forgiven, and all chance of mishap seemed to have passed.

LIII

THE GHOST WHO WAS FOILED

THERE are ghosts of many kinds, but the ghosts of those who have hung themselves are the worst. Such ghosts are always coaxing other living people to hang themselves from the beams of the roof. If they succeed in persuading some one to hang himself, then the road to the Nether World is open to them, and they can once more enter into the wheel of transformation. The following story of such a ghost is told by persons worthy of belief.

Once upon a time there lived a man in Tsing Tschoufu who had passed his military examination, and had been ordered to Tsinanfu to report for duty. It was at the season of rains. So it happened that evening came on before he could reach the town-inn where he had expected to pass the night. Just as the sun was setting he reached a small village and asked for a night's lodging. But there were only poor families in the village who had no room for him in their huts. So

GHOST STORIES

they directed him to an old temple which stood outside the village, and said he could spend the night there.

The images of the gods in the temple were all decayed, so that one could not distinguish one from the other. Thick spider-webs covered the entrance, and the dust lay inches high everywhere. So the soldier went out into the open, where he found an old flight of steps. He spread out his knapsack on a stone step, tied his horse to an old tree, took his flask from his pocket and drank—for it had been a hot day. There had been a heavy rain, but it had just cleared again. The new moon was on the decline. The soldier closed his eyes and tried to sleep.

Suddenly he heard a rustling sound in the temple, and a cool wind passed over his face and made him shudder. And he saw a woman come out of the temple, dressed in an old dirty red gown, and with a face as white as a chalk wall. She stole past quietly as though she were afraid of being seen. The soldier knew no fear. So he pretended to be asleep and did not move, but watched her with half-shut eyes. And he saw her draw a rope from her sleeve and disappear. Then he knew that she was the ghost of one who had hung herself. He got up softly and followed her, and, sure enough, she went into the village.

When she came to a certain house she slipped into the court through a crack in the door. The soldier leaped over the wall after her. It was a house with three rooms. In the rear room a lamp was burning dimly. The soldier looked through the window into the room, and there was a young woman of about twenty sitting on the bed, sighing deeply, and her kerchief was wet through with tears. Beside her lay a little child, asleep. The woman looked up toward the beam of the ceiling. One moment she would weep and the next she would stroke the child. When the soldier looked more closely, there was the ghost sitting up on the beam. She had passed the rope around her neck and was hanging herself in dumb show. And whenever she beckoned with her hand the woman looked up toward her. This went on for some time.

Finally the woman said: "You say it would be best for me to die. Very well, then, I will die; but I cannot part from my child!"

And once more she burst into tears. But the ghost merely laughed and coaxed her again.

So the woman said determinedly: "It is enough. I will die!"

With these words she opened her chest of clothes, put on new garments, and painted her face before the mirror. Then she drew up a bench and climbed up on it. She undid her girdle and knotted it to the beam. She had already stretched forth her neck and was about to leap from the bench, when the child suddenly awoke and began to cry. The woman climbed down again and soothed and quieted her child, and while she was petting it she wept, so that the tears fell from her eyes like a string of pearls. The ghost frowned and hissed, for it feared to lose its prey. In a short time the child had fallen asleep again, and the woman once more began to look aloft. Then she rose, again climbed on the bench, and was about to lay the noose about her neck when the soldier began to call out loudly and drum on the window-pane. Then he broke it and climbed into the room. The woman fell to the ground and the ghost disappeared. The soldier recalled the woman to consciousness, and then he saw something hanging down from the beam, like a cord without an end. Knowing that it belonged to the ghost of the hanged woman he took and kept it.

Then he said to the woman: "Take good care of your child! You have but one life to lose in this world!"

And with that he went out.

Then it occurred to him that his horse and his baggage were still in the temple. And he went there to get them. When he came out of the village there was the ghost, waiting for him in the road.

The ghost bowed and said: "I have been looking for a substitute for many years, and to-day, when it seemed as though I should really get one, you came along and spoiled my chances. So there is nothing more for me to do. Yet there is something which I left behind me in my hurry. You surely must have found it, and I will ask you to return it to me. If I only have this one thing, my not having found a substitute will not worry me."

Then the soldier showed her the rope and said with a laugh: "Is this the thing you mean? Why, if I were to give it back to you then some one is sure to hang themselves. And that I could not allow."

With these words he wound the rope around his arm, drove her off and said: "Now be off with you!"

But then the ghost grew angry. Her face turned greenish-black, her hair fell in wild disorder down her neck, her eyes grew bloodshot, and her tongue hung far out of her mouth. She stretched forth both hands and tried to seize the soldier, but he struck out at her with his clenched fist. By mistake he hit himself in the nose and it began to bleed. Then he sprinkled a few drops of blood in her direction and, since the ghosts cannot endure human blood, she ceased her attack, moved off a few paces and began to abuse him. This she did for some time, until the cock in the village began to crow. Then the ghost disappeared.

In the meantime the farmer-folk of the village had come to thank the soldier. It seems that after he had left the woman her husband had come home, and asked his wife what had happened. And then for the first time he had learned what had occurred. So they all set out together along the road in order to look for the soldier outside the village. When they found him he was still beating the air with his fists and talking wildly. So they called out to him and he told them what had taken place. The rope could still be seen on his bare arm; yet it had grown fast to it, and surrounded it in the shape of a red ring of flesh.

The day was just dawning, so the soldier swung himself into his saddle and rode away.

Note: This tale has been handed down traditionally, and is given as told among the people.

LIV

THE PUNISHMENT OF GREED

ONCE upon a time there lived a man south of the Yangtze-kiang. He had taken a position as a teacher in Sutschoufu, on the border of Shantung. But when he got there he found that the schoolhouse had not yet been completed. Yet a two-story building in the neighborhood had been rented, in which the teacher was to live and hold school in the meantime. This house stood outside the village, not far from the river bank. A broad plain, overgrown with tangled brush, stretched out from it on every side. The teacher was pleased with the view.

Well, one evening he was standing in the door of his house watching the sun go down. The smoke that rose from the village chimneys gradually merged with the twilight shadows. All the noises of the day had died away. Suddenly, off in the distance, along the river bank, he beheld a fiery gleam. He hurried away at once in order to see what it might be. And there, on the bank, he found a wooden coffin, from which came the radiance he had noticed. Thought the teacher to himself: "The jewels with which they adorn the dead on their journey shine by night. Perhaps there are gems in the coffin!" And greed awoke in his heart, and he forgot that a coffin is a resting-place of the dead and should be respected. He took up a large stone, broke the cover of the coffin, and bent over to look more closely. And there in the coffin lay a youth. His face was as white as paper, he wore a mourning turban on his head, his body was wrapped in hempen garments, and he wore straw sandals on his feet. The teacher was greatly frightened and turned to go away. But the corpse had already raised itself to a sitting posture. Then the teacher's fear got the better of him, and he began to run. And the corpse climbed out of its coffin and ran after him. Fortunately the house was not far away. The teacher ran as fast as he could, flew up the steps and locked the door after him. Gradually he caught his breath again. Outside there was not a sound to be heard. So he thought that perhaps the corpse had not followed him all the way. He opened the window and peered down. The corpse was leaning against the wall of the house. Suddenly it saw that the window had been opened, and with one leap it bounded up and in through it. Overcome by terror, the teacher fell down the stairs of the house, and rolled unconscious to the bottom of the flight. And when he did so the corpse fell down on the floor of the room above.

At the time the school children had all long since gone home. And the owner of the house lived in another dwelling, so that no one knew anything about what had happened. On the following morning the children came to school as usual. They found the door locked, and when they called no one answered. Then they broke down the door and found their teacher lying unconscious on the ground. They sprinkled him with ginger, but it took a long time before he woke from his coma. When they asked he told them all that had occurred. Then they all went upstairs and took away the corpse. It was taken outside the village limits and burned, and the bones which remained were once more laid in the coffin. But the teacher said, with a sigh: "Because of a moment's greed, I nearly lost my life!" He resigned his position, returned home and never, through all the days of his life, did he speak of gain again.

Note: The corpse wears a mourning turban and is dressed in mourning. According to local tradition, young people who die before their parents, are laid in their coffins clad in mourning, so that even in death they may do their duty and be able to mourn their parents when the latter shall have died. The tale is taken from the Sc Tsi Hia.

LV

THE NIGHT ON THE BATTLEFIELD

ONCE upon a time there was a merchant, who was wandering toward Shantung with his wares, along the road from the South. At about the second watch of the night, a heavy storm blew up from the

North. And he chanced to see an inn at one side of the road, whose lights were just being lit. He went in to get something to drink and order lodgings for the night, but the folk at the inn raised objections. Yet an old man among them took pity on his unhappy situation and said: "We have just prepared a meal for warriors who have come a long distance, and we have no wine left to serve you. But there is a little side room here which is still free, and there you may stay overnight." With these words he led him into it. But the merchant could not sleep because of his hunger and thirst. Outside he could hear the noise of men and horses. And since all these proceedings did not seem quite natural to him, he got up and looked through a crack in the door. And he saw that the whole inn was filled with soldiers, who were sitting on the ground, eating and drinking, and talking about campaigns of which he had never heard. After a time they began calling to each other: "The general is coming!" And far off in the distance could be heard the cries of his body-guard. All the soldiers hurried out to receive him. Then the merchant saw a procession with many paper lanterns, and riding in their midst a man of martial appearance with a long beard. He dismounted, entered the inn, and took his place at the head of the board. The soldiers mounted guard at the door, awaiting his commands, and the inn-keeper served food and drink, to which the general did full justice.

When he had finished his officers entered, and he said to them: "You have now been underway for some time. Go back to your men. I shall rest a little myself. It will be time enough to beat the assembly when the order to advance is given."

The officers received his commands and withdrew.

Then the general called out: "Send Asti in!" and a young officer entered from the left side of the house. The people of the inn locked the gates and withdrew for the night, while Asti conducted the long-haired general to a door at the left, through a crack of which shone the light of a lamp. The merchant stole from his room and looked through the crack in the door. Within the room was a bed of bamboo, without covers or pillows. The lamp stood on the ground. The long-bearded general took hold of his head. It came off and he placed it on the bed. Then Asti took hold of his arms. These also came off and were carefully placed beside the head. Then the old general threw himself down on the bed crosswise, and Asti took hold of his body, which came apart below the thighs, and the two legs fell to the ground. Then the lamp went out. Overcome by terror the merchant hurried back to his room as fast as he could, holding his sleeves before his eyes, and laid down on his bed, where he tossed about sleepless all night.

At last he heard a cock crow in the distance. He was shivering. He took his sleeves from his face and saw that dawn was stealing along the sky. And when he looked about him, there he was lying in the middle of a thick clump of brush. Round about him was a wilderness, not a house, not even a grave was to be seen anywhere. In spite of being chilled, he ran about three miles till he came to the nearest inn. The inn-keeper opened the door and asked him with astonishment where he came from at that early hour. So the merchant told him his experiences and inquired as to the sort of place at which he had spent the night. The inn-keeper shook his head: "The whole neighborhood is covered with old battlefields," was his reply, "and all sorts of supernatural things take place on them after dark."

Note: This tale is taken from the Sin Tsi Hia.

LVI

THE KINGDOM OF THE OGRES

IN the land of Annam there once dwelt a man named Su, who sailed the seas as a merchant. Once his ship was suddenly driven on a distant shore by a great storm. It was a land of hills broken by ravines and green with luxuriant foliage, yet he could see something along the hills which looked like human dwellings. So he took some food with him and went ashore. No sooner had he entered the hills than he could see at either hand the entrances to caves, one close beside the other, like a row of beehives. So he stopped and looked into one of the openings. And in it sat two ogres, with teeth like spears and eyes like fiery lamps. They were just devouring a deer. The merchant was terrified by this sight and turned to flee; but the ogres had already noticed him and they caught him and dragged him into their cave. Then they talked to each other with animal sounds, and were about to tear his clothes from his body and devour him. But the merchant hurriedly took a bag of bread and dried meat out and offered it to them. They divided it, ate it up and it seemed to taste good to them. Then they once more went through the bag; but he gestured with his hand to show them that he had no more.

Then he said: "Let me go! Aboard my ship I have frying-pans and cooking-pots, vinegar and spices. With these I could prepare your food."

The ogres did not understand what he was saying, however, and were still ferocious. So he tried to make them understand in dumb show, and finally they seemed to get an idea of his meaning. So they went to the ship with him, and he brought his cooking gear to the cave, collected brush-wood, made a fire and cooked the remains of the deer. When it was done to a turn he gave them some of it to eat, and the two creatures devoured it with the greatest satisfaction. Then they left the cave and closed the opening with a great rock. In a short space of time they returned with another deer they had caught. The merchant skinned it, fetched fresh water, washed the meat and cooked several kettles full of it. Suddenly in came a whole herd of ogres, who devoured all he had cooked, and became quite animated over their eating. They all kept pointing to the kettle which seemed too small to them. When three or four days had passed, one of the ogres dragged in an enormous cooking-pot on his back, which was thenceforth used exclusively.

Now the ogres crowded about the merchant, bringing him wolves and deer and antelopes, which he had to cook for them, and when the meat was done they would call him to eat it with them.

Thus a few weeks passed and they gradually came to have such confidence in him that they let him run about freely. And the merchant listened to the sounds which they uttered, and learned to understand them. In fact, before very long he was able to speak the language of the ogres himself. This pleased the latter greatly, and they brought him a young ogre girl and made her his wife. She gave him valuables and fruit to win his confidence, and in course of time they grew much attached to each other.

One day the ogres all rose very early, and each one of them hung a string of radiant pearls about his neck. They ordered the merchant to be sure and cook a great quantity of meat. The merchant asked his wife what it all meant.

"This will be a day of high festival," answered she, "we have invited the great king to a banquet."

But to the other ogres she said: "The merchant has no string of pearls!"

Then each of the ogres gave him five pearls and his wife added ten, so that he had fifty pearls in all. These his wife threaded and hung the pearl necklace about his neck, and there was not one of the pearls which was not worth at least several hundred ounces of silver.

Then the merchant cooked the meat, and having done so left the cave with the whole herd in order to receive the great king. They came to a broad cave, in the middle of which stood a huge block of stone, as smooth and even as a table. Round it were stone seats. The place of honor was covered with a leopard-skin, and the rest of the seats with deerskins. Several dozen ogres were sitting around the cave in rank and file.

Suddenly a tremendous storm blew up, whirling around the dust in columns, and a monster appeared who had the figure of an ogre. The ogres all crowded out of the cave in a high state of excitement to receive him. The great king ran into the cave, sat down with his legs outstretched, and glanced about him with eyes as round as an eagle's. The whole herd followed him into the cave, and stood at either hand of him, looking up to him and folding their arms across their breasts in the form of a cross in order to do him honor.

The great king nodded, looked around and asked: "Are all the folk of the Wo-Me hills present?"

The entire herd declared that they were.

Then he saw the merchant and asked: "From whence does he hail?"

His wife answered for him, and all spoke with praise of his art as a cook. A couple of ogres brought in the cooked meat and spread it out on the table. Then the great king ate of it till he could eat no more, praised it with his mouth full, and said that in the future they were always to furnish him with food of this kind.

Then he looked at the merchant and asked: "Why is your necklace so short?"

With these words he took ten pearls from his own necklace, pearls as large and round as bullets of a blunderbuss. The merchant's wife quickly took them on his behalf and hung them around his neck; and the merchant crossed his arms like the ogres and spoke his thanks. Then the great king went off again, flying away like lightning on the storm.

In the course of time heaven sent the merchant children, two boys and a girl. They all had a human form and did not resemble their mother. Gradually the children learned to speak and their father taught them the language of men. They grew up, and were soon so strong that they could run across the hills as though on level ground.

One day the merchant's wife had gone out with one of the boys and the girl and had been absent for half-a-day. The north wind was blowing briskly, and in the merchant's heart there awoke a longing for his old home. He took his son by the hand and went down to the sea-shore. There his old ship was still lying, so he climbed into it with his boy, and in a day and a night was back in Annam again.

When he reached home he loosened two of his pearls from his chain, and sold them for a great quantity of gold, so that he could keep house in handsome style. He gave his son the name of Panther, and when the boy was fourteen years of age he could lift thirty hundred weight with ease. Yet he was rough by nature and fond of fighting. The general of Annam, astonished at his bravery, appointed him a colonel, and in putting down a revolt his services were so meritorious that he was already a general of the second rank when but eighteen.

At about this time another merchant was also driven ashore by a storm on the island of Wo-Me. When he reached land he saw a youth who asked him with astonishment: "Are you not from the Middle Kingdom?"

The merchant told him how he had come to be driven ashore on the island, and the youth led him to a little cave in a secret valley. Then he brought deer-flesh for him to eat, and talked with him. He told him that his father had also come from Annam, and it turned out that his father was an old acquaintance of the man to whom he was talking.

"We will have to wait until the wind blows from the North," said the youth, "then I will come and escort you. And I will give you a message of greeting to take to my father and brother."

"Why do you not go along yourself and hunt up your father?" asked the merchant.

"My mother does not come from the Middle Kingdom," replied the youth. "She is different in speech and appearance, so it cannot well be."

One day the wind blew strongly from the North, and the youth came and escorted the merchant to his ship, and ordered him, at parting, not to forget a single one of his words.

When the merchant returned to Annam, he went to the palace of Panther, the general, and told him all that had happened. When Panther listened to him telling about his brother, he sobbed with bitter grief. Then he secured leave of absence and sailed out to sea with two soldiers. Suddenly a typhoon arose, which lashed the waves until they spurted sky-high. The ship turned turtle, and Panther fell into the sea. He was seized by a creature and flung up on a strand where there seemed to be dwellings. The creature who had seized him looked like an ogre, so Panther addressed him in the ogre tongue. The ogre, surprised, asked him who he was, and Panther told him his whole story.

The ogre was pleased and said: "Wo-Me is my old home, but it lies about eight thousand miles away from here. This is the kingdom of the poison dragons."

Then the ogre fetched a ship and had Panther seat himself in it, while he himself pushed the ship before him through the water so that it clove the waves like an arrow. It took a whole night, but in the morning a shoreline appeared to the North, and there on the strand stood a youth on look-out. Panther recognized his brother. He stepped ashore and they clasped hands and wept. Then Panther turned around to thank the ogre, but the latter had already disappeared.

Panther now asked after his mother and sister and was told that both were well and happy, so he wanted to go to them with his brother. But the latter told him to wait, and went off alone. Not long after he came back with their mother and sister. And when they saw Panther, both wept with emotion. Panther now begged them to return with him to Annam.

But his mother replied: "I fear that if I went, people would mock me because of my figure."

"I am a high officer," replied Panther, "and people would not dare to insult you."

So they all went down to the ship together with him. A favorable wind filled their sails and they sped home swiftly as an arrow flies. On the third day they reached land. But the people whom they encountered were all seized with terror and ran away. Then Panther took off his mantle and divided it among the three so that they could dress themselves.

When they reached home and the mother saw her husband again, she at once began to scold him violently because he had said not a word to her when he went away. The members of his family, who all came to greet the wife of the master of the house, did so with fear and trembling. But Panther advised his mother to learn the language of the Middle Kingdom, dress in silks, and accustom herself to human food. This she agreed to do; yet she and her daughter had men's clothing made for them. The brother and sister gradually grew more fair of complexion, and looked like the people of the Middle Kingdom. Panther's brother was named Leopard, and his sister Ogrechild. Both possessed great bodily strength.

But Panther was not pleased to think that his brother was so uneducated, so he had him study. Leopard was highly gifted; he understood a book at first reading; yet he felt no inclination to become a man of learning. To shoot and to ride was what he best loved to do. So he rose to high rank as a professional soldier, and finally married the daughter of a distinguished official.

It was long before Ogrechild found a husband, because all suitors were afraid of their mother-in-law to be. But Ogrechild finally married one of her brother's subordinates. She could draw the strongest bow, and strike the tiniest bird at a distance of a hundred paces. Her arrow never fell to earth without having scored a hit. When her husband went out to battle she always accompanied him, and that he finally became a general was largely due to her. Leopard was already a field marshal at the age of thirty, and his mother accompanied him on his campaigns. When a dangerous enemy drew near, she buckled on armor, and took a knife in her hand to meet him in place of her son. And among the enemies who encountered her there was not a single one who did not flee from her in terror. Because of her courage the emperor bestowed upon her the title of "The Superwoman."

Note: The ogres here mentioned are the primitive inhabitants of the Island of Ceylon, also called Rakshas, who appear in legend as man-devouring monsters.

LVII

THE MAIDEN WHO WAS STOLEN AWAY

IN the western portion of the old capital city of Lo Yang there was a ruined cloister, in which stood an enormous pagoda, several hundred stories high. Three or four people could still find room to stand on its very top.

Not far from it there lived a beautiful maiden, and one very hot summer's day she was sitting in the courtyard of her home, trying to keep cool. And as she sat there a sudden cyclone came up and carried her off. When she opened her eyes, there she was on top of the pagoda, and beside her stood a young man in the dress of a student.

He was very polite and affable, and said to her: "It seems as though heaven had meant to bring us together, and if you promise to marry me, we will be very happy." But to this the maiden would not agree. So the student said that until she changed her mind she would have to remain on the pagoda-top. Then he produced bread and wine for her to satisfy her hunger and thirst, and disappeared.

Thereafter he appeared each day and asked her whether she had changed her mind, and each day she told him she had not. When he went away he always carefully closed the openings in the pagoda-top with stones, and he had also removed some of the steps of the stairs, so that she could not climb down. And when he came to the pagoda-top he always brought her food and drink, and he also presented her with rouge and powder, dresses and mandarin-coats and all sorts of jewelry. He told her he had bought them in the market place. And he also hung up a great carbuncle-stone so that the pagoda-top was bright by night as well as by day. The maiden had all that heart could wish, and yet she was not happy.

But one day when he went away he forgot to lock the window. The maiden spied on him without his knowing it, and saw that from a youth he turned himself into an ogre, with hair as red as madder and a face as black as coal. His eyeballs bulged out of their sockets, and his mouth looked like a dish full of blood. Crooked white fangs thrust themselves from his lips, and two wings grew from his shoulders. Spreading them, he flew down to earth and at once turned into a man again.

The maiden was seized with terror and burst into tears. Looking down from her pagoda she saw a wanderer passing below. She called out, but the pagoda was so high that her voice did not carry down to him. She beckoned with her hand, but the wanderer did not look up. Then she could think of nothing else to do but to throw down the old clothes she had formerly worn. They fluttered through the air to the ground.

The wanderer picked up the clothes. Then he looked up at the pagoda, and quite up at the very top he saw a tiny figure which looked like that of a girl; yet he could not make out her features. For a long time he wondered who it might be, but in vain. Then he saw a light.

"My neighbor's daughter," said he to himself, "was carried away by a magic storm. Is it possible that she may be up there?"

So he took the clothes with him and showed them to the maiden's parents, and when they saw them they burst into tears.

But the maiden had a brother, who was stronger and braver than any one for miles around. When the tale had been told him he took a heavy ax and went to the pagoda. There he hid himself in the tall grass and waited for what would happen. When the sun was just going down, along came a youth, tramping the hill. Suddenly he turned into an ogre, spread his wings and was about to fly. But the brother flung his ax at him and struck him on the arm. He began to roar loudly, and then fled to the western hills. But when the brother saw that it was impossible to climb the pagoda, he went back and enlisted the aid of several neighbors. With them he returned the following morning and they climbed up into the pagoda. Most of the steps of the stairway were in good condition, for the ogre had only destroyed those at the top. But they were able to get up with a ladder, and then the brother fetched down his sister and brought her safely home again.

And that was the end of the enchantment.

Note: In this tale the ogre is a Yakscha or a Fe Tian Ya Tscha.

LVIII

THE FLYING OGRE

THERE once lived in Sianfu an old Buddhist monk, who loved to wander in lonely places. In the course of his wanderings he once came to the Kuku-Nor, and there he saw a tree which was a thousand feet high and many cords in breadth. It was hollow inside and one could see the sky shining down into it from above.

When he had gone on a few miles, he saw in the distance a girl in a red coat, barefoot, and with unbound hair, who was running as fast as the wind. In a moment she stood before him.

"Take pity on me and save my life!" said she to him.

When the monk asked her what was the trouble, she replied: "A man is pursuing me. If you will tell him you have not seen me, I will be grateful to you all my life long!"

With that she ran up to the hollow tree and crawled into it.

When the monk had gone a little further, he met one who rode an armored steed. He wore a garment of gold, a bow was slung across his shoulders, and a sword hung at his side. His horse ran with the speed of lightning, and covered a couple of miles with every step. Whether it ran in the air or on the ground, its speed was the same.

"Have you seen the girl in the red coat?" asked the stranger. And when the monk replied that he had seen nothing, the other continued: "Bonze, you should not lie! This girl is not a human being, but a flying ogre. Of flying ogres there are thousands of varieties, who bring ruin to people everywhere. I have already slain a countless number of them, and have pretty well done away with them. But this one is the worst of all. Last night the Lord of the Heavens gave me a triple command, and that is the reason I have hurried down from the skies. There are eight thousand of us under way in all directions to catch this monster. If you do not tell the truth, monk, then you are sinning against heaven itself!"

Upon that the monk did not dare deceive him, but pointed to the hollow tree. The messenger of the skies dismounted, stepped into the tree and looked about him. Then he once more mounted his horse, which carried him up the hollow trunk and out at the end of the tree. The monk looked up and could see a small, red flame come out of the tree-top. It was followed by the messenger of the skies. Both rose up to the clouds and disappeared. After a time there fell a rain of blood. The ogre had probably been hit by an arrow or captured.

Afterward the monk told the tale to the scholar who wrote it down.

Note: This flying ogre is also of the Yakscha tribe.

LIX

BLACK ARTS

THE wild people who dwell in the South-West are masters of many black arts. They often lure men of the Middle Kingdom to their country by promising them their daughters in marriage, but their promises are not to be trusted. Once there was the son of a poor family, who agreed to labor for three years for one of the wild men in order to become his son-in-law. At the end of that time the wedding was celebrated, and the couple were given a little house for a home. But no sooner had they entered it than the wife warned her husband to be on his guard, since her parents did not like him, and would seek to do him harm. In accordance with the custom she entered the house first with a lighted lantern, but when the bridegroom followed her she had disappeared. And thus it went, day by day. During the daytime she was there, but when evening came she disappeared.

And one day, not long after they had been married, his wife said to him: "To-morrow morning my mother celebrates her birthday, and you must go to congratulate her. They will offer you tea and food. The tea you may drink, but be sure not to touch any of the food. Keep this in mind!"

So the following day the wife and husband went to her mother's home and offered their congratulations. Her parents seemed highly pleased, and served them with tea and sweets. The son-in-law drank, but ate nothing, though his wife's parents, with kind words and friendly gestures, kept urging him to help himself. At last the son-in-law did not know what to do, and thought that surely they could mean him no ill. And seeing the fresh caught eels and crabs on the plate before him, he ate a little of them. His wife gave him a reproachful glance, and he offered some excuse for taking his leave.

But his mother-in-law said: "This is my birthday. You simply must taste my birthday noodles!"

With that she placed a great dish before him, filled with noodles that looked like threads of silver, mingled with fat meat, and spiced with fragrant mushrooms. During all the time he had been living in the country the son-in-law had never yet seen such an appetizing dish. Its pleasant odor rose temptingly to his nostrils, and he could not resist raising his chop-sticks. His wife glanced over at him, but he pretended that he did not see her.

She coughed significantly, but he acted as though he did not hear. Finally she trod on his foot under the table; and then he regained control of himself.

He had not as yet eaten half of the food and said: "My hunger is satisfied."

Then he took leave, and went off with his wife.

"This is a serious matter," said the latter. "You would not listen to my words, and now you will surely have to die!"

But still he did not believe her, until he suddenly felt terrible pains, which soon grew unbearable, so that he fell to the ground unconscious. His wife at once hung him up by the feet from the beam of the roof, and put a panful of glowing charcoal under his body, and a great jar of water, into which she had poured sesame oil, in front of the fire, directly below his mouth. And when the fire had heated him thoroughly, he suddenly opened his mouth—and can you imagine what came out of it? A squirming, crawling mass of poisonous worms, centipedes, toads and tadpoles, who all fell into the jar of water. Then his wife untied him, carried him to bed, and gave him wine mingled with realgar to drink. Then he recovered.

"What you ate in the belief that they were eels and crabs," said his wife, "were nothing but toads and tadpoles, and the birthday noodles were poisonous worms and centipedes. But you must continue to be careful. My parents know that you have not died, and they will think up other evil plans."

A few days later his father-in-law said to him: "There is a large tree growing on the precipice which juts over the cave. In it is the nest of the phœnix. You are still young and able to climb, so go there quickly and fetch me the eggs!"

His son-in-law went home and told his wife.

"Take long bamboo poles," said she, "and tie them together, and fasten a curved sword at the top. And take these nine loaves of bread and these hens' eggs, there are seven times seven of them. Carry them along with you in a basket. When you come to the spot you will see a large nest up in the branches. Do not climb the tree, but chop it down with the curved sword. Then throw away your poles, and run for dear life. Should a monster appear and follow you, throw him the loaves of bread, three loaves at a time, and finally throw down the eggs on the ground and make for home as quickly as you can. In this way you may escape the danger which threatens you."

The man noted all she said exactly and went. And sure enough he saw the bird's nest—it was as large as a round pavilion. Then he tied his curved sword to the poles, chopped at the tree with all his strength, laid down his poles on the ground and never looked around but ran for dear life. Suddenly he heard the roaring of a thunder-storm rising above him. When he looked up he saw a great dragon, many fathoms long and some ten feet across. His eyes gleamed like two lamps and he was spitting fire and flame from his maw. He had stretched out two feelers and was feeling along the ground. Then the man swiftly flung the loaves into the air. The dragon caught them, and it took a little time before he had devoured them. But no sooner had the man gained a few steps than the dragon once more came flying after him. Then he flung him more loaves and when the loaves came to an end, he turned over his basket so that the eggs rolled over the ground. The dragon had not yet satisfied his hunger and opened his greedy jaws wide. When he suddenly caught sight of the eggs, he descended from the air, and since the eggs were scattered round about, it took some time before he had sucked them all. In the meantime the man succeeded in escaping to his home.

When he entered the door and saw his wife, he said to her, amid sobs: "It was all I could do to escape, and I am lucky not to be in the dragon's stomach! If this sort of thing keeps up much longer I am bound to die!"

With these words he kneeled and begged his wife pitifully to save his life.

"Where is your home?" asked his wife.

"My home is about a hundred miles away from here, in the Middle Kingdom, and my old mother is still living. The only thing that worries me is that we are so poor."

His wife said: "I will flee with you, and we will find your mother. And waste no regrets on your poverty."

With that she gathered up all the house held in the

way of pearls and precious stones, put them in a bag and had her husband tie it around his waist. Then she also gave him an umbrella, and in the middle of the night they climbed the wall with the aid of a ladder, and stole away.

His wife had also said to him: "Take the umbrella on your back and run as fast as ever you can! Do not open it, and do not look around! I will follow you in secret."

So he turned North and ran with all his might and main. He had been running for a day and a night, had covered nearly a hundred miles, and passed the boundaries of the wild people's country, when his legs gave out and he grew hungry. Before him lay a mountain village. He stopped at the village gate to rest, drew some food from his pocket and began to eat. And he looked around without being able to see his wife.

Said he to himself: "Perhaps she has deceived me after all, and is not coming with me!"

After he had finished eating, he took a drink from a spring, and painfully dragged himself further. When the heat of the day was greatest a violent mountain rain suddenly began to fall. In his haste he forgot what his wife had told him and opened his umbrella. And out fell his wife upon the ground.

She reproached him: "Once more you have not listened to my advice. Now the damage has been done!"

Quickly she told him to go to the village, and there to buy a white cock, seven black tea-cups, and half a length of red nettlecloth.

"Do not be sparing of the silver pieces in your pocket!" she cried after him as he went off.

He went to the village, attended to everything,

and came back. The woman tore the cloth apart, made a coat of it and put it on. No sooner had they walked a few miles before they could see a red cloud rising up in the South, like a flying bird.

"That is my mother," said the woman.

In a moment the cloud was overhead. Then the woman took the black tea-cups and threw them at it. Seven she threw and seven fell to earth again. And then they could hear the mother in the cloud weeping and scolding, and thereupon the cloud disappeared.

They went on for about four hours. Then they heard a sound like the noise of silk being torn, and could see a cloud as black as ink, which was rushing up against the wind.

"Alas, that is my father!" said the woman. "This is a matter of life and death, for he will not let us be! Because of my love for you I will now have to disobey the holiest of laws!"

With these words she quickly seized the white cock, separated its head from its body, and flung the head into the air. At once the black cloud dissolved, and her father's body, the head severed from the trunk, fell down by the edge of the road. Then the woman wept bitterly, and when she had wept her fill they buried the corpse. Thereupon they went together to her husband's home, where they found his old mother still living. They then undid the bag of pearls and jewels, bought a piece of good ground, built a fine house, and became wealthy and respected members of the community.

Note: Realgar: The Chinese believe that realgar is a mithridate and tonic.

HISTORIC LEGENDS

LX

THE SORCERER OF THE WHITE LOTUS LODGE

ONCE upon a time there was a sorcerer who belonged to the White Lotus Lodge. He knew how to deceive the multitude with his black arts, and many who wished to learn the secret of his enchantments became his pupils.

One day the sorcerer wished to go out. He placed a bowl which he covered with another bowl in the hall of his house, and ordered his pupils to watch it. But he warned them against uncovering the bowl to see what might be in it.

No sooner had he gone than the pupils uncovered the bowl and saw that it was filled with clear water. And floating on the water was a little ship made of straw, with real masts and sails. They were surprised and pushed it with their fingers till it upset. Then they quickly righted it again and once more covered the bowl. By that time the sorcerer was already standing among them. He was angry and scolded them, saying: "Why did you disobey my command?"

His pupils rose and denied that they had done so.

But the sorcerer answered: "Did not my ship turn turtle at sea, and yet you try to deceive me?"

On another evening he lit a giant candle in his room, and ordered his pupils to watch it lest it be blown out by the wind. It must have been at the second watch of the night and the sorcerer had not yet come back.

The pupils grew tired and sleepy, so they went to bed and gradually fell asleep. When they woke up again the candle had gone out. So they rose quickly and re-lit it. But the sorcerer was already in the room, and again he scolded them.

"Truly we did not sleep! How could the light have gone out?"

Angrily the sorcerer replied: "You let me walk fifteen miles in the dark, and still you can talk such nonsense!"

Then his pupils were very much frightened.

In the course of time one of his pupils insulted the sorcerer. The latter made note of the insult, but said nothing. Soon after he told the pupil to feed the swine, and no sooner had he entered the sty than his master turned him into a pig. The sorcerer then at once called in a butcher, sold the pig to the man, and he went the way of all pigs who go to the butcher.

One day this pupil's father turned up to ask after his son, for he had not come back to his home for a long time. The sorcerer told him that his son had left him long ago. The father returned home and inquired everywhere for his son without success. But one of his son's fellow-pupils, who knew of the matter, informed the father. So the father complained to the district mandarin. The latter, however, feared that the sorcerer might make himself invisible. He did not dare to have him arrested, but informed his superior and begged for a thousand well-armed soldiers. These surrounded the sorcerer's home and seized him, together with his wife and child. All three were put into wooden cages to be transported to the capital.

The road wound through the mountains, and in the midst of the hills up came a giant as large as a tree,

HISTORIC LEGENDS

with eyes like saucers, a mouth like a plate, and teeth a foot long. The soldiers stood there trembling and did not dare to move.

Said the sorcerer: "That is a mountain spirit. My wife will be able to drive him off."

They did as he suggested, unchained the woman, and she took a spear and went to meet the giant. The latter was angered, and he swallowed her, tooth and nail. This frightened the rest all the more.

The sorcerer said: "Well, if he has done away with my wife, then it is my son's turn!"

So they let the son out of his cage. But the giant swallowed him in the same way. The rest all looked on without knowing what to do.

The sorcerer then wept with rage and said: "First he destroys my wife, and then my son. If only he might be punished for it! But I am the only one who can punish him!"

And, sure enough, they took him out of his cage, too, gave him a sword, and sent him out against the giant. The sorcerer and the giant fought with each other for a time, and at last the giant seized the sorcerer, thrust him into his maw, stretched his neck and swallowed him. Then he went his way contentedly.

And now when it was too late, the soldiers realized that the sorcerer had tricked them.

Note: The Lodge of the White Lotus is one of the secret revolutionary societies of China. It harks back to Tung Tian Giau Dschu as its founder. Compare note to No. 18. The "mountain spirit," of course, is an optical illusion called up by the sorcerer, by means of which he frees his family and himself from the soldiers.

LXI

THE THREE EVILS

ONCE upon a time, in the old days, there lived a young man by the name of Dschou Tschu. He was of more than ordinary strength, and no one could withstand him. He was also wild and undisciplined, and wherever he was, quarrels and brawls arose. Yet the village elders never ventured to punish him seriously. He wore a high hat on his head, adorned with two pheasants' wings. His garments were woven of embroidered silk, and at his side hung the Dragonspring sword. He was given to play and to drinking, and his hand was inclined to take that which belonged to others. Whoever offended him had reason to dread the consequences, and he always mixed into disputes in which others were engaged. Thus he kept it up for years, and was a pest throughout the neighborhood.

Then a new mandarin came to that district. When he had arrived, he first went quietly about the country and listened to the people's complaints. And they told him that there were three great evils in that district.

Then he clothed himself in coarse garments, and wept before Dschou Tschu's door. Dschou Tschu was just coming from the tavern, where he had been drinking. He was slapping his sword and singing in a loud voice.

When he reached his house he asked: "Who is weeping here so pitifully?"

And the mandarin replied: "I am weeping because of the people's distress."

HISTORIC LEGENDS

Then Dschou Tschu saw him and broke out into loud laughter.

"You are mistaken, my friend," said he. "Revolt is seething round about us like boiling water in a kettle. But here, in our little corner of the land, all is quiet and peaceful. The harvest has been abundant, corn is plentiful, and all go happily about their work. When you talk to me about distress I have to think of the man who groans without being sick. And who are you, tell me that, who instead of grieving for yourself, are grieving for others? And what are you doing before my door?"

"I am the new mandarin," replied the other. "Since I left my litter I have been looking about in the neighborhood. I find the people are honest and simple in their way of life, and every one has sufficient to wear and to eat. This is all just as you state. Yet, strange to say, when the elders come together, they always sigh and complain. And if they are asked why, they answer: 'There are three great evils in our district!' I have come to ask you to do away with two of them, as to the third, perhaps I had better remain silent. And this is the reason I weep before your door."

"Well, what are these evils?" answered Dschou Tschu. "Speak freely, and tell me openly all that you know!"

"The first evil," said the mandarin, "is the evil dragon at the long bridge, who causes the water to rise so that man and beast are drowned in the river. The second evil is the tiger with the white forehead, who dwells in the hills. And the third evil, Dschou Tschu—is yourself!"

Then the blush of shame mounted to the man's cheek, and he bowed and said: "You have come here from afar to be the mandarin of this district, and yet you feel such sympathy for the people? I was born in this place and yet I have only made our elders grieve. What sort of a creature must I be? I beg that you will return home again. I will see to it that matters improve!"

Then he ran without stopping to the hills, and hunted the tiger out of his cave. The latter leaped into the air so that the whole forest was shaken as though by a storm. Then he came rushing up, roaring, and stretching out his claws savagely to seize his enemy. Dschou Tschu stepped back a pace, and the tiger lit on the ground directly in front of him. Then he thrust the tiger's neck to the ground with his left hand, and beat him without stopping with his right, until he lay dead on the earth. Dschou Tschu loaded the tiger on his back and went home.

Then he went to the long bridge. He undressed, took his sword in his hand, and thus dived into the water. No sooner had he disappeared, than there was a boiling and hissing, and the waves began to foam and billow. It sounded like the mad beating of thousands of hoofs. After a time a stream of blood shot up from the depths, and the water of the river turned red. Then Dschou Tschu, holding the dragon in his hand, rose out of the waves.

He went to the mandarin and reported, with a bow: "I have cut off the dragon's head, and have also done away with the tiger. Thus I have happily accomplished your command. And now I shall wander away so that you may be rid of the third evil as well. Lord, watch over my country, and tell the elders that they need sorrow no more!"

When he had said this he enlisted as a soldier. In combat against the robbers he gained a great reputation and once, when the latter were pressing him hard, and he saw that he could not save himself, he bowed to the East and said: "The day has come at last when I can atone for my sin with my life!" Then he offered his neck to the sword and died.

Note: A legendary tale rather than a folk-story, with a fine moral.

LXII

HOW THREE HEROES CAME BY THEIR DEATHS BECAUSE OF TWO PEACHES

AT the beginning of his reign Duke Ging of Tsi loved to draw heroes about him. Among those whom he attached to him were three of quite extraordinary bravery. The first was named Gung Sun Dsia, the second Tian Kai Gang, the third Gu I Dsi. All three were highly honored by the prince, but the honor paid them made them presumptuous, they kept the court in a turmoil, and overstepped the bounds of respect which lie between a prince and his servants.

At the time Yan Dsi was chancellor of Tsi. The duke consulted him as to what would be best to do. And the chancellor advised him to give a great court banquet and invite all his courtiers. On the table, the choicest dish of all, stood a platter holding four magnificent peaches.

Then, in accordance with his chancellor's advice, the Duke rose and said: "Here are some magnificent peaches, but I cannot give one to each of you. Only those most worthy may eat of them. I myself reign over the land, and am the first among the princes of the empire. I have been successful in holding my possessions and power, and that is my merit. Hence one of the peaches falls to me. Yan Dsi sits here as my chancellor. He regulates communications with foreign lands and keeps the peace among the people. He has made my kingdom powerful among the kingdoms of the earth. That is his merit, and hence the second peach falls to him. Now there are but two peaches left; yet I cannot tell which ones among you are the worthiest. You may rise yourselves and tell us of your merits. But whoever has performed no great deeds, let him hold his tongue!"

Then Gung Sun Dsia beat upon his sword, rose up and said: "I am the prince's captain general. In the South I besieged the kingdom of Lu, in the West I conquered the kingdom of Dsin, in the North I captured the army of Yan. All the princes of the East come to the Duke's court and acknowledge the overlordship of Tsi. That is my merit. I do not know whether it deserves a peach."

The Duke replied: "Great is your merit! A peach is your just due!"

Then Tian Kai Giang rose, beat on the table, and cried: "I have fought a hundred battles in the army of the prince. I have slain the enemy's general-in-chief, and captured the enemy's flag. I have extended the borders of the Duke's land till the size of his realm has been increased by a thousand miles. How is it with my merit?"

The Duke said: "Great is your merit! A peach is your just due!"

Then Gu I Dsi arose; his eyes started from their sockets, and he shouted with a loud voice: "Once, when the Duke was crossing the Yellow River, wind and waters rose. A river-dragon snapped up one of the steeds of the chariot and tore it away. The ferryboat rocked like a sieve and was about to capsize. Then I took my sword and leaped into the stream. I fought with the dragon in the midst of the foaming waves. And by reason of my strength I managed to kill him, though my eyes stood out of my head with my exertions. Then I came to the surface with the dragon's head in one hand, and holding the rein of the rescued horse in the other, and I had saved my prince from drowning. Whenever our country was at war with neighboring states, I refused no service. I commanded the van, I fought in single combat. Never did I turn my back on the foe. Once the prince's chariot stuck fast in the swamp, and the enemy hurried up on all sides. I pulled the chariot out, and drove off the hostile mercenaries. Since I have been in the prince's service I have saved his life more than once. I grant that my merit is not to be compared with that of the prince and that of the chancellor, yet it is greater than that of my two companions. Both have received peaches, while I must do without. This means that real merit is not rewarded, and that the Duke looks on me with disfavor. And in such case how may I ever show myself at court again!''

With these words he drew his sword and killed himself.

Then Gung Sun Dsia rose, bowed twice, and said with a sigh: ''Both my merit and that of Tian Kai Giang does not compare with Gu I Dsi's and yet the peaches were given us. We have been rewarded beyond our deserts, and such reward is shameful. Hence it is better to die than to live dishonored!''

He took his sword and swung it, and his own head rolled on the sand.

Tian Kai Giang looked up and uttered a groan of

disgust. He blew the breath from his mouth in front of him like a rainbow, and his hair rose on end with rage. Then he took sword in hand and said: "We three have always served our prince bravely. We were like the same flesh and blood. The others are dead, and it is my duty not to survive them!"

And he thrust his sword into his throat and died.

The Duke sighed incessantly, and commanded that they be given a splendid burial. A brave hero values his honor more than his life. The chancellor knew this, and that was why he purposely arranged to incite the three heroes to kill themselves by means of the two peaches.

Note: Duke Ging of Tsi (Eastern Shantung) was an older contemporary of Confucius. The chancellor Yan Dsi, who is the reputed author of a work on philosophy, is the same who prevented the appointment of Confucius at the court of Tsi.

LXIII

HOW THE RIVER-GOD'S WEDDING WAS BROKEN OFF

AT the time of the seven empires there lived a man by the name of Si-Men Bau, who was a governor on the Yellow River. In this district the river-god was held in high honor. The sorcerers and witches who dwelt there said: "Every year the river-god looks for a bride, who must be selected from among the people. If she be not found then wind and rain will not come at the proper seasons, and there will be scanty crops and floods!" And then, when a girl came of age in some wealthy family, the sorcerers would say that she should be selected. Whereupon her parents, who

HISTORIC LEGENDS

wished to protect their daughter, would bribe them with large sums of money to look for some one else, till the sorcerers would give in, and order the rich folk to share the expense of buying some poor girl to be cast into the river. The remainder of the money they would keep for themselves as their profit on the transaction. But whoever would not pay, their daughter was chosen to be the bride of the river-god, and was forced to accept the wedding gifts which the sorcerers brought her. The people of the district chafed grievously under this custom.

Now when Si-Men entered into office, he heard of this evil custom. He had the sorcerers come before him and said: "See to it that you let me know when the day of the river-god's wedding comes, for I myself wish to be present to honor the god! This will please him, and in return he will shower blessings on my people." With that he dismissed them. And the sorcerers were full of praise for his piety.

So when the day arrived they gave him notice. Si-Men dressed himself in his robes of ceremony, entered his chariot and drove to the river in festival procession. The elders of the people, as well as the sorcerers and the witches were all there. And from far and near men, women and children had flocked together in order to see the show. The sorcerers placed the river-bride on a couch, adorned her with her bridal jewels, and kettledrums, snaredrums and merry airs vied with each other in joyful sound.

They were about to thrust the couch into the stream, and the girl's parents said farewell to her amid tears. But Si-Men bade them wait and said: "Do not be in such a hurry! I have appeared in person to escort the bride, hence everything must be done solemnly and in order. First some one must go to the river-god's castle, and let him know that he may come himself and fetch his bride.''

And with these words he looked at a witch and said: "You may go!" the witch hesitated, but he ordered his servants to seize her and thrust her into the stream. After which about an hour went by.

"That woman did not understand her business," continued Si-Men, "or else she would have been back long ago!" And with that he looked at one of the sorcerers and added: "Do you go and do better!" The sorcerer paled with fear, but Si-Men had him seized and cast into the river. Again half-an-hour went by.

Then Si-Men pretended to be uneasy. "Both of them have made a botch of their errand," said he, "and are causing the bride to wait in vain!" Once more he looked at a sorcerer and said: "Do you go and hunt them up!" But the sorcerer flung himself on the ground and begged for mercy. And all the rest of the sorcerers and witches knelt to him in a row, and pleaded for grace. And they took an oath that they would never again seek a bride for the river-god.

Then Si-Men held his hand, and sent the girl back to her home, and the evil custom was at an end forever.

Note: Si-Men Bau was an historical personage, who lived five centuries before Christ.

LXIV

DSCHANG LIANG

DSCHANG LIANG was a native of one of those states which had been destroyed by the Emperor Tsin Schi Huang. And Dschang Liang determined to do a deed for his dead king's sake, and to that end gathered followers with whom to slay Tsin Schi Huang.

Once Tsin Schi Huang was making a progress through the country. When he came to the plain of Bo Lang, Dschang Liang armed his people with iron maces in order to kill him. But Tsin Schi Huang always had two traveling coaches which were exactly alike in appearance. In one of them he sat himself, while in the other was seated another person. Dschang Liang and his followers met the decoy wagon, and Dschang Liang was forced to flee from the Emperor's rage. He came to a ruined bridge. An icy wind was blowing, and the snowflakes were whirling through the air. There he met an old, old man wearing a black turban and a yellow gown. The old man let one of his shoes fall into the water, looked at Dschang Liang and said: "Fetch it out, little one!"

Dschang Liang controlled himself, fetched out the shoe and brought it to the old man. The latter stretched out his foot to allow Dschang Liang to put it on, which he did in a respectful manner. This pleased the old man and he said: "Little one, something may be made of you! Come here to-morrow morning early, and I will have something for you."

The following morning at break of dawn, Dschang Liang appeared. But the old man was already there and reproached him: "You are too late. To-day I will tell you nothing. To-morrow you must come earlier."

So it went on for three days, and Dschang Liang's patience was not exhausted. Then the old man was satisfied, brought forth the Book of Hidden Complements, and gave it to him. "You must read it," said he, "and then you will be able to rule a great emperor. When your task is completed, seek me at the foot of the Gu Tschong Mountain. There you will find a yellow stone, and I will be by that yellow stone.''

Dschang Liang took the book and aided the ancestor of the Han dynasty to conquer the empire. The emperor made him a count. From that time forward Dschang Liang ate no human food and concentrated in spirit. He kept company with the four whitebeards of the Shang Mountain, and with them shared the sunset roses in the clouds. Once he met two boys who were singing and dancing:

> "Geen the garments you should wear,
> If to heaven's gate you'd fare;
> There the Golden Mother greet,
> Bow before the Wood Lord's feet!"

When Dschang Liang heard this, he bowed before the youths, and said to his friends: "Those are angel children of the King Father of the East. The Golden Mother is the Queen of the West. The Lord of Wood is the King Father of the East. They are the two primal powers, the parents of all that is male and female, the root and fountain of heaven and earth, to whom all that has life is indebted for its creation and nourishment. The Lord of Wood is the master of all the male saints, the Golden Mother is the mistress of all the female saints. Whoever would gain immortality, must first greet the Golden Mother and then bow before the King Father. Then he may rise up to the three Pure Ones and stand in the presence of the Highest. The song of the angel children shows the manner in which the hidden knowledge may be acquired."

At about that time the emperor was induced to have some of his faithful servants slain. Then Dschang Liang left his service and went to the Gu Tschong Mountain. There he found the old man by the yellow stone, gained the hidden knowledge, returned home, and feigning illness loosed his soul from his body and disappeared.

Later, when the rebellion of the "Red Eyebrows" broke out, his tomb was opened. But all that was found within it was a yellow stone. Dschang Liang was wandering with Laotsze in the invisible world.

Once his grandson Dschang Dau Ling went to Kunlun Mountain, in order to visit the Queen Mother of the West. There he met Dschang Liang. Dschang Dau Ling gained power over demons and spirits, and became the first Taoist pope. And the secret of his power has been handed down in his family from generation to generation.

Note: "In a yellow robe," is an indication of Taoism: compare with No. 38. "The Book of Hidden Complements" (Yin Fu Ging). Compare with Lia Dsi, Introduction.

LXV

OLD DRAGONBEARD

AT the time of the last emperor of the Sui dynasty, the power was in the hands of the emperor's uncle, Yang Su. He was proud and extravagant. In his halls stood choruses of singers and bands of dancing girls, and serving-maids stood ready to obey his least sign. When the great lords of the empire came to visit him he remained comfortably seated on his couch while he received them.

In those days there lived a bold hero named Li Dsing. He came to see Yang Su in humble clothes in order to bring him a plan for the quieting of the empire.

He made a low bow to which Yang Su did not reply, and then he said: "The empire is about to be troubled by dissension and heroes are everywhere taking up arms. You are the highest servant of the imperial house. It should be your duty to gather the bravest around the throne. And you should not rebuff people by your haughtiness!"

When Yang Su heard him speak in this fashion he collected himself, rose from his place, and spoke to him in a friendly manner.

Li Dsing handed him a memorial, and Yang Su entered into talk with him concerning all sorts of things. A serving-maid of extraordinary beauty stood beside them. She held a red flabrum in her hand, and kept her eyes fixed on Li Dsing. The latter at length took his leave and returned to his inn.

Later in the day some one knocked at his door. He looked out, and there, before the door, stood a person turbaned and gowned in purple, and carrying a bag slung from a stick across his shoulder.

Li Dsing asked who it was and received the answer: "I am the fan-bearer of Yang Su!"

With that she entered the room, threw back her mantle and took off her turban. Li Dsing saw that she was a maiden of eighteen or nineteen.

She bowed to him, and when he had replied to her greeting she began: "I have dwelt in the house of Yang Su for a long time and have seen many famous people, but none who could equal you. I will serve you wherever you go!"

Li Dsing answered: "The minister is powerful. I am afraid that we will plunge ourselves into misfortune."

"He is a living corpse, in whom the breath of life

grows scant," said the fan-bearer, "and we need not fear him."

He asked her name, and she said it was Dschang, and that she was the oldest among her brothers and sisters.

And when he looked at her, and considered her courageous behavior and her sensible words, he realized that she was a girl of heroic cast, and they agreed to marry and make their escape from the city in secret. The fan-bearer put on men's clothes, and they mounted horses and rode away. They had determined to go to Taiyuanfu.

On the following day they stopped at an inn. They had their room put in order and made a fire on the hearth to cook their meal. The fan-bearer was combing her hair. It was so long that it swept the ground, and so shining that you could see your face in it. Li Dsing had just left the room to groom the horses. Suddenly a man who had a long curling mustache like a dragon made his appearance. He came along riding on a lame mule, threw down his leather bag on the ground in front of the hearth, took a pillow, made himself comfortable on a couch, and watched the fan-bearer as she combed her hair. Li Dsing saw him and grew angry; but the fan-bearer had at once seen through the stranger. She motioned Li Dsing to control himself, quickly finished combing her hair and tied it in a knot.

Then she greeted the guest and asked his name.

He told her that he was named Dschang.

"Why, my name is also Dschang," said she, "so we must be relatives!"

Thereupon she bowed to him as her elder brother.

"How many are there of you brothers?" she then inquired.

"I am the third," he answered, "and you?"

"I am the oldest sister."

"How fortunate that I should have found a sister to-day," said the stranger, highly pleased.

Then the fan-bearer called to Li Dsing through the door and said: "Come in! I wish to present my third brother to you!"

Then Li Dsing came in and greeted him.

They sat down beside each other and the stranger asked: "What have you to eat?"

"A leg of mutton," was the answer.

"I am quite hungry," said the stranger.

So Li Dsing went to the market and brought bread and wine. The stranger drew out his dagger, cut the meat, and they all ate in company. When they had finished he fed the rest of the meat to his mule.

Then he said: "Sir Li, you seem to be a moneyless knight. How did you happen to meet my sister?"

Li Dsing told him how it had occurred.

"And where do you wish to go now?"

"To Taiyuanfu," was the answer.

Said the stranger: "You do not seem to be an ordinary fellow. Have you heard anything regarding a hero who is supposed to be in this neighborhood?"

Li Dsing answered: "Yes, indeed, I know of one, whom heaven seems destined to rule."

"And who might he be?" inquired the other.

"He is the son of Duke Li Yuan of Tang, and he is no more than twenty years of age."

"Could you present him to me some time?" asked the stranger.

And when Li Dsing has assured him he could, he continued: "The astrologers say that a special sign has been noticed in the air above Taiyuanfu. Perhaps it is caused by the very man. To-morrow you may await me at the Fenyang Bridge!"

With these words he mounted his mule and rode away, and he rode so swiftly that he seemed to be flying.

The fan-bearer said to him: "He is not a pleasant customer to deal with. I noticed that at first he had no good intentions. That is why I united him to us by bonds of relationship."

Then they set out together for Taiyuanfu, and at the appointed place, sure enough, they met Dragonbeard. Li Dsing had an old friend, a companion of the Prince of Tang.

He presented the stranger to this friend, named Liu Wendsing, saying: "This stranger is able to foretell the future from the lines of the face, and would like to see the prince."

Thereupon Liu Wendsing took him in to the prince. The prince was clothed in a simple indoor robe, but there was something impressive about him, which made him remarked among all others. When the stranger saw him, he fell into a profound silence, and his face turned gray. After he had drunk a few flagons of wine he took his leave.

"That man is a true ruler," he told Li Dsing. "I am almost certain of the fact, but to be sure my friend must also see him."

Then he arranged to meet Li Dsing on a certain day at a certain inn.

"When you see this mule before the door, together with a very lean jackass, then you may be certain I am there with my friend."

On the day set Li Dsing went there and, sure enough he saw the mule and the jackass before the door. He gathered up his robe and descended to the upper story of the inn. There sat old Dragonbeard and a Taoist priest over their wine. When the former saw Li Dsing he was much pleased, bade him sit down and offered him wine. After they had pledged each other, all three returned to Lui Wendsing. He was engaged in a game of chess with the prince. The prince rose with respect and asked them to be seated.

As soon as the Taoist priest saw his radiant and heroic countenance he was disconcerted, and greeted him with a low bow, saying: "The game is up!"

When they took their leave Dragonbeard said to Li Dsing: "Go on to Sianfu, and when the time has come, ask for me at such and such a place."

And with that he went away snorting.

Li Dsing and the fan-bearer packed up their belongings, left Taiyuanfu and traveled on toward the West. At that time Yang Su died, and great disturbance arose throughout the empire.

In the course of a few days Li Dsing and his wife reached the meeting-place appointed by Dragonbeard. They knocked at a little wooden door, and out came a servant, who led them through long passages. When they emerged magnificent buildings arose before them, in front of which stood a crowd of slave girls. Then they entered a hall in which the most valuable dowry that could be imagined had been piled up: mirrors, clothes, jewelry, all more beautiful than earth is wont to show. Handsome slave girls led them to the bath, and when they had changed their garments their friend was announced. He stepped in clad in silks and foxpelts, and looking almost like a dragon or a tiger. He greeted his guests with pleasure and also called in his wife, who was of exceptional loveliness. A festive banquet was served, and all four sat down to it. The table was covered with the most expensive viands, so rare that they did not even know their names. Flagons and dishes and all the utensils were made of gold and jade, and ornamented with pearls and precious stones.

Two companies of girl musicians alternately blew flutes and chalameaus. They sang and danced, and it seemed to the visitors that they had been transported to the palace of the Lady of the Moon. The rainbow garments fluttered, and the dancing girls were beautiful beyond all the beauty of earth.

After they had banqueted, Dragonbeard commanded his servitors to bring in couches upon which embroidered silken covers had been spread. And after they had seen everything worth seeing, he presented them with a book and a key.

Then he said: "In this book are listed the valuables and the riches which I possess. I make you a wedding-present of them. Nothing great may be undertaken without wealth, and it is my duty to endow my sister properly. My original intention had been to take the Middle Kingdom in hand and do something with it. But since a ruler has already arisen to reign over it, what is there to keep me in this country? For Prince Tang of Taiyuanfu is a real hero, and will have restored order within a few years' time. You must both of you aid him, and you will be certain to rise to high honors. You, my sister, are not alone beautiful, but you have also the right way of looking at things. None other than yourself would have been able to recognize the true worth of Li Dsing, and none other than Li Dsing would have had the good fortune to encounter you. You will share the honors which will be your husband's portion, and your name will be recorded in history. The treasures which I bestow upon you, you are to use to help the true ruler. Bear this in mind! And in ten years' time a glow will rise far away to the South-east, and it shall be a sign that I have reached my goal. Then you may pour a libation of wine in the direction of the South-east, to wish me good fortune!"

Then, one after another, he had his servitors and slave-girls greeted Li Dsing and the fan-bearer, and said to them: "This is your master and your mistress!"

When he had spoken these words, he took his wife's hand, they mounted three steeds which were held ready, and rode away.

Li Dsing and his wife now established themselves in the house, and found themselves possessed of countless wealth. They followed Prince Tang, who restored order to the empire, and aided him with their money. Thus the great work was accomplished, and after peace had been restored throughout the empire, Li Dsing was made Duke of We, and the fan-bearer became a duchess.

Some ten years later the duke was informed that in the empire beyond the sea a thousand ships had landed an army of a hundred thousand armored soldiers. These had conquered the country, killed its prince, and set up their leader as its king. And order now reigned in that empire.

Then the duke knew that Dragonbeard had accomplished his aim. He told his wife, and they robed themselves in robes of ceremony and offered wine in order to wish him good fortune. And they saw a radiant crimson ray flash up on the South-eastern horizon. No doubt Dragonbeard had sent it in answer. And both of them were very happy.

Note: Yang Su died in the year 606 A.D. The Li Dsing of this tale has nothing in common with Li Dsing, the father of Notschka (No. 18). He lived as a historical personage, 571-649 A.D. Li Yuan was the founder of the Tang dynasty, 565-635 A.D. His famous son, to whom he owed the throne, the "Prince of Tang," was named Li Schi Min. His father abdicated in 618 in his favor. This tale is not, of course, historical, but legendary. Compare with the introduction of the following one.

LXVI

HOW MOLO STOLE THE LOVELY ROSE-RED

AT the time when the Tang dynasty reigned over the Middle Kingdom, there were master swordsmen of various kinds. Those who came first were the saints of the sword. They were able to take different shapes at will, and their swords were like strokes of lightning. Before their opponents knew they had been struck their heads had already fallen. Yet these master swordsmen were men of lofty mind, and did not lightly mingle in the quarrels of the world. The second kind of master swordsmen were the sword heroes. It was their custom to slay the unjust, and to come to the aid of the oppressed. They wore a hidden dagger at their side and carried a leather bag at their belt. By magic means they were able to turn human heads into flowing water. They could fly over roofs and walk up and down walls, and they came and went and left no trace. The swordsmen of the lowest sort were the mere bought slayers. They hired themselves out to those who wished to do away with their enemies. And death was an everyday matter to them.

Old Dragonbeard must have been a master swordsman standing midway between those of the first and of the second order. Molo, however, of whom this story tells, was a sword hero.

At that time there lived a young man named Tsui, whose father was a high official and the friend of the prince. And the father once sent his son to visit his princely friend, who was ill. The son was young, handsome and gifted. He went to carry out his father's instructions. When he entered the prince's palace, there stood three beautiful slave girls, who piled rosy peaches into a golden bowl, poured sugar over them and presented them to him. After he had eaten he took his leave, and his princely host ordered one of the slave girls, Rose-Red by name, to escort him to the gate. As they went along the young man kept looking back at her. And she smiled at him and made signs with her fingers. First she would stretch out three fingers, then she would turn her hand around three times, and finally she would point to a little mirror which she wore on her breast. When they parted she whispered to him: "Do not forget me!"

When the young man reached home his thoughts were all in confusion. And he sat down absent-mindedly like a wooden rooster. Now it happened that he had an old servant named Molo, who was an extraordinary being.

"What is the trouble, master," said he. "Why are you so sad? Do you not want to tell your old slave about it?"

So the boy told him what had occurred, and also mentioned the signs the girl had made to him in secret.

Said Molo: "When she stretched out three fingers, it meant that she is quartered in the third court of the palace. When she turned round her hand three times, it meant the sum of three times five fingers, which is fifteen. When she pointed at the little mirror, she meant to say that on the fifteenth, when the moon is round as a mirror, at midnight, you are to go for her."

Then the young man was roused from his confused thoughts, and was so happy he could hardly control himself.

But soon he grew sad again and said: "The prince's palace is shut off as though by an ocean. How would it be possible to win into it?"

"Nothing easier," said Molo. "On the fifteenth we will take two pieces of dark silk and wrap ourselves up in them, and thus I will carry you there. Yet there is a wild dog on guard at the slave girl's court, who is strong as a tiger and watchful as a god. No one can pass by him, so he must be killed."

When the appointed day had come, the servant said: "There is no one else in the world who can kill this dog but myself!"

Full of joy the youth gave him meat and wine, and the old man took a chain-hammer and disappeared with it.

And after no more time had elapsed than it takes to eat a meal he was back again and said: "The dog is dead, and there is nothing further to hinder us!"

At midnight they wrapped themselves in dark silk, and the old man carried the youth over the tenfold walls which surrounded the palace. They reached the third gateway and the gate stood ajar. Then they saw the glow of a little lamp, and heard Rose-Red sigh deeply. The entire court was silent and deserted. The youth raised the curtain and stepped into the room. Long and searchingly Rose-Red looked at him, then seized his hand.

"I knew that you were intelligent, and would understand my sign language. But what magic power have you at your disposal, that you were able to get here?"

The youth told her in detail how Molo had helped him.

"And where is Molo?" she asked.

"Outside, before the curtain," was his answer.

Then she called him in and gave him wine to drink from a jade goblet and said: "I am of good family and have come here from far away. Force alone has made me a slave in this palace. I long to leave it.

For though I have jasper chop-sticks with which to eat, and drink my wine from golden flagons, though silk and satin rustle around me and jewels of every kind are at my disposal, all these are but so many chains and fetters to hold me here. Dear Molo, you are endowed with magic powers. I beg you to save me in my distress! If you do, I will be glad to serve your master as a slave, and will never forget the favor you do me."

The youth looked at Molo. Molo was quite willing. First he asked permission to carry away Rose-Red's gear and jewels in sacks and bags. Three times he went away and returned until he had finished. Then he took his master and Rose-Red upon his back, and flew away with them over the steep walls. None of the watchmen of the prince's palace noticed anything out of the way. At home the youth hid Rose-Red in a distant room.

When the prince discovered that one of his slave-girls was missing, and that one of his wild dogs had been killed, he said: "That must have been some powerful sword hero!" And he gave strict orders that the matter should not be mentioned, and that investigations should be made in secret.

Two years passed, and the youth no longer thought of any danger. Hence, when the flowers began to bloom in the spring, Rose-Red went driving in a small wagon outside the city, near the river. And there one of the prince's servants saw her, and informed his master. The latter sent for the youth, who, since he could not conceal the matter, told him the whole story exactly as it had happened.

Said the prince: "The whole blame rests on Rose-Red. I do not reproach you. Yet since she is now your wife I will let the whole matter rest. But Molo will have to suffer for it!"

"THEN HE TOOK HIS MASTER AND ROSE-RED UPON HIS
BACK AND FLEW WITH THEM OVER THE STEEP WALLS"

So he ordered a hundred armored soldiers, with bows and swords, to surround the house of the youth, and under all circumstances to take Molo captive. But Molo drew his dagger and flew up the high wall. Thence he looked about him like a hawk. The arrows flew as thick as rain, but not one hit him. And in a moment he had disappeared, no one knew where.

Yet ten years later one of his former master's servants ran across him in the South, where he was selling medicine. And he looked exactly as he had looked ten years before.

Note: This fairy-tale has many features in common with the fairy-tales of India, noticeably the use of the sign language, which the hero himself does not understand, but which is understood by his companion.

LXVII

THE GOLDEN CANISTER

IN the days of the Tang dynasty there lived a certain count in the camp at Ludschou. He had a slave who could play the lute admirably, and was also so well versed in reading and writing that the count employed her to indite his confidential letters.

Once there was a great feast held in the camp. Said the slave-girl: "The large kettledrum sounds so sad to-day; some misfortune must surely have happened to the kettledrummer!"

The count sent for the kettledrummer and questioned him.

"My wife has died," he replied, "yet I did not venture to ask for leave of absence. That is why, in spite of me, my kettledrum sounded so sad."

The count allowed him to go home.

At that time there was much strife and jealousy among the counts along the Yellow River. The emperor wished to put an end to their dissensions by allying them to each other by marriages. Thus the daughter of the Count of Ludschou had married the son of the old Count of Webo. But this did not much improve matters. The old Count of Webo had lung trouble, and when the hot season came it always grew worse, and he would say: "Yes, if I only had Ludschou! It is cooler and I might feel better there!"

So he gathered three thousand warriors around him, gave them good pay, questioned the oracle with regard to a lucky day, and set out to take Ludschou by force.

The Count of Ludschou heard of it. He worried day and night, but could see no way out of his difficulties. One night, when the water-clock had already been set up, and the gate of the camp had been locked, he walked about the courtyard, leaning on his staff. Only his slave-girl followed him.

"Lord," said she, "it is now more than a month since sleep and appetite have abandoned you! You live sad and lonely, wrapped up in your grief. Unless I am greatly deceived it is on account of Webo."

"It is a matter of life and death," answered the count, "of which you women understand nothing."

"I am no more than a slave-girl," said she, "and yet I have been able to guess the cause of your grief."

The count realized that there was meaning in her words and replied: "You are in truth an extraordinary girl. It is a fact that I am quietly reflecting on some way of escape."

The slave-girl said: "That is easily done! You need not give it a thought, master! I will go to Webo and see how things are. This is the first watch of the night. If I go now, I can be back by the fifth watch."

"Should you not succeed," said the count, "you merely bring misfortune upon me the more quickly."

"A failure is out of the question," answered the slave-girl.

Then she went to her room and prepared for her journey. She combed her raven hair, tied it in a knot on the top of her head, and fastened it with a golden pin. Then she put on a short garment embroidered with purple, and shoes woven of dark silk. In her breast she hid a dagger with dragon-lines graved on it, and upon her forehead she wrote the name of the Great God. Then she bowed before the count and disappeared.

The count poured wine for himself and waited for her, and when the morning horn was blown, the slave-girl floated down before him as light as a leaf.

"Did all go well?" asked the count.

"I have done no discredit to my mission," replied the girl.

"Did you kill any one?"

"No, I did not have to go to such lengths. Yet I took the golden canister at the head of Webo's couch along as a pledge."

The count asked what her experience had been, and she began to tell her story:

"I set out when the drums were beating their first tattoo and reached Webo three hours before midnight. When I stepped through the gate, I could see the sentries asleep in their guard-rooms. They snored so that it sounded like thunder. The camp sentinels were pacing their beats, and I went in through the left entrance into the room in which the Count of Webo slept. There lay your relative on his back behind the curtain, plunged in sweet slumber. A costly sword showed from beneath his pillow; and beside it stood an open canister of gold. In the canister were various slips. On one of them was set down his age and the day of his birth, on another the name of the Great Bear God. Grains of incense and pearls were scattered over it. The candles in the room burned dimly, and the incense in the censers was paling to ash. The slave-girls lay huddled up, round about, asleep. I could have drawn out their hair-pins and raised their robes and they would not have awakened. Your relative's life was in my hand, but I could not bring myself to kill him. So I took the golden canister and returned. The water-clock marked the third hour when I had finished my journey. Now you must have a swift horse saddled quickly, and must send a man to Webo to take back the golden canister. Then the Lord of Webo will come to his senses, and will give up his plans of conquest."

The Count of Ludschou at once ordered an officer to ride to Webo as swiftly as possible. He rode all day long and half the night and finally arrived. In Webo every one was excited because of the loss of the golden canister. They were searching the whole camp rigorously. The messenger knocked at the gate with his riding-whip, and insisted on seeing the Lord of Webo. Since he came at so unusual an hour the Lord of Webo guessed that he was bringing important information, and left his room to receive the messenger. The latter handed him a letter which said: "Last night a stranger from Webo came to us. He informed us that with his own hands he had taken a golden canister from beside your bed. I have not ventured to keep it and hence am sending it back to you by messenger." When the Lord of Webo saw the golden canister he was much frightened. He took the messenger into his own room, treated him to a splendid meal, and rewarded him generously.

On the following day he sent the messenger back again, and gave him thirty thousand bales of silk and a team of four horses along as a present for his master. He also wrote a letter to the Count of Ludschou:

"My life was in your hand. I thank you for having spared me, regret my evil intentions and will improve. From this time forward peace and friendship shall ever unite us, and I will let no thought to the contrary enter my mind. The citizen soldiery I have gathered I will use only as a protection against robbers. I have already disarmed the men and sent them back to their work in the fields."

And thenceforward the heartiest friendship existed between the two relatives North and South of the Yellow River.

One day the slave-girl came and wished to take leave of her master.

"In my former existence," said the slave-girl, "I was a man. I was a physician and helped the sick. Once upon a time I gave a little child a poison to drink by mistake instead of a healing draught, and the child died. This led the Lord of Death to punish me, and I came to earth again in the shape of a slave-girl. Yet I remembered my former life, tried to do well in my new surroundings, and even found a rare teacher who taught me the swordsman's art. Already I have served you for nineteen years. I went to Webo for you in order to repay your kindness. And I have succeeded in shaping matters so that you are living at peace with your relatives again, and thus have saved the lives of thousands of people. For a weak woman this is a real service, sufficient to absolve me of my original fault. Now I shall retire from the world and dwell among the silent hills, in order to labor for sanctity with a clean heart. Perhaps I may thus succeed in returning to my former condition of life. So I beg of you to let me depart!"

The count saw that it would not be right to detain her any longer. So he prepared a great banquet, invited a number of guests to the farewell meal, and many a famous knight sat down to the board. And all honored her with toasts and poems.

The count could no longer hide his emotion, and the slave-girl also bowed before him and wept. Then she secretly left the banquet-hall, and no human being ever discovered whither she had gone.

Note: This motive of the intelligent slave-girl also occurs in the story of the three empires. "On her forehead she wrote the name of the Great God:" Regarding this god, Tai I, the Great One, compare annotation to No. 18. The God of the Great Bear, i. e., of the constellation. The letters which are exchanged are quite as noticeable for what is implied between the lines, as for what is actually set down.

LXVIII

YANG GUI FE

THE favorite wife of the emperor Ming Huang of the Tang dynasty was the celebrated Yang Gui Fe. She so enchanted him by her beauty that he did whatever she wished him to do. But she brought her cousin to the court, a gambler and a drinker, and because of him the people began to murmur against the emperor. Finally a revolt broke out, and the emperor was obliged to flee. He fled with his entire court to the land of the four rivers.

But when they reached a certain pass his own soldiers mutinied. They shouted that Yang Gui Fe's cousin was to blame for all, and that he must die or they would go no further. The emperor did not know what to do. At last the cousin was delivered up to the soldiers and was slain. But still they were not satisfied.

"As long as Yang Gui Fe is alive she will do all in her power to punish us for the death of her cousin, so she must die as well!"

Sobbing, she fled to the emperor. He wept bitterly and endeavored to protect her; but the soldiers grew more and more violent. Finally she was hung from a pear-tree by a eunuch.

The emperor longed so greatly for Yang Gui Fe that he ceased to eat, and could no longer sleep. Then one of his eunuchs told him of a man named Yang Shi Wu, who was able to call up the spirits of the departed. The emperor sent for him and Yang Shi Wu appeared.

That very evening he recited his magic incantations, and his soul left its body to go in search of Yang Gui Fe. First he went to the Nether World, where the shades of the departed dwell. Yet no matter how much he looked and asked he could find no trace of her. Then he ascended to the highest heaven, where sun, moon and stars make their rounds, and looked for her in empty space. Yet she was not to be found there, either. So he came back and told the emperor of his experience. The emperor was dissatisfied and said: "Yang Gui Fe's beauty was divine. How can it be possible that she had no soul!"

The magician answered: "Between hill and valley and amid the silent ravines dwell the blessed. I will go back once more and search for her there."

So he wandered about on the five holy hills, by the four great rivers and through the islands of the sea. He went everywhere, and finally came to fairyland.

The fairy said: "Yang Gui Fe has become a blessed spirit and dwells in the great south palace!"

So the magician went there and knocked on the door. A maiden came out and asked what he wanted, and he told her that the emperor had sent him to look for her mistress. She let him in. The way led through broad gardens filled with flowers of jade and trees of coral, giving forth the sweetest of odors. Finally they reached a high tower, and the maiden raised the curtain hanging before a door. The magician knelt and looked up. And there he saw Yang Gui Fe sitting on a throne, adorned with an emerald headdress and furs of yellow swans' down. Her face glowed with rosy color, yet her forehead was wrinkled with care.

She said: "Well do I know the emperor longs for me! But for me there is no path leading back to the world of men! Before my birth I was a blessed sky-fairy, and the emperor was a blessed spirit as well. Even then we loved each other dearly. Then, when the emperor was sent down to earth by the Lord of the Heavens, I, too, descended to earth and found him there among men. In twelve years' time we will meet again. Once, on the evening of the seventh day, when we stood looking up at the Weaving Maiden and the Herd Boy, we swore eternal love. The emperor had a ring, which he broke in two. One half he gave to me, the other he kept himself. Take this half of mine, bring it to the emperor, and tell him not to forget the words we said to each other in secret that evening. And tell him not to grieve too greatly because of me!"

With that she gave him the ring, with difficulty suppressing her sobs. The magician brought back the ring with him. At sight of it the emperor's grief broke out anew.

He said: "What we said to each other that evening no one else has ever learned! And now you bring me back her ring! By that sign I know that your words are true and that my beloved has really become a blessed spirit."

Then he kept the ring and rewarded the magician lavishly.

Note: The emperor Ming Huang of the Tang dynasty ruled from 713 to 756 A.D. The introduction to the tale is historical. The "land of the four rivers" is Setchuan.

LXIX

THE MONK OF THE YANGTZE-KIANG

BUDDHISM took its rise in southern India, on the island of Ceylon. It was there that the son of a Brahminic king lived, who had left his home in his youth, and had renounced all wishes and all sensation. With the greatest renunciation of self he did penance so that all living creatures might be saved. In the course of time he gained the hidden knowledge and was called Buddha.

In the days of the Emperor Ming Di, of the dynasty of the Eastern Hans, a golden glow was seen in the West, a glow which flashed and shone without interruption.

One night the emperor dreamed that he saw a golden saint, twenty feet in height, barefoot, his head shaven, and clothed in Indian garb enter his room, who said to him: "I am the saint from the West! My gospel must be spread in the East!"

When the ruler awoke he wondered about this dream, and sent out messengers to the lands of the West in order to find out what it meant.

Thus it was that the gospel of Buddha came to China, and continued to gain in influence up to the time of the Tang dynasty. At that time, from emperors and kings down to the peasants in the villages, the wise and the ignorant alike were filled with reverence for Buddha. But under the last two dynasties his gospel came to be more and more neglected. In these days the Buddhist monks run to the houses of the rich, read their sutras and pray for pay. And one hears nothing of the great saints of the days gone by.

At the time of the Emperor Tai Dsung, of the Tang dynasty, it once happened that a great drought reigned in the land, so that the emperor and all his officials erected altars everywhere in order to plead for rain.

Then the Dragon-King of the Eastern Sea talked with the Dragon of the Milky Way and said: "To-day they are praying for rain on earth below. The Lord of the Heavens has granted the prayer of the King of Tang. To-morrow you must let three inches of rain fall!"

"No, I must let only two inches of rain fall," said the old dragon.

So the two dragons made a wager, and the one who lost promised as a punishment to turn into a mud salamander.

The following day the Highest Lord suddenly issued an order saying that the Dragon of the Milky Way was to instruct the wind and cloud spirits to send down three inches of rain upon the earth.

To contradict this command was out of the question.

But the old dragon thought to himself: "It seems that the Dragon-King had a better idea of what was going to happen than I had, yet it is altogether too humiliating to have to turn into a mud salamander!" So he let only two inches of rain fall, and reported back to the heavenly court that the command had been carried out.

Yet the Emperor Tai Dsung then offered a prayer of thanks to heaven. In it he said: "The precious fluid was bestowed upon us to the extent of two inches of depth. We beg submissively that more may be sent down, so that the parched crops may recover!"

When the Lord of the Heavens read this prayer he was very angry and said: "The criminal Dragon of the Milky Way has dared diminish the rain which I had ordered. He cannot be suffered to continue his guilty life. So We Dschong, who is a general among men on earth, shall behead him, as an example for all living beings."

In the evening the Emperor Tai Dsung had a dream. He saw a giant enter his room, who pleaded with hardly restrained tears: "Save me, O Emperor! Because of my own accord I diminished the rainfall, the Lord of the Heavens, in his anger, has commanded that We Dschong behead me to-morrow at noon. If you will only prevent We Dschong from falling asleep at that time, and pray that I may be saved, misfortune once more may pass me by!"

The emperor promised, and the other bowed and left him.

The following day the emperor sent for We Dschong. They drank tea together and played chess.

Toward noon We Dschong suddenly grew tired and sleepy; but he did not dare take his leave. The emperor, however, since one of his pawns had been taken, fixed his gaze for a moment on the chess-board and pondered, and before he knew it We Dschong was already snoring with a noise like a distant thunder. The emperor was much frightened, and hastily called out to him; but he did not awake. Then he had two eunuchs shake him, but a long time passed before he could be aroused.

"How did you come to fall asleep so suddenly?" asked the emperor.

"I dreamed," replied We Dschong, "that the Highest God had commanded me to behead the old dragon. I have just hewn off his head, and my arm still aches from the exertion."

And before he had even finished speaking a dragon's head, as large as a bushel-measure, suddenly fell down out of the air. The emperor was terribly frightened and rose.

"I have sinned against the old dragon," said he. Then he retired to the inner chambers of his palace and was confused in mind. He remained lying on his couch, closed his eyes, said not a word, and breathed but faintly.

Suddenly he saw two persons in purple robes who had a summons in their hands. They spoke to him as follows: "The old Dragon of the Milky Way has complained against the emperor in the Nether World. We beg that you will have the chariot harnessed!"

Instinctively the emperor followed them, and in the courtyard there stood his chariot before the castle, ready and waiting. The emperor entered it, and off they went flying through the air. In a moment they had reached the city of the dead. When he entered he saw the Lord of the High Mountain sitting in the midst of the city, with the ten princes of the Nether World in rows at his right and left. They all rose, bowed to him and bade him be seated.

Then the Lord of the High Mountain said: "The old Dragon of the Milky Way has really committed a deed which deserved punishment. Yet Your Majesty has promised to beg the Highest God to spare him, which prayer would probably have saved the old dragon's life. And that this matter was neglected over the chess-board might well be accounted a mistake. Now the old dragon complains to me without ceasing. When I think of how he has striven to gain sainthood for more than a thousand years, and must now fall back into the cycle of transformations, I am really depressed. It is for this reason I have called together the princes of the ten pits of the Nether World, to find a way out of the difficulty, and have invited Your Majesty to come here to discuss the matter. In heaven, on earth and in the Nether World only the gospel of Buddha has no limits. Hence, when you return to earth great sacrifices should be made to the three and thirty lords of the heavens. Three thousand six hundred holy priests of Buddha must read the sutras in order to deliver the old dragon so that he may rise again to the skies, and keep his original form. But the writings and readings of men will not be enough to ensure this. It will be necessary to go to the Western Heavens and thence bring words of truth."

This the emperor agreed to, and the Lord of the Great Mountain and the ten princes of the Nether World rose and said as they bowed to him: "We beg that you will now return!"

Suddenly Tai Dsung opened his eyes again, and there he was lying on his imperial couch. Then he made public the fact that he was at fault, and had the holiest among the priests of Buddha sent for to fetch the sutras from the Western Heavens. And it was Huan Dschuang, the Monk of the Yangtze-kiang, who in obedience to this order, appeared at court.

The name of this Huan Dschuang had originally been Tschen. His father had passed the highest examinations during the reign of the preceding emperor, and had been intrusted with the office of district mandarin on the Yangtze-kiang. He set out with his wife for this new district, but when their ship reached the Yellow River it fell in with a band of robbers. Their captain slew the whole retinue, threw father Tschen into the river, took his wife and the document appointing him mandarin, went to the district capital under an assumed name and took charge of it. All the serving-men whom he took along were members of his robber-band. Tschen's wife, however, together with her little boy, he imprisoned in a tower room. And all the servants who attended her were in the confidence of the robbers.

Now below the tower was a little pond, and in this pond rose a spring which flowed beneath the walls to the Yellow River. So one day Tschen's wife took a little basket of bamboo, pasted up the cracks and laid her little boy in the basket. Then she cut her finger, wrote down the day and hour of the boy's birth on a strip of silk paper with the blood, and added that the boy must come and rescue her when he had reached the age of twelve. She placed the strip of silk paper beside the boy in the basket, and at night, when no one was about, she put the basket in the pond. The current carried it away to the Yangtze-kiang, and once there it drifted on as far as the monastery on the Golden Hill, which is an island lying in the middle of the river. There a priest who had come to draw water found it. He fished it out and took it to the monastery.

When the abbot saw what had been written in blood, he ordered his priests and novices to say nothing about it to any one. And he brought up the boy in the monastery.

When the latter had reached the age of five, he was taught to read the holy books. The boy was more intelligent than any of his fellow-students, soon grasped the meaning of the sacred writings, and entered more and more deeply into their secrets. So he was allowed to take the vows, and when his head had been shaven was named: "The Monk of the Yangtze-kiang."

By the time he was twelve he was as large and strong as a grown man. The abbot, who knew of the duty he still had to perform, had him called to a quiet room. There he drew forth the letter written in blood and gave it to him.

When the monk had read it he flung himself down on the ground and wept bitterly. Thereupon he thanked the abbot for all that the latter had done for him. He set out for the city in which his mother dwelt, ran around the yamen of the mandarin, beat upon the wooden fish and cried: "Deliverance from all suffering! Deliverance from all suffering!"

After the robber who had slain his father had slipped into the post he held by false pretences, he had taken care to strengthen his position by making powerful friends. He even allowed Tschen's wife, who had now been a prisoner for some ten years, a little more liberty.

On that day official business had kept him abroad. The woman was sitting at home, and when she heard the wooden fish beaten so insistently before the door and heard the words of deliverance, the voice of her heart cried out in her. She sent out the serving-maid to call in the priest. He came in by the back door, and when she saw that he resembled his father in every feature, she could no longer restrain herself, but burst into tears. Then the monk of the Yangtze-kiang realized that this was his mother and he took the bloody writing out and gave it to her.

She stroked it and said amid sobs: "My father is a high official, who has retired from affairs and dwells in the capital. But I have been unable to write to him, because this robber guarded me so closely. So I kept alive as well as I could, waiting for you to come. Now hurry to the capital for the sake of your father's memory, and if his honor is made clear then I can die in peace. But you must hasten so that no one finds out about it."

The monk then went off quickly. First he went back to his cloister to bid farewell to his abbot; and then he set out for Sianfu, the capital.

Yet by that time his grandfather had already died. But one of his uncles, who was known at court, was still living. He took soldiers and soon made an end of the robbers. But the monk's mother had died in the meantime.

From that time on, the Monk of the Yangtze-kiang lived in a pagoda in Sianfu, and was known as Huan Dschuang. When the emperor issued the order calling the priests of Buddha to court, he was some twenty years of age. He came into the emperor's presence, and the latter honored him as a great teacher. Then he set out for India.

He was absent for seventeen years. When he returned he brought three collections of books with him, and each collection comprised five-hundred and forty

HISTORIC LEGENDS

rolls of manuscript. With these he once more entered the presence of the emperor. The emperor was overjoyed, and with his own hand wrote a preface of the holy teachings, in which he recorded all that had happened. Then the great sacrifice was held to deliver the old Dragon of the Milky Way.

Note: The emperor Tai Dsung is Li Shi Min, the Prince of Tang mentioned in No. 64. He was the most glorious and splendid of all Chinese rulers. The "Dragon-King of the Eastern Sea" has appeared frequently in these fairy-tales. As regards the "Lord of the High Mountain," and the ten princes of the Nether World, comp. Nos. 38 and 49. The Highest Lord is Yu Huang, the Lord of Jade or of Nephrite. Huan Dschuang was originally known as Tschen. Regarding his father's fate subsequent to his being drowned, and that of his sons in the spirit-world see No. 24. The "bamboo basket" is a Moses motive which occurs in other Chinese fairy-tales. The Monk of the Yangtze-kiang" is, literally, (in Chinese, Giang Liu Ho Schang) "The monk washed ashore by the stream." "Wooden fish:" A hollow piece of wood in the form of a fish, which is beaten by the Buddhists as sign of watchfulness. Three collections of books—the Tripitaka. As regards one of the legendary companions of Huan Dschuang on his journey, see No. 73.

LITERARY FAIRY TALES

LXX

THE HEARTLESS HUSBAND

IN olden times Hanchow was the capital of Southern China, and for that reason a great number of beggars had gathered there. These beggars were in the habit of electing a leader, who was officially entrusted with the supervision of all begging in the town. It was his duty to see that the beggars did not molest the townsfolk, and he received a tenth of their income from all his beggar subjects. When it snowed or rained, and the beggars could not go out to beg, he had to see to it that they had something to eat, and he also had to conduct their weddings and funerals. And the beggars obeyed him in all things.

Well, it happened that there was a beggar king of this sort in Hanchow by the name of Gin, in whose family the office had been handed down from father to son for seven generations. What they had taken in by way of beggars' pence they had lent out on interest, and so the family had gradually become well-to-do, and finally even rich.

The old beggar-king had lost his wife at the age of fifty. But he had an only child, a girl who was called "Little Golden Daughter." She had a face of rare beauty and was the jewel of his love. She had been versed in the lore of books from her youth up, and could write, improvise poems and compose essays. She was also experienced in needlework, a skilled dancer and singer, and could play the flute and zither.

The old beggar-king above all else wanted her to have a scholar for a husband. Yet because he was a beggar-king the distinguished families avoided him, and with those who were of less standing than himself he did not wish to have anything to do. So it came about that Little Golden Daughter had reached the age of eighteen without being betrothed.

Now at that time there dwelt in Hanchow, near the Bridge of Peace, a scholar by the name of Mosu. He was twenty years of age, and universally popular because of his beauty and talent. His parents were both dead, and he was so poor that he could hardly manage to keep alive. His house and lot had long since been mortgaged or sold, and he lived in an abandoned temple, and many a day passed at whose end he went hungry to bed.

A neighbor took pity on him and said to him one day: "The beggar-king has a child named Little Golden Daughter, who is beautiful beyond all telling. And the beggar-king is rich and has money, but no son to inherit it. If you wish to marry into his family his whole fortune would in the end come to you. Is that not better than dying of hunger as a poor scholar?"

At that time Mosu was in dire extremity. Hence, when he heard these words he was greatly pleased. He begged the neighbor to act as a go-between in the matter.

So the latter visited the old beggar-king and talked with him, and the beggar-king talked over the matter with Little Golden Daughter, and since Mosu came from a good family and was, in addition, talented and learned, and had no objection to marrying into their family, they were both much pleased with the

LITERARY FAIRY TALES

prospect. So they agreed to the proposal, and the two were married.

So Mosu became a member of the beggar-king's family. He was happy in his wife's beauty, always had enough to eat and good clothes to wear. So he thought himself lucky beyond his deserts, and lived with his wife in peace and happiness.

The beggar-king and his daughter, to whom their low estate was a thorn in the flesh, admonished Mosu to be sure to study hard. They hoped that he would make a name for himself and thus reflect glory on their family as well. They bought books for him, old and new, at the highest prices, and they always supplied him liberally with money so that he could move in aristocratic circles. They also paid his examination expenses. So his learning increased day by day, and the fame of it spread through the entire district. He passed one examination after another in rapid succession, and at the age of twenty-three was appointed mandarin of the district of Wu We. He returned from his audience with the emperor in ceremonial robes, high on horseback.

Mosu had been born in Hanchow, so the whole town soon knew that he had passed his examination successfully, and the townsfolk crowded together on both sides of the street to look at him as he rode to his father-in-law's house. Old and young, women and children gathered to enjoy the show, and some idle loafer called out in a loud voice:

"The old beggar's son-in-law has become a mandarin!"

Mosu blushed with shame when he heard these words. Speechless and out of sorts he seated himself in his room. But the old beggar-king in the joy of his heart did not notice his ill humor. He had a great festival banquet prepared, to which he invited all his neighbors and good friends. But most of the invited guests were beggars and poor folk, and he insisted that Mosu eat with them. With much difficulty Mosu was induced to leave his room. Yet when he saw the guests gathered around the table, as ragged and dirty as a horde of hungry devils, he retired again with disdain. Little Golden Daughter, who realized how he felt, tried to cheer him up again in a hundred and one ways, but all in vain.

A few days later Mosu, with his wife and servants, set out for the new district he was to govern. One goes from Hanchow to Wu We by water. So they entered a ship and sailed out to the Yangtze-kiang. At the end of the first day they reached a city where they anchored. The night was clear and the moonrays glittered on the water, and Mosu sat in the front part of the ship enjoying the moonlight. Suddenly he chanced to think of the old beggar-king. It was true that his wife was wise and good, but should heaven happen to bless them with children, these children would always be the beggar's nephews and nieces, and there was no way of preventing such a disgrace. And thus thinking a plan occurred to him. He called Little Golden Daughter out of the cabin to come and enjoy the moonlight, and she came out to him happily. Men servants and maid servants and all the sailors had long since gone to sleep. He looked about him on all sides, but there was no one to be seen. Little Golden Daughter was standing at the front of the ship, thinking no evil, when a hand suddenly thrust her into the water. Then Mosu pretended to be frightened, and began to call out: "My wife made a misstep and has fallen into the water!"

And when they heard his words, the servants hurried up and wanted to fish her out.

But Mosu said: "She has already been carried away by the current, so you need not trouble yourselves!" Then he gave orders to set sail again as soon as possible.

Now who would have thought that owing to a fortunate chance, Sir Hu, the mandarin in charge of the transportation system of the province, was also about to take charge of his department, and had anchored in the same place. He was sitting with his wife at the open window of the ship's cabin, enjoying the moonlight and the cool breeze.

Suddenly he heard some one crying on the shore, and it sounded to him like a girl's voice. He quickly sent people to assist her, and they brought her aboard. It was Little Golden Daughter.

When she had fallen into the water, she had felt something beneath her feet which held her up so that she did not sink. And she had been carried along by the current to the river-bank, where she crept out of the water. And then she realized that her husband, now that he had become distinguished, had forgotten how poor he had been, and for all she had not been drowned, she felt very lonely and abandoned, and before she knew it her tears began to flow. So when Sir Hu asked her what was the matter, she told him the whole story. Sir Hu comforted her.

"You must not shed another tear," said he. "If you care to become my adopted daughter, we will take care of you."

Little Golden Daughter bowed her thanks. But Hu's wife ordered her maids to bring other clothes to take the place of the wet ones, and to prepare a bed for her. The servants were strictly bidden to call her "Miss," and to say nothing of what had occurred.

So the journey continued and in a few days' time Sir Hu entered upon his official duties. Wu We, where Mosu was district mandarin, was subject to his rule, and the latter made his appearance in order to visit his official superior. When Sir Hu saw Mosu he thought to himself: "What a pity that so highly gifted a man should act in so heartless a manner!"

When a few months had passed, Sir Hu said to his subordinates: "I have a daughter who is very pretty and good, and would like to find a son-in-law to marry into my family. Do you know of any one who might answer?"

His subordinates all knew that Mosu was young and had lost his wife. So they unanimously suggested him.

Sir Hu replied: "I have also thought of that gentleman, but he is young and has risen very rapidly. I am afraid he has loftier ambitions, and would not care to marry into my family and become my son-in-law."

"He was originally poor," answered his people, "and he is your subordinate. Should you care to show him a kindness of this sort, he will be sure to accept it joyfully, and will not object to marrying into your family."

"Well, if you all believe it can be done," said Sir Hu, "then pay him a visit and find out what he thinks about it. But you must not say that I have sent you."

Mosu, who was just then reflecting how he might win Sir Hu's favor, took up the suggestion with pleasure, and urgently begged them to act as his go-between in the matter, promising them a rich reward when the connection was established.

So they went back again and reported to Sir Hu.

He said: "I am much pleased that the gentleman in question does not disdain this marriage. But my wife and I are extremely fond of this daughter of ours, and we can hardly resign ourselves to giving her up. Sir Mosu is young and aristocratic, and our little daughter has been spoiled. If he were to ill-treat her, or at some future time were to regret having married into our family, my wife and I would be inconsolable. For this reason everything must be clearly understood in advance. Only if he positively agrees to do these things would I be able to receive him into my family."

Mosu was informed of all these conditions, and declared himself ready to accept them. Then he brought gold and pearls and colored silks to Sir Hu's daughter as wedding gifts, and a lucky day was chosen for the wedding. Sir Hu charged his wife to talk to Little Golden Daughter.

"Your adopted father," said she, "feels sorry for you, because you are lonely, and therefore has picked out a young scholar for you to marry."

But Little Golden Daughter replied: "It is true that I am of humble birth, yet I know what is fitting. It chances that I agreed to cast my lot with Mosu for better or for worse. And though he has shown me but little kindness, I will marry no other man so long as he lives. I cannot bring myself to form another union and break my troth."

And thus speaking the tears poured from her eyes. When Sir Hu's wife saw that nothing would alter her resolve, she told her how matters really stood.

"Your adopted father," said she, "is indignant at Mosu's heartlessness. And although he will see to it that you meet again, he has said nothing to Mosu which would lead him to believe that you are not our own daughter. Therefore Mosu was delighted to marry you. But when the wedding is celebrated this evening, you must do thus and so, in order that he may taste your just anger."

When she had heard all this, Little Golden Daughter dried her tears, and thanked her adopted parents. Then she adorned herself for the wedding.

The same day, late at evening, Mosu came to the house wearing golden flowers on his hat, and a red scarf across his breast, riding on a gaily trapped horse, and followed by a great retinue. All his friends and acquaintances came with him in order to be present at the festival celebration.

In Sir Hu's house everything had been adorned with colored cloths and lanterns. Mosu dismounted from his horse at the entrance of the hall. Here Sir Hu had spread a festival banquet to which Mosu and his friends were led. And when the goblet had made the rounds three times, serving-maids came and invited Mosu to follow them to the inner rooms. The bride, veiled in a red veil, was led in by two maidservants. Following the injunctions of the master of the ceremony, they worshiped heaven and earth together, and then the parents-in-law. Thereupon they went into another apartment. Here brightly colored candles were burning, and a wedding dinner had been prepared. Mosu felt as happy as though he had been raised to the seventh heaven.

But when he wanted to leave the room, seven or eight maids with bamboo canes in their hands appeared at each side of the door, and began to beat him without mercy. They knocked his bridal hat from his head, and then the blows rained down upon his back and shoulders. When Mosu cried for help he heard a delicate voice say: "You need not kill that heartless bridegroom of mine completely! Ask him to come in and greet me!"

Then the maids stopped beating him, and gathered about the bride, who removed her bridal veil.

Mosu bowed with lowered head and said: "But what have I done?"

Yet when he raised his eyes he saw that none other than his wife, Little Golden Daughter, was standing before him.

He started with fright and cried: "A ghost, a ghost!" But all the servants broke out into loud laughter.

At last Sir Hu and his wife came in, and the former said: "My dear son-in-law, you may rest assured that my adopted daughter, who came to me while I was on my way to this place, is no ghost."

Then Mosu hastily fell on his knees and answered: "I have sinned and beg for mercy!" And he kowtowed without end.

"With that I have nothing to do," remarked Sir Hu, "if our little daughter only gets along well with you, then all will be in order."

But Little Golden Daughter said: "You heartless scoundrel! In the beginning you were poor and needy. We took you into our family, and let you study so that you might become somebody, and make a name for yourself. But no sooner had you become a mandarin and a man of standing, than your love turned into enmity, and you forgot your duty as a husband and pushed me into the river. Fortunately, I found my dear adopted parents thereby. They fished me out, and made me their own child, otherwise I would have found a grave in the bellies of the fishes. How can I honorably live again with such a man as you?"

With these words she began to lament loudly, and she called him one hard-hearted scoundrel after another.

Mosu lay before her, speechless with shame, and begged her to forgive him.

Now when Sir Hu noticed that Little Golden Daughter had sufficiently relieved herself by her scolding, he helped Mosu up and said to him: "My dear son-in-law, if you repent of your misdeed, Little Golden Daughter will gradually cease to be angry. Of course you are an old married couple; yet as you have renewed your vows this evening in my house, kindly do me a favor and listen to what I have to say: You, Mosu, are weighed with a heavy burden of guilt, and for that reason you must not resent your wife's being somewhat indignant, but must have patience with her. I will call in my wife to make peace between you."

With these words Sir Hu went out and sent in his wife who finally, after a great deal of difficulty, succeeded in reconciling the two, so that they agreed once more to take up life as husband and wife.

And they esteemed and loved each other twice as much as they had before. Their life was all happiness and joy. And later, when Sir Hu and his wife died, they mourned for them as if in truth they had been their own parents.

Note: "To marry into": as a rule the wife enters the home of her husband's parents. But when there is no male heir, it is arranged that the son-in-law continues the family of his wife's parents, and lives in their home. The custom is still very prevalent in Japan, but it is not considered very honorable in China to enter into a strange family in this way. It is characteristic that Mosu, as a punishment for disdaining to "marry into" a family the first time, is obliged to "marry into" a second time, the family of Sir Hu.

The costume here described is still the wedding-costume of China. "Little Golden Daughter" said: "You heartless scoundrel!"; despite her faithfulness, in accordance with Chinese custom, she is obliged to show her anger over his faithlessness; this is necessary before the matter can be properly adjusted, so that she may "preserve her face."

LXXI

GIAUNA THE BEAUTIFUL

ONCE upon a time there was a descendant of Confucius. His father had a friend, and this friend held an official position in the South and offered the young man a place as secretary. But when the latter reached the town where he was to have been active, he found that his father's friend had already died. Then he was much embarrassed, seeing that he did not have the means to return home again. So he was glad to take refuge in the Monastery of Puto, where he copied holy books for the abbot.

About a hundred paces west of the monastery stood a deserted house. One day there had been a great snowfall, and as young Kung accidentally passed by the door of the house, he noticed a well dressed and prepossessing youth standing there who bowed to him and begged him to approach. Now young Kung was a scholar, and could appreciate good manners. Finding that the youth and himself had much in common, he took a liking to him, and followed him into the house. It was immaculately clean; silk curtains hung before the doors, and on the walls were pictures of good old masters. On a table lay a book entitled: "Tales of the Coral Ring." Coral Ring was the name of a cavern.

Once upon a time there lived a monk at Puto who

was exceedingly learned. An aged man had led him into the cave in question, where he had seen a number of volumes on the book stands. The aged man had said: "These are the histories of the various dynasties." In a second room were to be found the histories of all the peoples on earth. A third was guarded by two dogs. The aged man explained: "In this room are kept the secret reports of the immortals, telling the arts by means of which they gained eternal life. The two dogs are two dragons." The monk turned the pages of the books, and found that they were all works of ancient times, such as he had never seen before. He would gladly have remained in the cave, but the old man said: "That would not do!" and a boy led him out again. The name of that cave, however, was the Coral Ring, and it was described in the volume which lay on the table.

The youth questioned Kung regarding his name and family, and the latter told him his whole history. The youth pitied him greatly and advised him to open a school.

Kung answered with a sigh: "I am quite unknown in the neighborhood, and have no one to recommend me!"

Said the youth: "If you do not consider me altogether too unworthy and stupid, I should like to be your pupil myself."

Young Kung was overjoyed. "I should not dare to attempt to teach you," he replied, "but together we might dedicate ourselves to the study of science." He then asked why the house had been standing empty for so long.

The youth answered: "The owner of the house has gone to the country. We come from Shensi, and have taken the house for a short time. We only moved in a few days ago."

They chatted and joked together gaily, and the young man invited Kung to remain overnight, ordering a small boy to light a pan of charcoal.

Then he stepped rapidly into the rear room and soon returned saying: "My father has come."

As Kung rose an aged man with a long, white beard and eyebrows stepped into the room and said, greeting him: "You have already declared your willingness to instruct my son, and I am grateful for your kindness. But you must be strict with him and not treat him as a friend."

Then he had garments of silk, a fur cap, and shoes and socks of fur brought in, and begged Kung to change his clothes. Wine and food were then served. The cushions and covers of the tables and chairs were made of stuffs unknown to Kung, and their shimmering radiance blinded the eye. The aged man retired after a few beakers of wine, and then the youth showed Kung his essays. They were all written in the style of the old masters and not in the new-fangled eight-section form.

When he was asked about this, the youth said with a smile: "I am quite indifferent to winning success at the state examinations!" Then he turned to the small boy and said: "See whether the old gentleman has already fallen asleep. If he has, you may quietly bring in little Hiang-Nu."

The boy went off, and the youth took a lute from an embroidered case. At once a serving-maid entered, dressed in red, and surpassingly beautiful. The youth bade her sing "The Lament of the Beloved," and her melting tones moved the heart. The third watch of the night had passed before they retired to sleep.

On the following morning all rose early and study began. The youth was exceptionally gifted. Whatever he had seen but once was graven in his memory. Hence he made surprising progress in the course of a few months. The old custom was followed of writing an essay every five days, and celebrating its completion with a little banquet. And at each banquet Hiang-Nu was sent for.

One evening Kung could not remove his glance from Hiang-Nu. The youth guessed his thoughts and said to him: "You are as yet unmarried. Early and late I keep thinking as to how I can provide you with a charming life companion. Hiang-Nu is the serving-maid of my father, so I cannot give her to you."

Said Kung: "I am grateful to you for your friendly thought. But if the girl you have in mind is not just as beautiful as Hiang-Nu, then I would rather do without."

The youth laughed: "You are indeed inexperienced if you think that Hiang-Nu is beautiful. Your wish is easily fulfilled."

Thus half a year went by and the monotonous rainy season had just began. Then a swelling the size of a peach developed in young Kung's breast, which increased over night until it was as large as a tea-cup. He lay on his couch groaning with pain, and unable to eat or to sleep. The youth was busy day and night nursing him, and even the old gentleman asked how he was getting along.

Then the youth said: "My little sister Giauna alone is able to cure this illness. Please send to grandmother, and have her brought here!"

The old gentleman was willing, and he sent off his boy.

The next day the boy came back with the news that Giauna would come, together with her aunt and her cousin A-Sung.

Not long after the youth led his sister into the room. She was not more than thirteen or fourteen years of age, enchantingly beautiful, and slender as a willow-tree. When the sick man saw her he forgot all his pain and his spirits rose.

The youth said to his sister Giauna: "This is my best friend, whom I love as a brother! I beg of you, little sister, to cure him of his illness!"

The maiden blushed with confusion; then she stepped up to the sick-bed. While she was feeling his pulse, it seemed to him as though she brought the fragrance of orchards with her.

Said the maiden with a smile: "No wonder that this illness has befallen him. His heart beats far too stormily. His illness is serious but not incurable. Now the blood which has flowed has already gathered, so we will have to cut to cure."

With that she took her golden armlet from her arm and laid it on the aching place. She pressed it down very gently, and the swelling rose a full inch above the armlet so that it enclosed the entire swelling. Then she loosed a pen-knife with a blade as thin as paper from her silken girdle. With one hand she held the armlet, and with the other she took the knife and lightly passed it around the bottom of the ring. Black blood gushed forth and ran over mattress and bed. But young Kung was so enchanted by the presence of the beautiful Giauna that not only did he feel no pain, but his one fear was that the whole affair might end too soon, and that she would disappear from his sight. In a moment the diseased flesh had been cut away, and Giauna had fresh water brought and cleansed the wound. Then she took a small red pellet from her mouth, and laid it on the wound, and when she turned around in a circle, it seemed to Kung as though she drew out all the inflammation in steam and flames. Once more she turned in a circle, and he felt his wound itch and quiver, and when she turned for the third time, he was completely cured.

The maiden took the pellet into her mouth again and said: "Now all is well!" Then she hastened into the inner room. Young Kung leaped up in order to thank her.

True, he was now cured of his illness, but his thoughts continued to dwell on Giauna's pretty face. He neglected his books and sat lost in day-dreams.

His friend had noticed it and said to him: "I have at last succeeded, this very day, in finding an attractive life companion for you."

Kung asked who she might be.

"The daughter of my aunt, A-Sung. She is seventeen years of age, and anything but homely."

"I am sure she is not as beautiful as Giauna," thought Kung. Then he hummed the lines of a song to himself:

> "Who once has seen the sea close by,
> All rivers shallow streams declares;
> Who o'er Wu's hill the clouds watched fly,
> Says nothing with that view compares."

The youth smiled. "My little sister Giauna is still very young," said he. "Besides, she is my father's only daughter, and he would not like to see her marry some one from afar. But my cousin A-Sung is not homely either. If you do not believe me, wait until they go walking in the garden, and then you may take a look at them without their knowing it."

Kung posted himself at the open window on the lookout, and sure enough, he saw Giauna come along leading another girl by the hand, a girl so beautiful that

LITERARY FAIRY TALES

there was none other like her. Giauna and she seemed to be sisters, only to be told apart by a slight difference in age.

Then young Kung was exceedingly happy and begged his friend to act for him in arranging the marriage, which the latter promised to do. The next day he came to Kung, and told him amid congratulations that everything was arranged. A special court was put in order for the young pair, and the wedding was celebrated. Young Kung felt as though he had married a fairy, and the two became very fond of each other.

One day Kung's friend came to him in a state of great excitement and said: "The owner of this house is coming back, and my father now wishes to return to Shensi. The time for us to part draws near, and I am very sad!"

Kung wished to accompany them, but his friend advised him to return to his own home.

Kung mentioned the difficulties in the way, but the youth replied: "That need not worry you, because I will accompany you."

After a time the father came, together with A-Sung, and made Kung a present of a hundred ounces of gold. Then the youth took Kung and his wife by the hand, and told them to close their eyes. As soon as they did so off they went through the air like a storm-wind. All Kung could notice was that the gale roared about his ears.

When some time had passed the youth cried: "Now we have arrived!" Kung opened his eyes and saw his old home, and then he knew that his friend was not of human kind.

Gaily they knocked at the door of his home. His mother opened it and when she saw that he had brought along so charming a wife she was greatly pleased. Then Kung turned around to his friend, but the latter had already disappeared.

A-Sung served her mother-in-law with great devotion, and her beauty and virtue was celebrated far and near. Soon after young Kung gained the doctorate, and was appointed inspector of prisons in Shensi. He took his wife along with him, but his mother remained at home, since Shensi was too far for her to travel. And heaven gave A-Sung and Kung a little son.

But Kung became involved in a dispute with a traveling censor. The latter complained about Kung and he was dismissed from his post.

So it happened that one day he was idling about before the city, when he saw a handsome youth riding a black mule. When he looked more closely he saw that it was his old friend. They fell into each others' arms, laughing and weeping, and the youth led him to a village. In the midst of a thick grove of trees which threw a deep shade, stood a house whose upper stories rose to the skies. One could see at a glance that people of distinction lived there. Kung now inquired after sister Giauna, and was told that she had married. He remained over night and then went off to fetch his wife.

In the meantime Giauna arrived. She took A-Sung's little son in her arms and said: "Cousin, this is a little stranger in our family!"

Kung greeted her, and again thanked her for the kindness she had shown him in curing his illness.

She answered with a smile: "Since then you have become a distinguished man, and the wound has long since healed. Have you still not forgotten your pain?"

Then Giauna's husband arrived, and every one became acquainted. And after that they parted.

One day the youth came sadly to Kung and said: "We are threatened by a great misfortune to-day. I do not know whether you would be willing to save us!"

Kung did not know what it might be; but he gladly promised his aid. Then the youth called up the entire family and they bowed down in the outer court.

He began: "I will tell you the truth just as it is. We are foxes. This day we are threatened by the danger of thunder. If you care to save us, then there is a hope that we may manage to stay alive; if not, then take your child and go, so that you are not involved in our danger."

But Kung vowed that he would share life and death with them.

Then the youth begged him to stand in the door with a sword in his hand, and said: "Now when the thunder begins to roll you must stand there and never stir."

Suddenly dark clouds rose in the sky, and the heavens grew gloomy as if night were closing down. Kung looked about him, but the buildings had all disappeared, and behind him he could only see a high barrow, in which was a large cave whose interior was lost in darkness. In the midst of his fright he was surprised by a thunderbolt. A heavy rain poured down in streams, and a storm wind arose which rooted up the tallest trees. Everything glimmered before his eyes and his ears were deafened. But he held his sword in his hand, and stood as firm as a rock. Suddenly in the midst of black smoke and flashes of lightning, he saw a monster with a pointed beak and long claws, which was carrying off a human body. When he looked more closely he recognized by the dress that it was Giauna. He leaped up at the monster and struck at him with his sword, and at once Giauna fell to the ground. A tremendous crash of thunder shook the earth, and Kung fell down dead.

Then the tempest cleared away, and the blue sky appeared once more.

Giauna had regained consciousness, and when she saw Kung lying dead beside her she said amid sobs: "He died for my sake! Why should I continue to live?"

A-Sung also came out, and together they carried him into the cave. Giauna told A-Sung to hold his head while her brother opened his mouth. She herself took hold of his chin, and brought out her little red pellet. She pressed it against his lips with her own, and breathed into his lungs. Then the breath came back to his throat with a rattling noise, and in a short time he was himself once more.

So there was the whole family reunited again, and none of its members had come to harm. They gradually recovered from their fright, and were quite happy: when suddenly a small boy brought the news that Giauna's husband and his whole family had been killed by the thunder. Giauna broke down, weeping, and the others tried to comfort her.

Finally Kung said: "It is not well to dwell too long amid the graves of the dead. Will you not come home with me?"

Thereupon they packed up their belongings and went with him. He assigned a deserted garden, which he carefully walled off, to his friend and his family as a dwelling-place. Only when Kung and A-Sung came to visit them was the bolt drawn. Then Giauna and her brother played chess, drank tea and chatted with them like members of the same family.

But Kung's little son had a somewhat pointed face, which resembled a fox's, and when he went along the street, the people would turn around and say: "There goes the fox-child!"

Note: "Not in the new-fangled eight-section form:" Ba Gu Wen Dschang, i. e., essays in eight-section form, divided according to strict rules, were the customary theses in the governmental examinations in China up to the time of the great educational reform. To-day there is a general return to the style of the old masters, the free form of composition. "The danger of thunder": Three times the foxes must have escaped the mortal danger of thunder.

LXXII

THE FROG PRINCESS

THERE where the Yangtze-kiang has come about halfway on its course to the sea, the Frog King is worshiped with great devotion. He has a temple there and frogs by the thousand are to be found in the neighborhood, some of them of enormous size. Those who incur the wrath of the god are apt to have strange visitations in their homes. Frogs hop about on tables and beds, and in extreme cases they even creep up the smooth walls of the room without falling. There are various kinds of omens, but all indicate that some misfortune threatens the house in question. Then the people living in it become terrified, slaughter a cow and offer it as a sacrifice. Thus the god is mollified and nothing further happens.

In that part of the country there once lived a youth named Sia Kung-Schong. He was handsome and intelligent. When he was some six or seven years of age, a serving-maid dressed in green entered his home. She said that she was a messenger from the Frog King, and declared that the Frog King wished to have his daughter marry young Sia. Old Sia was an honest man, not very bright, and since this did not suit him, he declined the offer on the plea that his son was still too young to marry. In spite of this, however, he did not dare look about for another mate for him.

Then a few years passed and the boy gradually grew up. A marriage between him and a certain Mistress Giang was decided upon.

But the Frog King sent word to Mistress Giang: "Young Sia is my son-in-law. How dare you undertake to lay claim to what does not belong to you!" Then Father Giang was frightened, and took back his promise.

This made Old Sia very sad. He prepared a sacrifice and went to his temple to pray. He explained that he felt unworthy of becoming the relation of a god. When he had finished praying a multitude of enormous maggots made their appearance in the sacrificial meat and wine, and crawled around. He poured them out, begged forgiveness, and returned home filled with evil forebodings. He did not know what more he could do, and had to let things take their course.

One day young Sia went out into the street. A messenger stepped up to him and told him, on the part of the Frog King that the latter urgently requested Sia to come to him. There was no help for it; he had to follow the messenger. He led him through a red gateway into some magnificent, high-ceilinged rooms. In the great hall sat an ancient man who might have been some eighty years of age. Sia cast himself down on the ground before him in homage. The old man bade him rise, and assigned him a place at the table. Soon a number of girls and women came crowding in to look at him. Then the old man turned to them and said: "Go to the room of the bride and tell her that the bride-groom has arrived!"

Quickly a couple of maids ran away, and shortly after an old woman came from the inner apartments, leading a maiden by the hand, who might have been sixteen years of age, and was incomparably beautiful. The old man pointed to her and said: "This is my tenth little daughter. It seemed to me that you would make a good pair. But your father has scorned us because of our difference in race. Yet one's marraige is a matter that is of life-long importance. Our parents can determine it only in part. In the end it rests mainly with one's self."

Sia looked steadily at the girl, and a fondness for her grew in his heart. He sat there in silence. The old man continued: "I knew very well that the young gentleman would agree. Go on ahead of us, and we will bring you your bride!"

Sia said he would, and hurried to inform his father. His father did not know what to do in his excitement. He suggested an excuse and wanted to send Sia back to decline his bride with thanks. But this Sia was not willing to do. While they were arguing the matter, the bride's carriage was already at the door. It was surrounded by a crowd of greencoats, and the lady entered the house, and bowed politely to her parents-in-law. When the latter saw her they were both pleased, and the wedding was announced for that very evening.

The new couple lived in peace and good understanding. And after they had been married their divine parents-in-law often came to their house. When they appeared dressed in red, it meant that some good fortune was to befall them; when they came dressed in white, it signified that they were sure to make some gain. Thus, in the course of time, the family became wealthy.

But since they had become related to the gods the

rooms, courtyards and all other places were always crowded with frogs. And no one ventured to harm them. Sia Kung-Schong alone was young and showed no consideration. When he was in good spirits he did not bother them, but when he got out of sorts he knew no mercy, and purposely stepped on them and killed them.

In general his young wife was modest and obedient; yet she easily lost her temper. She could not approve her husband's conduct. But Sia would not do her the favor to give up his brutal habit. So she scolded him because of it and he grew angry.

"Do you imagine," he told her, "that because your parents can visit human beings with misfortune, that a real man would be afraid of a frog?"

His wife carefully avoided uttering the word "frog," hence his speech angered her and she said: "Since I have dwelt in your house your fields have yielded larger crops, and you have obtained the highest selling prices. And that is something after all. But now, when young and old, you are comfortably established, you wish to act like the fledgling owl, who picks out his own mother's eyes as soon as he is able to fly!"

Sia then grew still more angry and answered: "These gifts have been unwelcome to me for a long time, for I consider them unclean. I could never consent to leave such property to sons and grandsons. It would be better if we parted at once!"

So he bade his wife leave the house, and before his parents knew anything about it, she was gone. His parents scolded him and told him to go at once and bring her back. But he was filled with rage, and would not give in to them.

That same night he and his mother fell sick. They

felt weak and could not eat. The father, much worried, went to the temple to beg for pardon. And he prayed so earnestly that his wife and son recovered in three days' time. And the Frog Princess also returned, and they lived together happily and contented as before.

But the young woman sat in the house all day long, occupied solely with her ornaments and her rouge, and did not concern herself with sewing and stitching. So Sia Kung-Schong's mother still had to look out for her son's clothes.

One day his mother was angry and said: "My son has a wife, and yet I have to do all the work! In other homes the daughter-in-law serves her mother-in-law. But in our house the mother-in-law must serve the daughter-in-law."

This the princess accidentally heard. In she came, much excited, and began: "Have I ever omitted, as is right and proper, to visit you morning and evening? My only fault is that I will not burden myself with all this toil for the sake of saving a trifling sum of money!" The mother answered not a word, but wept bitterly and in silence because of the insult offered her.

Her son came along and noticed that his mother had been weeping. He insisted on knowing the reason, and found out what had happened. Angrily he reproached his wife. She raised objections and did not wish to admit that she had been in the wrong. Finally Sia said: "It is better to have no wife at all than one who gives her mother-in-law no pleasure. What can the old frog do to me after all, if I anger him, save call misfortunes upon me and take my life!" So he once more drove his wife out of the house.

The princess left her home and went away. The following day fire broke out in the house, and spread to several other buildings. Tables, beds, everything was burned.

Sia, in a rage because of the fire, went to the temple to complain: "To bring up a daughter in such a way that she does not please her parents-in-law shows that there is no discipline in a house. And now you even encourage her in her faults. It is said the gods are most just. Are there gods who teach men to fear their wives? Incidentally, the whole quarrel rests on me alone. My parents had nothing to do with it. If I was to be punished by the ax and cord, well and good. You could have carried out the punishment yourself. But this you did not do. So now I will burn your own house in order to satisfy my own sense of justice!"

With these words he began piling up brush-wood before the temple, struck sparks and wanted to set it ablaze. The neighbors came streaming up, and pleaded with him. So he swallowed his rage and went home.

When his parents heard of it, they grew pale with a great fear. But at night the god appeared to the people of a neighboring village, and ordered them to rebuild the house of his son-in-law. When day began to dawn they dragged up building-wood and the workmen all came in throngs to build for Sia. No matter what he said he could not prevent them. All day long hundreds of workmen were busy. And in the course of a few days all the rooms had been rebuilt, and all the utensils, curtains and furniture were there as before. And when the work had been completed the princess also returned. She climbed the stairs to the great room, and acknowledged her fault with many tender and loving words. Then she turned to Sia Kung-

Schong, and smiled at him sideways. Instead of resentment joy now filled the whole house. And after that time the princess was especially peaceable. Two whole years passed without an angry word being said.

But the princess had a great dislike for snakes. Once, by way of a joke, young Sia put a small snake into a parcel, which he gave her and told her to open. She turned pale and reproached him. Then Sia-Kung-Schong also took his jest seriously, and angry words passed.

At last the princess said: "This time I will not wait for you to turn me out. Now we are finally done with one another!" And with that she walked out of the door.

Father Sia grew very much alarmed, beat his son himself with his staff, and begged the god to be kind and forgive. Fortunately there were no evil consequences. All was quiet and not a sound was heard.

Thus more than a year passed. Sia-Kung-Schong longed for the princess and took himself seriously to task. He would creep in secret to the temple of the god, and lament because he had lost the princess. But no voice answered him. And soon afterward he even heard that the god had betrothed his daughter to another man. Then he grew hopeless at heart, and thought of finding another wife for himself. Yet no matter how he searched he could find none who equalled the princess. This only increased his longing for her, and he went to the home of the Yuans, to a member of which family it was said she had been promised. There they had already painted the walls, and swept the courtyard, and all was in readiness to receive the bridal carriage. Sia was overcome with remorse and discontent. He no longer ate, and fell ill. His parents were quite stunned by the anxiety they felt on his account, and were incapable of helpful thought.

Suddenly while he was lying there only half-conscious, he felt some one stroke him, and heard a voice say: "And how goes it with our real husband, who insisted on turning out his wife?"

He opened his eyes and it was the princess.

Full of joy he leaped up and said: "How is it you have come back to me?" The princess answered: "To tell the truth, according to your own habit of treating people badly, I should have followed my father's advice and taken another husband. And, as a matter of fact, the wedding gifts of the Yuan family have been lying in my home for a long time. But I thought and thought and could not bring myself to do so. The wedding was to have been this evening and my father thought it shameful to have the wedding gifts carried back. So I took the things myself and placed them before the Yuan's door. When I went out my father ran out beside me: 'You insane girl,' he said, 'so you will not listen to what I say! If you are ill-treated by Sia in the future I wash my hands of it. Even if they kill you you shall not come home to me again!'"

Moved by her faithfulness the tears rolled from Sia's eyes. The servants, full of joy, hurried to the parents to acquaint them with the good news. And when they heard it they did not wait for the young people to come to them, but hastened themselves to their son's rooms, took the princess by the hand and wept. Young Sia, too, had become more settled by this time, and was no longer so mischievous. So he and his wife grew to love each other more sincerely day by day.

Once the princess said to him: "Formerly, when you always treated me so badly, I feared that we would not keep company into our old age. So I never asked heaven to send us a child. But now that all has changed, and I will beg the gods for a son.''

And, sure enough, before long Sia's parents-in-law appeared in the house clad in red garments, and shortly after heaven sent the happy pair two sons instead of one.

From that time on their intercourse with the Frog-King was never interrupted. When some one among the people had angered the god, he first tried to induce young Sia to speak for him, and sent his wife and daughter to the Frog Princess to implore her aid. And if the princess laughed, then all would be well.

The Sia family has many descendants, whom the people call "the little frog men." Those who are near them do not venture to call them by this name, but those standing further off do so.

Note: "Little frog men," Wa Dsi, is the derogatory name which the North Chinese give the Chinese of the South on occasion.

LXXIII

ROSE OF EVENING

ON the fifth day of the fifth month the festival of the Dragon Junk is held along the Yangtzekiang. A dragon is hollowed out of wood, painted with an armor of scales, and adorned with gold and bright colors. A carved red railing surrounds this ship, and its sails and flags are made of silks and brocade. The after part of the vessel is called the dragon's tail. It rises ten feet above the water, and a board which floats in the water is tied to it by means of a cloth. Upon this board sit boys who turn somersaults, stand on their heads, and perform all sorts of tricks. Yet, being so close to the water their danger is very great. It is the custom, therefore, when a boy is hired for this purpose, to give his parents money before he is trained. Then, if he falls into the water and is drowned, no one has him on their conscience. Farther South the custom differs in so much that instead of boys, beautiful girls are chosen for this purpose.

In Dschen-Giang there once lived a widow named Dsiang, who had a son called Aduan. When he was no more than seven years of age he was extraordinarily skilful, and no other boy could equal him. And his reputation increasing as he grew, he earned more and more money. So it happened that he was still called upon at the Dragon Junk Festival when he was already sixteen.

But one day he fell into the water below the Gold Island and was drowned. He was the only son of his mother, and she sorrowed over him, and that was the end of it.

Yet Aduan did not know that he had been drowned. He met two men who took him along with them, and he saw a new world in the midst of the waters of the Yellow River. When he looked around, the waves of the river towered steeply about him like walls, and a palace was visible, in which sat a man wearing armor and a helmet. His two companions said to him: "That is the Prince of the Dragon's Cave!" and bade him kneel.

The Prince of the Dragon's Cave seemed to be of a mild and kindly disposition and said: "We can make use of such a skilful lad. He may take part in the dance of the willow branches!"

So he was brought to a spot surrounded by extensive buildings. He entered, and was greeted by a crowd of boys who were all about fourteen years of age.

An old woman came in and they all called out: "This is Mother Hia!" And she sat down and had Aduan show his tricks. Then she taught him the dance of the flying thunders of Tsian-Tang River, and the music that calms the winds on the sea of Dung-Ting. When the cymbals and kettle-drums reechoed through all the courts, they deafened the ear. Then, again, all the courts would fall silent. Mother Hia thought that Aduan would not be able to grasp everything the very first time; so she taught him with great patience. But Aduan had understood everything from the first, and that pleased old Mother Hia. "This boy," said she, "equals our own Rose of Evening!"

The following day the Prince of the Dragon's Cave held a review of his dancers. When all the dancers had assembled, the dance of the Ogres was danced first. Those who performed it all wore devil-masks and garments of scales. They beat upon enormous cymbals, and their kettle-drums were so large that four men could just about span them. Their sound was like the sound of a mighty thunder, and the noise was so great that nothing else could be heard. When the dance began, tremendous waves spouted up to the very skies, and then fell down again like star-glimmer which scatters in the air.

The Prince of the Dragon Cave hastily bade the dance cease, and had the dancers of the nightingale round step forth. These were all lovely young girls of sixteen. They made a delicate music with flutes, so that the breeze blew and the roaring of the waves was stilled in a moment. The water gradually became as quiet as a crystal world, transparent to its lowest depths. When the nightingale dancers had finished, they withdrew and posted themselves in the western courtyard.

Then came the turn of the swallow dancers. These were all little girls. One among them, who was about fifteen years of age, danced the dance of the giving of flowers with flying sleeves and waving locks. And as their garments fluttered, many-colored flowers dropped from their folds, and were caught up by the wind and whirled about the whole courtyard. When the dance had ended, this dancer also went off with the rest of the girls to the western courtyard. Aduan looked at her from out the corner of his eye, and fell deeply in love with her. He asked his comrades who she might be and they told him she was named "Rose of Evening."

But the willow-spray dancers were now called out. The Prince of the Dragon Cave was especially desirous of testing Aduan. So Aduan danced alone, and he danced with joy or defiance according to the music. When he looked up and when he looked down his glances held the beat of the measure. The Dragon Prince, enchanted with his skill, presented him with a garment of five colors, and gave him a carbuncle set in golden threads of fish-beard for a hair-jewel. Aduan bowed his thanks for the gift, and then also hastened to the western courtyard. There all the dancers stood in rank and file. Aduan could only look at Rose of Evening from a distance, but still Rose of Evening returned his glances.

After a time Aduan gradually slipped to the end of his file and Rose of Evening also drew near to him, so that they stood only a few feet away from each other. But the strict rules allowed no confusion in the ranks, so they could only gaze and let their souls go out to each other.

Now the butterfly dance followed the others. This was danced by the boys and girls together, and the pairs were equal in size, age and the color of their garments. When all the dances had ended, the dancers marched out with the goose-step. The willow-spray dancers followed the swallow dancers, and Aduan hastened in advance of his company, while Rose of Evening lingered along after hers. She turned her head, and when she spied Aduan she purposely let a coral pin fall from her hair. Aduan hastily hid it in his sleeve.

When he had returned, he was sick with longing, and could neither eat nor sleep. Mother Hia brought him all sorts of dainties, looked after him three or four times a day, and stroked his forehead with loving care. But his illness did not yield in the least. Mother Hia was unhappy, and yet helpless.

"The birthday of the King of the Wu River is at hand," said she. "What is to be done?"

In the twilight there came a boy, who sat down on the edge of Aduan's bed and chatted with him. He belonged to the butterfly dancers, said he, and asked casually: "Are you sick because of Rose of Evening?" Aduan, frightened, asked him how he came to guess it. The other boy said, with a smile: "Well, because Rose of Evening is in the same case as yourself."

Disconcerted, Aduan sat up and begged the boy to advise him. "Are you able to walk?" asked the latter. "If I exert myself," said Aduan, "I think I could manage it."

So the boy led him to the South. There he opened a gate and they turned the corner, to the West. Once more the doors of the gate flew open, and now Aduan saw a lotus field about twenty acres in size. The lotus flowers were all growing on level earth, and their leaves were as large as mats and their flowers like umbrellas. The fallen blossoms covered the ground beneath the stalks to the depth of a foot or more. The boy led Aduan in and said. "Now first of all sit down for a little while!" Then he went away.

After a time a beautiful girl thrust aside the lotus flowers and came into the open. It was Rose of Evening. They looked at each other with happy timidity, and each told how each had longed for the other. And they also told each other of their former life. Then they weighted the lotus-leaves with stones so that they made a cozy retreat, in which they could be together, and promised to meet each other there every evening. And then they parted.

Aduan came back and his illness left him. From that time on he met Rose of Evening every day in the lotus field.

After a few days had passed they had to accompany the Prince of the Dragon Cave to the birthday festival of the King of the Wu River. The festival came to an end, and all the dancers returned home. Only, the King had kept back Rose of the Evening and one of the nightingale dancers to teach the girls in his castle.

Months passed and no news came from Rose of Evening, so that Aduan went about full of longing and despair. Now Mother Hia went every day to the castle of the god of the Wu River. So Aduan told her that Rose of Evening was his cousin, and entreated her to take him along with her so that he could at least see her a single time. So she took him along, and let him stay at the lodge-house of the river-god for a few days. But the indwellers of the castle were so strictly watched that he could not see Rose of Evening even a single time. Sadly Aduan went back again.

Another month passed and Aduan, filled with gloomy thoughts, wished that death might be his portion.

One day Mother Hia came to him full of pity, and began to sympathize with him. "What a shame," said she, "that Rose of Evening has cast herself into the river!"

Aduan was extremely frightened, and his tears flowed resistlessly. He tore his beautiful garments, took his gold and his pearls, and went out with the sole idea of following his beloved in death. Yet the waters of the river stood up before him like walls, and no matter how often he ran against them, head down, they always flung him back.

He did not dare return, since he feared he might be questioned about his festival garments, and severely punished because he had ruined them. So he stood there and knew not what to do, while the perspiration ran down to his ankles. Suddenly, at the foot of the water-wall he saw a tall tree. Like a monkey he climbed up to its very top, and then, with all his might, he shot into the waves.

And then, without being wet, he found himself suddenly swimming on the surface of the river. Unexpectedly the world of men rose up once more before his dazzled eyes. He swam to the shore, and as he walked along the river-bank, his thoughts went back to his old mother. He took a ship and traveled home.

When he reached the village, it seemed to him as though all the houses in it belonged to another world. The following morning he entered his mother's house, and as he did so, heard a girl's voice beneath the window saying: "Your son has come back again!" The voice sounded like the voice of Rose of Evening, and when she came to greet him at his mother's side, sure enough, it was Rose of Evening herself.

And in that hour the joy of these two who were so fond of each other overcame all their sorrow. But in the mother's mind sorrow and doubt, terror and joy mingled in constant succession in a thousand different ways.

When Rose of Evening had been in the palace of the river-king, and had come to realize that she would never see Aduan again, she determined to die, and flung herself into the waters of the stream. But she was carried to the surface, and the waves carried and cradled her till a ship came by and took her aboard. They asked whence she came. Now Rose of Evening had originally been a celebrated singing girl of Wu, who had fallen into the river and whose body had never been found. So she thought to herself that, after all, she could not return to her old life again. So she answered: "Madame Dsiang, in Dschen-Giang is my mother-in-law." Then the travelers took passage for her in a ship which brought her to the place she had mentioned. The widow Dsiang first said she must be mistaken, but the girl insisted that there was no mistake, and told Aduan's mother her whole story. Yet, though the latter was charmed by her surpassing loveliness, she feared that Rose of Evening was too young to live a widow's life. But the girl was respectful and industrious, and when she saw that poverty ruled in her new home, she took her pearls and sold them for a high price. Aduan's old mother was greatly pleased to see how seriously the girl took her duties.

Now that Aduan had returned again Rose of Evening could not control her joy. And even Aduan's old mother cherished the hope that, after all, perhaps her son had not died. She secretly dug up her son's grave, yet all his bones were still lying in it. So she questioned Aduan. And then, for the first time, the latter realized that he was a departed spirit. Then he feared that Rose of Evening might regard him with disgust because he was no longer a human being. So he ordered his mother on no account to speak of it, and this his mother promised. Then she spread the report in the village that the body which had been found in the river had not been that of her son at all. Yet she could not rid herself of the fear that, since Aduan was a departed spirit, heaven might refuse to send him a child.

In spite of her fear, however, she was able to hold a grandson in her arms in course of time. When she looked at him, he was no different from other children, and then her cup of joy was filled to overflowing.

Rose of Evening gradually became aware of the fact that Aduan was not really a human being. "Why did you not tell me at once?" said she. "Departed spirits who wear the garments of the dragon castle, surround themselves with a soul-casing so heavy in texture that they can no longer be distinguished from the living.

And if one can obtain the lime made of dragon-horn which is in the castle, then the bones may be glued together in such wise that flesh and blood will grow over them again. What a pity that we could not obtain the lime while we were there!"

Aduan sold his pearl, for which a merchant from foreign parts gave him an enormous sum. Thus his family grew very wealthy. Once, on his mother's birthday, he danced with his wife and sang, in order to please her. The news reached the castle of the Dragon Prince and he thought to carry off Rose of Evening by force. But Aduan, alarmed, went to the Prince, and declared that both he and his wife were departed spirits. They examined him and since he cast no shadow, his word was taken, and he was not robbed of Rose of Evening.

Note: "Rose of Evening" is one of the most idyllic of Chinese art fairy-tales. The idea that the departed spirit throws no shadow has analogies in Norse and other European fairy-tales.

LXXIV

THE APE SUN WU KUNG

FAR, far away to the East, in the midst of the Great Sea there is an island called the Mountain of Flowers and Fruits. And on this mountain there is a high rock. Now this rock, from the very beginning of the world, had absorbed all the hidden seed power of heaven and earth and sun and moon, which endowed it with supernatural creative gifts. One day the rock burst, and out came an egg of stone. And out of this stone egg a stone ape was hatched by magic power.

When he broke the shell he bowed to all sides. Then he gradually learned to walk and to leap, and two streams of golden radiance broke from his eyes which shot up to the highest of the castles of heaven, so that the Lord of the Heavens was frightened. So he sent out the two gods, Thousandmile-Eye and Fine-Ear, to find out what had happened. The two gods came back and reported: "The rays shine from the eyes of the stone ape who was hatched out of the egg which came from the magic rock. There is no reason for uneasiness."

Little by little the ape grew up, ran and leaped about, drank from the springs in the valleys, ate the flowers and fruits, and time went by in unconstrained play.

One day, during the summer, when he was seeking coolness, together with the other apes on the island, they went to the valley to bathe. There they saw a waterfall which plunged down a high cliff. Said the apes to each other: "Whoever can force his way through the waterfall, without suffering injury, shall be our king." The stone ape at once leaped into the air with joy and cried: "I will pass through!" Then he closed his eyes, bent down low and leaped through the roar and foam of the waters. When he opened his eyes once more he saw an iron bridge, which was shut off from the outer world by the waterfall as though by a curtain.

At its entrance stood a tablet of stone on which were graven the words: "This is the heavenly cave behind the water-curtain on the Blessed Island of Flowers and Fruits." Filled with joy, the stone ape leaped out again through the waterfall and told the other apes what he had found. They received the news with great content, and begged the stone ape to take them there. So the tribe of apes leaped through the water on the iron bridge, and then crowded into the cave castle where they found a hearth with a profusion of pots, cups and platters. But all were made of stone. Then the apes paid homage to the stone ape as their king, and he was given the name of Handsome King of the Apes. He appointed long-tailed, ring-tailed and other monkeys to be his officials and counselors, servants and retainers, and they led a blissful life on the Mountain, sleeping by night in their cave castle, keeping away from birds and beasts, and their king enjoyed untroubled happiness. In this way some three hundred years went by.

One day, when the King of the Apes sat with his subjects at a merry meal, he suddenly began to weep. Frightened, the apes asked him why he so suddenly grew sad amid all his bliss. Said the King: "It is true that we are not subject to the law and rule of man, that birds and beasts do not dare attack us, yet little by little we grow old and weak, and some day the hour will strike when Death, the Ancient, will drag us off! Then we are gone in a moment, and can no longer dwell upon earth!" When the apes heard these words, they hid their faces and sobbed. But an old ape, whose arms were connected in such a way that he could add the length of one to that of the other, stepped forth from the ranks. In a loud tone of voice he said: "That you have hit upon this thought, O King, shows the desire to search for truth has awakened you! Among all living creatures, there are but three kinds who are exempt from Death's power: the Buddhas, the blessed spirits and the gods. Whoever attains one of these three grades escapes the rod of re-birth, and lives as long as the Heavens themselves."

The King of the Apes said: "Where do these three kinds of beings live?" And the old ape replied:

"They live in caves and on holy mountains in the great world of mortals." The King was pleased when he heard this, and told his apes that he was going to seek out gods and sainted spirits in order to learn the road to immortality from them. The apes dragged up peaches and other fruits and sweet wine to celebrate the parting banquet, and all made merry together.

On the following morning the Handsome King of the Apes rose very early, built him a raft of old pine trees and took a bamboo staff for a pole. Then he climbed on the raft, quite alone, and poled his way through the Great Sea. Wind and waves were favorable and he reached Asia. There he went ashore. On the strand he met a fisherman. He at once stepped up to him, knocked him down, tore off his clothes and put them on himself. Then he wandered around and visited all famous spots, went into the market-places, the densely populated cities, learned how to conduct himself properly, and how to speak and act like a well-bred human being. Yet his heart was set on learning the teaching of the Buddhas, the blessed spirits and the holy gods. But the people of the country in which he was were only concerned with honors and wealth. Not one of them seemed to care for life. Thus he went about until nine years had passed by unnoticed. Then he came to the strand of the Western Sea and it occurred to him: "No doubt there are gods and saints on the other side of the sea!" So he built another raft, floated it over the Western Sea and reached the land of the West. There he let his raft drift, and went ashore. After he had searched for many days, he suddenly saw a high mountain with deep, quiet valleys. As the Ape King went toward it, he heard a man singing in the woods, and the song sounded like one the blessed spirits might sing. So he hastily entered the wood to see who might be singing. There he met a wood-chopper at work. The Ape King bowed to him and said: "Venerable, divine master, I fall down and worship at your feet!" Said the wood-chopper: "I am only a workman; why do you call me divine master?" "Then, if you are no blessed god, how comes it you sing that divine song?" The wood-chopper laughed and said: "You are at home in music. The song I was singing was really taught me by a saint." "If you are acquainted with a saint," said the Ape King, "he surely cannot live far from here. I beg of you to show me the way to his dwelling." The wood-chopper replied: "It is not far from here. This mountain is known as the Mountain of the Heart. In it is a cave where dwells a saint who is called "The Discerner." The number of his disciples who have attained blessedness is countless. He still has some thirty to forty disciples gathered about him. You need only follow this path which leads to the South, and you cannot miss his dwelling." The Ape King thanked the wood-chopper and, sure enough, he came to the cave which the latter had described to him. The gate was locked and he did not venture to knock. So he leaped up into a pine tree, picked pine-cones and devoured the seed. Before long one of the saint's disciples came and opened the door and said: "What sort of a beast is it that is making such a noise?" The Ape King leaped down from his tree, bowed, and said: "I have come in search of truth. I did not venture to knock." Then the disciple had to laugh and said: "Our master was seated lost in meditation, when he told me to lead in the seeker after truth who stood without the gate, and here you really are. Well, you may come along with me!" The Ape King smoothed his clothes, put his hat on straight, and stepped in. A long passage led past magnificent buildings and quiet hidden huts to the place where the master was sitting upright on a seat of white marble. At his right and left stood his disciples, ready to serve him. The Ape King flung himself down on the ground and greeted the master humbly. In answer to his questions he told him how he had found his way to him. And when he was asked his name, he said: "I have no name. I am the ape who came out of the stone." So the master said: "Then I will give you a name. I name you Sun Wu Kung." The Ape King thanked him, full of joy, and thereafter he was called Sun Wu Kung. The master ordered his oldest disciple to instruct Sun Wu Kung in sweeping and cleaning, in going in and out, in good manners, how to labor in the field and how to water the gardens. In the course of time he learned to write, to burn incense and read the sutras. And in this way some six or seven years went by.

One day the master ascended the seat from which he taught, and began to speak regarding the great truth. Sun Wu Kung understood the hidden meaning of his words, and commenced to jerk about and dance in his joy. The master reproved him: "Sun Wu Kung, you have still not laid aside your wild nature! What do you mean by carrying on in such an unfitting manner?" Sun Wu Kung bowed and answered: "I was listening attentively to you when the meaning of your words was disclosed to my heart, and without thinking I began to dance for joy. I was not giving way to my wild nature." Said the master: "If your spirit has really awakened, then I will announce the great truth to you. But there are three hundred and sixty ways by means of which one may reach this truth. Which way shall I teach you?" Said Sun Wu Kung: "Whichever you will, O Master!" Then the Master asked: "Shall I teach you the way of magic?" Said Sun Wu Kung: "What does magic teach one?" The Master replied: "It teaches one to raise up spirits, to question oracles, and to foretell fortune and misfortune." "Can one secure eternal life by means of it?" inquired Sun Wu Kung. "No," was the answer. "Then I will not learn it." "Shall I teach you the sciences?" "What are the sciences?" "They are the nine schools of the three faiths. You learn how to read the holy books, pronounce incantations, commune with the gods, and call the saints to you." "Can one gain eternal life by means of them?" "No." "Then I will not learn them." "The way of repose is a very good way." "What is the way of repose?" "It teaches how to live without nourishment, how to remain quiescent in silent purity, and sit lost in meditation." "Can one gain eternal life in this way?" "No." "Then I will not learn it." "The way of deeds is also a good way." "What does that teach?" "It teaches one to equalize the vital powers, to practice bodily exercise, to prepare the elixir of life and to hold one's breath." "Will it give one eternal life?" "Not so." "Then I will not learn it! I will not learn it!" Thereupon the Master pretended to be angry, leaped down from his stand, took his cane and scolded: "What an ape! This he will not learn, and that he will not learn! What are you waiting to learn, then?" With that he gave him three blows across the head, retired to his inner chamber, and closed the great door after him.

The disciples were greatly excited, and overwhelmed Sun Wu Kung with reproaches. Yet the latter paid no attention to them, but smiled quietly to himself, for he had understood the riddle which the Master had given him to solve. And in his heart he thought:

"His striking me over the head three times meant that I was to be ready at the third watch of the night. His withdrawing to his inner chamber and closing the great door after him, meant that I was to go in to him by the back door, and that he would make clear the great truth to me in secret." Accordingly he waited until evening, and made a pretense of lying down to sleep with the other disciples. But when the third watch of the night had come he rose softly and crept to the back door. Sure enough it stood ajar. He slipped in and stepped before the Master's bed. The Master was sleeping with his face turned toward the wall, and the ape did not venture to wake him, but knelt down in front of the bed. After a time the Master turned around and hummed a stanza to himself:

"A hard, hard grind,
 Truth's lesson to expound.
One talks oneself deaf, dumb and blind.
 Unless the right man's found."

Then Sun Wu Kung replied: "I am waiting here reverentially!"

The Master flung on his clothes, sat up in bed and said harshly: "Accursed ape! Why are you not asleep? What are you doing here?"

Sun Wu Kung answered: "Yet you pointed out to me yesterday that I was to come to you at the third watch of the night, by the back door, in order to be instructed in the truth. Therefore I have ventured to come. If you will teach me in the fulness of your grace, I will be eternally grateful to you."

Thought the Master to himself: "There is real intelligence in this ape's head, to have made him understand me so well." Then he replied: "Sun Wu Kung, it shall be granted you! I will speak freely with you. Come quite close to me, and then I will show you the way to eternal life."

With that he murmured into his ear a divine, magical incantation to further the concentration of his vital powers, and explained the hidden knowledge word for word. Sun Wu Kung listened to him eagerly, and in a short time had learned it by heart. Then he thanked his teacher, went out again and lay down to sleep. From that time forward he practised the right mode of breathing, kept guard over his soul and spirit, and tamed the natural instincts of his heart. And while he did so three more years passed by. Then the task was completed.

One day the Master said to him: "Three great dangers still threaten you. Every one who wishes to accomplish something out of the ordinary is exposed to them, for he is pursued by the envy of demons and spirits. And only those who can overcome these three great dangers live as long as the heavens."

Then Sun Wu Kung was frightened and asked: "Is there any means of protection against these dangers?"

Then the Master again murmured a secret incantation into his ear, by means of which he gained the power to transform himself seventy-two times.

And when no more than a few days had passed Sun Wu Kung had learned the art.

One day the Master was walking before the cave in the company of his disciples. He called Sun Wu Kung up to him and asked: "What progress have you made with your art? Can you fly already?"

"Yes, indeed," said the ape.

"Then let me see you do so."

The ape leaped into the air to a distance of five or six feet from the ground. Clouds formed beneath his feet, and he was able to walk on them for several hundred yards. Then he was forced to drop down to earth again.

The Master said with a smile: "I call that crawling around on the clouds, not floating on them, as do the gods and saints who fly over the whole world in a single day. I will teach you the magic incantation for turning somersaults on the clouds. If you turn one of those somersaults you advance eighteen thousand miles at a clip."

Sun Wu Kung thanked him, full of joy, and from that time on he was able to move without limitation of space in any direction.

One day Sun Wu Kung was sitting together with the other disciples under the pine-tree by the gate, discussing the secrets of their teachings. Finally they asked him to show them some of his transforming arts. Sun Wu Kung could not keep his secret to himself, and agreed to do so.

With a smile he said: "Just set me a task! What do you wish me to change myself into?"

They said: "Turn yourself into a pine-tree."

So Sun Wu Kung murmured a magic incantation, turned around—and there stood a pine-tree before their very eyes. At this they all broke out into a horse-laugh. The Master heard the noise and came out of the gate, dragging his cane behind him.

"Why are you making such a noise?" he called out to them harshly.

Said they: "Sun Wu Kung has turned himself into a pine-tree, and this made us laugh."

"Sun Wu Kung, come here!" said the Master. "Now just tell me what tricks you are up to? Why do you have to turn yourself into a pine-tree? All the work you have done means nothing more to you than a chance to make magic for your companions to wonder at. That shows that your heart is not yet under control."

Humbly Sun Wu Kung begged his forgiveness.

But the Master said: "I bear you no ill will, but you must go away."

With tears in his eyes Sun Wu Kung asked him: "But where shall I go?"

"You must go back again whence you came," said the Master. And when Sun Wu Kung sadly bade him farewell, he threatened him: "Your savage nature is sure to bring down evil upon you some time. You must tell no one that you are my pupil. If you so much as breathe a word about it, I will fetch your soul and lock it up in the nethermost hell, so that you cannot escape for a thousand eternities."

Sun Wu Kung replied: "I will not say a word! I will not say a word!"

Then he once more thanked him for all the kindness shown him, turned a somersault and climbed up to the clouds.

Within the hour he had passed the seas, and saw the Mountain of Flowers and Fruits lying before him. Then he felt happy and at home again, let his cloud sink down to earth and cried: "Here I am back again, children!" And at once, from the valley, from behind the rocks, out of the grass and from amid the trees came his apes. They came running up by thousands, surrounded and greeted him, and inquired as to his adventures. Sun Wu Kung said: "I have now found the way to eternal life, and need fear Death the Ancient no longer." Then all the apes were overjoyed, and competed with each other in bringing flowers and fruits, peaches and wine, to welcome him. And again they honored Sun Wu Kung as the Handsome Ape King.

Sun Wu Kung now gathered the apes about him and questioned them as to how they had fared during his absence.

Said they: "It is well that you have come back again, great king! Not long ago a devil came here who wanted to take possession of our cave by force. We fought with him, but he dragged away many of your children and will probably soon return."

Sun Wu Kung grew very angry and said: "What sort of a devil is this who dares be so impudent?"

The apes answered: "He is the Devil-King of Chaos. He lives in the North, who knows how many miles away. We only saw him come and go amid clouds and mist."

Sun Wu Kung said: "Wait, and I will see to him!" With that he turned a somersault and disappeared without a trace.

In the furthest North rises a high mountain, upon whose slope is a cave above which is the inscription: "The Cave of the Kidneys." Before the door little devils were dancing. Sun Wu Kung called harshly to them: "Tell your Devil-King quickly that he had better give me my children back again!" The little devils were frightened, and delivered the message in the cave. Then the Devil-King reached for his sword and came out. But he was so large and broad that he could not even see Sun Wu Kung. He was clad from head to foot in black armor, and his face was as black as the bottom of a kettle. Sun Wu Kung shouted at him: "Accursed devil, where are your eyes, that you cannot see the venerable Sun?" Then the devil looked to the ground and saw a stone ape standing before him, bare-headed, dressed in red, with a yellow girdle and black boots. So the Devil-King laughed and said: "You are not even four feet high, less than thirty years of age, and weaponless, and yet you venture to make such a commotion." Said Sun Wu Kung: "I am not too small for you; and I can make myself large at will. You scorn me because I am without a weapon, but my two fists can thresh to the very skies." With that he stooped, clenched his fists and began to give the devil a beating. The devil was large and clumsy, but Sun Wu Kung leaped about nimbly. He struck him between the ribs and between the wind and his blows fell ever more fast and furious. In his despair the devil raised his great knife and aimed a blow at Sun Wu Kung's head. But the latter avoided the blow, and fell back on his magic powers of transformation. He pulled out a hair, put it in his mouth, chewed it, spat it out into the air and said: "Transform yourself!" And at once it turned into many hundreds of little apes who began to attack the devil. Sun Wu Kung, be it said, had eighty-four thousand hairs on his body, every single one of which he could transform. The little apes with their sharp eyes, leaped around with the greatest rapidity. They surrounded the Devil-King on all sides, tore at his clothes, and pulled at his legs, until he finally measured his length on the ground. Then Sun Wu Kung stepped up, tore his knife from his hand, and put an end to him. After that he entered the cave and released his captive children, the apes. The transformed hairs he drew to him again, and making a fire, he burned the evil cave to the ground. Then he gathered up those he had released, and flew back with them like a storm-wind to his cavern on the Mountain of Flowers and Fruits, joyfully greeted by all the apes.

After Sun Wu Kung had obtained possession of the Devil-King's great knife, he exercised his apes every day. They had wooden swords and lances of bamboo, and played their martial music on reed pipes. He had them build a camp so that they would be prepared for all dangers. Suddenly the thought came to Sun Wu Kung: "If we go on this way, perhaps we may incite some human or animal king to fight with us, and then we would not be able to withstand him with our wooden swords and bamboo lances!" And to his apes he said: "What should be done?" Four baboons stepped forward and said: "In the capital city of the Aulai empire there are warriors without number. And there coppersmiths and steelsmiths are also to be found. How would it be if we were to buy steel and iron and have those smiths weld weapons for us?"

A somersault and Sun Wu Kung was standing before the city moat. Said he to himself: "To first buy the weapons would take a great deal of time. I would rather make magic and take some." So he blew on the ground. Then a tremendous storm-wind arose which drove sand and stones before it, and caused all the soldiers in the city to run away in terror. Then Sun Wu Kung went to the armory, pulled out one of his hairs, turned it into thousands of little apes, cleared out the whole supply of weapons, and flew back home on a cloud.

Then he gathered his people about him and counted them. In all they numbered seventy-seven thousand. They held the whole Mountain in terror, and all the magic beasts and spirit princes who dwelt on it. And these came forth from seventy-two caves and honored Sun Wu Kung as their head.

One day the Ape King said: "Now you all have weapons; but this knife which I took from the Devil-King is too light, and no longer suits me. What should be done?"

Then the four baboons stepped forward and said:

"In view of your spirit powers, O king, you will find no weapon fit for your use on all the earth! Is it possible for you to walk through the water?"

The Ape King answered: "All the elements are subject to me and there is no place where I cannot go."

Then the baboons said: "The water at our cave here flows into the Great Sea, to the castle of the Dragon-King of the Eastern Sea. If your magic power makes it possible, you could go to the Dragon-King and let him give you a weapon."

This suited the Ape King. He leaped on the iron bridge and murmured an incantation. Then he flung himself into the waves, which parted before him and ran on till he came to the palace of water-crystal. There he met a Triton who asked who he was. He mentioned his name and said: "I am the Dragon-King's nearest neighbor, and have come to visit him." The Triton took the message to the castle, and the Dragon-King of the Eastern Sea came out hastily to receive him. He bade him be seated and served him with tea.

Sun Wu Kung said: "I have learned the hidden knowledge and gained the powers of immortality. I have drilled my apes in the art of warfare in order to protect our mountain; but I have no weapon I can use, and have therefore come to you to borrow one."

The Dragon-King now had General Flounder bring him a great spear. But Sun Wu Kung was not satisfied with it. Then he ordered Field-Marshal Eel to fetch in a nine-tined fork, which weighed three thousand six hundred pounds. But Sun Wu Kung balanced it in his hand and said: "Too light! Too light! Too light!"

Then the Dragon-King was frightened, and had the heaviest weapon in his armory brought in. It weighed seven thousand two hundred pounds. But this was still too light for Sun Wu Kung. The Dragon-King assured him that he had nothing heavier, but Sun Wu Kung would not give in and said: "Just look around!"

Finally the Dragon-Queen and her daughter came out, and said to the Dragon-King: "This saint is an unpleasant customer with whom to deal. The great iron bar is still lying here in our sea; and not so long ago it shone with a red glow, which is probably a sign it is time for it to be taken away."

Said the Dragon-King: "But that is the rod which the Great Yu used when he ordered the waters, and determined the depth of the seas and rivers. It cannot be taken away."

The Dragon-Queen replied: "Just let him see it! What he then does with it is no concern of ours."

So the Dragon-King led Sun Wu Kung to the measuring rod. The golden radiance that came from it could be seen some distance off. It was an enormous iron bar, with golden clamps on either side.

Sun Wu Kung raised it with the exertion of all his strength, and then said: "It is too heavy, and ought to be somewhat shorter and thinner!"

No sooner had he said this than the iron rod grew less. He tried it again, and then he noticed that it grew larger or smaller at command. It could be made to shrink to the size of a pin. Sun Wu Kung was overjoyed and beat about in the sea with the rod, which he had let grow large again, till the waves spurted mountain-high and the dragon-castle rocked on its foundations. The Dragon-King trembled with fright, and all his tortoises, fishes and crabs drew in their heads.

Sun Wu Kung laughed, and said: "Many thanks for the handsome present!" Then he continued: "Now I have a weapon, it is true, but as yet I have no armor. Rather than hunt up two or three other households, I think you will be willing to provide me with a suit of mail."

The Dragon-King told him that he had no armor to give him.

Then the ape said: "I will not leave until you have obtained one for me." And once more he began to swing his rod.

"Do not harm me!" said the terrified Dragon-King, "I will ask my brothers."

And he had them beat the iron drum and strike the golden gong, and in a moment's time all the Dragon-King's brothers came from all the other seas. The Dragon-King talked to them in private and said: "This is a terrible fellow, and we must not rouse his anger! First he took the rod with the golden clamps from me, and now he also insists on having a suit of armor. The best thing to do would be to satisfy him at once, and complain of him to the Lord of the Heavens later."

So the brothers brought a magic suit of golden mail, magic boots and a magic helmet.

Then Sun Wu Kung thanked them and returned to his cave. Radiantly he greeted his children, who had come to meet him, and showed them the rod with the golden clamps. They all crowded up and wished to pick it up from the ground, if only a single time; but it was just as though a dragon-fly had attempted to overthrow a stone column, or an ant were trying to carry a great mountain. It would not move a hair's breadth. Then the apes opened their mouths and stuck out their tongues, and said: "Father, how is it possible for you to carry that heavy thing?" So he told them the secret of the rod and showed them its effects. Then he set his empire in order, and appointed the four baboons field-marshals; and the seven beast-spirits, the ox-spirit, the dragon-spirit, the bird-spirit, the lion-spirit and the rest also joined him.

One day he took a nap after dinner. Before he did so he had let the bar shrink, and had stuck it in his ear. While he was sleeping he saw two men come along in his dream, who had a card on which was written "Sun Wu Kung." They would not allow him to resist, but fettered him and led his spirit away. And when they reached a great city the Ape King gradually came to himself. Over the city gate he saw a tablet of iron on which was engraved in large letters: "The Nether World."

Then all was suddenly clear to him and he said: "Why, this must be the dwelling-place of Death! But I have long since escaped from his power, and how dare he have me dragged here!" The more he reflected the wilder he grew. He drew out the golden rod from his ear, swung it and let it grow large. Then he crushed the two constables to mush, burst his fetters, and rolled his bar before him into the city. The ten Princes of the Dead were frightened, bowed before him and asked: "Who are you?"

Sun Wu Kung answered: "If you do not know me then why did you send for me and have me dragged to this place? I am the heaven-born saint Sun Wu Kung of the Mountain of Flowers and Fruits. And now, who are you? Tell me your names quickly or I will strike you!"

The ten Princes of the Dead humbly gave him their names.

Sun Wu Kung said: "I, the Venerable Sun, have gained the power of eternal life! You have nothing to say to me! Quick, let me have the Book of Life!"

They did not dare defy him, and had the scribe bring in the Book. Sun Wu Kung opened it. Under the head of "Apes," No. 1350, he read: "Sun Wu Kung, the heaven-born stone ape. His years shall be three hundred and twenty-four. Then he shall die without illness."

Sun Wu Kung took the brush from the table and struck out the whole ape family from the Book of Life, threw the Book down and said: "Now we are even! From this day on I will suffer no impertinences from you!"

With that he cleared a way for himself out of the Nether World by means of his rod, and the ten Princes of the Dead did not venture to stay him, but only complained of him afterward to the Lord of the Heavens.

When Sun Wu Kung had left the city he slipped and fell to the ground. This caused him to wake, and he noticed he had been dreaming. He called his four baboons to him and said: "Splendid, splendid! I was dragged to Death's castle and I caused considerable uproar there. I had them give me the Book of Life, and I struck out the mortal hour of all the apes!" And after that time the apes on the Mountain no longer died, because their names had been stricken out in the Nether World.

But the Lord of the Heavens sat in his castle, and had all his servants assembled about him. And a saint stepped forward and presented the complaint of the Dragon-King of the Eastern Sea. And another stepped forward and presented the complaint of the ten Princes of the Dead. The Lord of the Heavens glanced through the two memorials. Both told of the wild, unmannerly conduct of Sun Wu Kung. So the Lord of the Heavens ordered a god to descend to earth and take him prisoner. The Evening Star came forward, however, and said: "This ape was born of the purest powers of heaven and earth and sun and moon. He has gained the hidden knowledge and has become an immortal. Recall, O Lord, your great love for all that which has life, and forgive him his sin! Issue an order that he be called up to the heavens, and be given a charge here, so that he may come to his senses. Then, if he again oversteps your commands, let him be punished without mercy." The Lord of the Heavens was agreeable, had the order issued, and told the Evening Star to take it to Sun Wu Kung. The Evening Star mounted a colored cloud and descended on the Mountain of Flowers and Fruits.

He greeted Sun Wu Kung and said to him: "The Lord had heard of your actions and meant to punish you. I am the Evening Star of the Western Skies, and I spoke for you. Therefore he has commissioned me to take you to the skies, so that you may be given a charge there."

Sun Wu Kung was overjoyed and answered: "I had just been thinking I ought to pay Heaven a visit some time, and sure enough, Old Star, here you have come to fetch me!"

Then he had his four baboons come and said to them impressively: "See that you take good care of our Mountain! I am going up to the heavens to look around there a little!"

Then he mounted a cloud together with the Evening Star and floated up. But he kept turning his somersaults, and advanced so quickly that the Evening Star on his cloud was left behind. Before he knew it he had reached the Southern Gate of Heaven and was about to step carelessly through. The gatekeeper did not wish to let him enter, but he did not let this stop him. In the midst of their dispute the Evening Star came up and explained matters, and then he was allowed to enter the heavenly gate. When he came to the castle of the Lord of the Heavens, he stood upright before it, without bowing his head.

The Lord of the Heavens asked: "Then this hairy face with the pointed lips is Sun Wu Kung?"

He replied: "Yes, I am the Venerable Sun!"

All the servants of the Lord of the Heavens were shocked and said: "This wild ape does not even bow, and goes so far as to call himself the Venerable Sun. His crime deserves a thousand deaths!"

But the Lord said: "He has come up from the earth below, and is not as yet used to our rules. We will forgive him."

Then he gave orders that a charge be found for him. The marshal of the heavenly court reported: "There is no charge vacant anywhere, but an official is needed in the heavenly stables." Thereupon the Lord made him stablemaster of the heavenly steeds. Then the servants of the Lord of the Heavens told him he should give thanks for the grace bestowed on him. Sun Wu Kung called out aloud: "Thanks to command!" took possession of his certificate of appointment, and went to the stables in order to enter upon his new office.

Sun Wu Kung attended to his duties with great zeal. The heavenly steeds grew sleek and fat, and the stables were filled with young foals. Before he knew it half a month had gone by. Then his heavenly friends prepared a banquet for him.

While they were at table Sun Wu Kung asked accidentally: "Stablemaster? What sort of a title is that?"

"Why, that is an official title," was the reply.

"What rank has this office?"

"It has no rank at all," was the answer.

"Ah," said the ape, "is it so high that it outranks all other dignities?"

"No, it is not high, it is not high at all," answered his friends. "It is not even set down in the official roster, but is quite a subordinate position. All you have to do is to attend to the steeds. If you see to it that they grow fat, you get a good mark; but if they grow thin or ill, or fall down, your punishment will be right at hand."

Then the Ape King grew angry: "What, they treat me, the Venerable Sun, in such a shameful way!" and he started up. "On my Mountain I was a king, I was a father! What need was there for him to lure me into his heaven to feed horses? I'll do it no longer! I'll do it no longer!"

Hola, and he had already overturned the table, drawn the rod with the golden clamps from his ear, let it grow large and beat a way out for himself to the Southern gate of Heaven. And no one dared stop him.

Already he was back in his island Mountain and his people surrounded him and said: "You have been gone for more than ten years, great king! How is it you do not return to us until now?"

The Ape King said: "I did not spend more than about ten days in Heaven. This Lord of the Heavens does not know how to treat his people. He made me his stablemaster, and I had to feed his horses. I am so ashamed that I am ready to die. But I did not put up with it, and now I am here once more!"

His apes eagerly prepared a banquet to comfort him. While they sat at table two horned devil-kings came and brought him a yellow imperial robe as a present. Filled with joy he slipped into it, and appointed the two devil-kings leaders of the vanguard. They thanked him and began to flatter him: "With your power and wisdom, great king, why should you have to serve the Lord of the Heavens? To call you the Great Saint who is Heaven's Equal would be quite in order.''

The ape was pleased with this speech and said: "Good, good!" Then he ordered his four baboons to have a flag made quickly, on which was to be inscribed: "The Great Saint Who Is Heaven's Equal." And from that time on he had himself called by that title.

When the Lord of the Heavens learned of the flight of the ape, he ordered Li Dsing, the pagoda-bearing god, and his third son, Notscha, to take the Ape King prisoner. They sallied forth at the head of a heavenly warrior host, laid out a camp before his cave, and sent a brave warrior to challenge him to single combat. But he was easily beaten by Sun Wu Kung and obliged to flee, and Sun Wu Kung even shouted after him, laughing: "What a bag of wind! And he calls himself a heavenly warrior! I'll not slay you. Run along quickly and send me a better man!"

When Notscha saw this he himself hurried up to do battle.

Said Sun Wu Kung to him: "To whom do you belong, little one? You must not play around here, for something might happen to you!"

But Notscha cried out in a loud voice: "Accursed ape! I am Prince Notscha, and have been ordered to take you prisoner!" And with that he swung his sword in the direction of Sun Wu Kung.

"Very well," said the latter, "I will stand here and never move."

Then Notscha grew very angry, and turned into a three-headed god with six arms, in which he held six different weapons. Thus he rushed on to the attack.

Sun Wu Kung laughed. "The little fellow knows

the trick of it! But easy, wait a bit! I will change shape, too!"

And he also turned himself into a figure with three heads and with six arms, and swung three gold-clamp rods. And thus they began to fight. Their blows rained down with such rapidity that it seemed as though thousands of weapons were flying through the air. After thirty rounds the combat had not yet been decided. Then Sun Wu Kung hit upon an idea. He secretly pulled out one of his hairs, turned it into his own shape, and let it continue the fight with Notscha. He himself, however, slipped behind Notscha, and gave him such a blow on the left arm with his rod that his knees gave way beneath him with pain, and he had to withdraw in defeat.

So Notscha told his father Li Dsing: "This devil-ape is altogether too powerful! I cannot get the better of him!" There was nothing left to do but to return to the Heavens and admit their overthrow. The Lord of the Heavens bowed his head, and tried to think of some other hero whom he might send out.

Then the Evening Star once more came forward and said: "This ape is so strong and so courageous, that probably not one of us here is a match for him. He revolted because the office of stablemaster appeared too lowly for him. The best thing would be to temper justice with mercy, let him have his way, and appoint him Great Saint Who Is Heaven's Equal. It will only be necessary to give him the empty title, without combining a charge with it, and then the matter would be settled." The Lord of the Heavens was satisfied with this suggestion, and once more sent the Evening Star to summon the new saint. When Sun Wu Kung heard that he had arrived, he said: "The old Evening Star is a good fellow!" and he had his army draw up in line to give him a festive reception. He himself donned his robes of ceremony and politely went out to meet him.

Then the Evening Star told him what had taken place in the Heavens, and that he had his appointment as Great Saint Who Is Heaven's Equal with him.

Thereupon the Great Saint laughed and said: "You also spoke in my behalf before, Old Star! And now you have again taken my part. Many thanks! Many thanks!"

Then when they appeared together in the presence of the Lord of the Heavens the latter said: "The rank of Great Saint Who Is Heaven's Equal is very high. But now you must not cut any further capers."

The Great Saint expressed his thanks, and the Lord of the Heavens ordered two skilled architects to build a castle for him East of the peach-garden of the Queen-Mother of the West. And he was led into it with all possible honors.

Now the Saint was in his element. He had all that heart could wish for, and was untroubled by any work. He took his ease, walked about in the Heavens as he chose, and paid visits to the gods. The Three Pure Ones and the Four Rulers he treated with some little respect; but the planetary gods and the lords of the twenty-eight houses of the moon, and of the twelve zodiac signs, and the other stars he addressed familiarly with a "Hey, you!" Thus he idled day by day, without occupation among the clouds of the Heavens. On one occasion one of the wise said to the Lord of the Heavens: "The holy Sun is idle while day follows day. It is to be feared that some mischievous thoughts may occur to him, and it might be better to give him some charge."

So the Lord of the Heavens summoned the Great

Saint and said to him: "The life-giving peaches in the garden of the Queen-Mother will soon be ripe. I give you the charge of watching over them. Do your duty conscientiously!"

This pleased the Saint and he expressed his thanks. Then he went to the garden, where the caretakers and gardeners received him on their knees.

He asked them: "How many trees in all are there in the garden?"

"Three thousand six hundred," replied the gardener. "There are twelve-hundred trees in the foremost row. They have red blossoms and bear small fruit, which ripens every three thousand years. Whoever eats it grows bright and healthy. The twelve hundred trees in the middle row have double blossoms and bear sweet fruit, which ripens every six thousand years. Whoever eats of it is able to float in the rose-dawn without aging. The twelve hundred trees in the last row bear red-striped fruit with small pits. They ripen every nine thousand years. Whoever eats their fruit lives eternally, as long as the Heavens themselves, and remains untouched for thousands of eons."

The Saint heard all this with pleasure. He checked up the lists and from that time on appeared every day or so to see to things. The greater part of the peaches in the last row were already ripe. When he came to the garden, he would on each occasion send away the caretakers and gardeners under some pretext, leap up into the trees, and gorge himself to his heart's content with the peaches.

At that time the Queen-Mother of the West was preparing the great peach banquet to which she was accustomed to invite all the gods of the Heavens. She sent out the fairies in their garments of seven colors with baskets, that they might pick the peaches. The caretaker said to them: "The garden has now been entrusted to the guardianship of the Great Saint Who is Heaven's Equal, so you will first have to announce yourselves to him." With that he led the seven fairies into the garden. There they looked everywhere for the Great Saint, but could not find him. So the fairies said: "We have our orders and must not be late. We will begin picking the peaches in the meantime!" So they picked several baskets full from the foremost row. In the second row the peaches were already scarcer. And in the last row there hung only a single half-ripe peach. They bent down the bough and picked it, and then allowed it to fly up again.

Now it happened that the Great Saint, who had turned himself into a peach-worm, had just been taking his noon-day nap on this bough. When he was so rudely awakened, he appeared in his true form, seized his rod and was about to strike the fairies.

But the fairies said: "We have been sent here by the Queen-Mother. Do not be angry, Great Saint!"

Said the Great Saint: "And who are all those whom the Queen-Mother has invited?"

They answered: "All the gods and saints in the Heavens, on the earth and under the earth."

"Has she also invited me?" said the Saint.

"Not that we know of," said the fairies.

Then the Saint grew angry, murmured a magic incantation and said: "Stay! Stay! Stay!"

With that the seven fairies were banned to the spot. The Saint then took a cloud and sailed away on it to the palace of the Queen-Mother.

On the way he met the Bare-Foot God and asked him: "Where are you going?"

"To the peach banquet," was the answer.

Then the Saint lied to him, saying: "I have been

LITERARY FAIRY TALES

commanded by the Lord of the Heavens to tell all the gods and saints that they are first to come to the Hall of Purity, in order to practise the rites, and then go together to the Queen-Mother."

Then the Great Saint changed himself into the semblance of the Bare-Foot God and sailed to the palace of the Queen-Mother. There he let his cloud sink down and entered quite unconcerned. The meal was ready, yet none of the gods had as yet appeared. Suddenly the Great Saint caught the aroma of wine, and saw well-nigh a hundred barrels of the precious nectar standing in a room to one side. His mouth watered. He tore a few hairs out and turned them into sleep-worms. These worms crept into the nostrils of the cup-bearers so that they all fell asleep. Thereupon he enjoyed the delicious viands to the full, opened the barrels and drank until he was nearly stupefied. Then he said to himself: "This whole affair is beginning to make me feel creepy. I had better go home first of all and sleep a bit." And he stumbled out of the garden with uncertain steps. Sure enough, he missed his way, and came to the dwelling of Laotzse. There he regained consciousness. He arranged his clothing and went in. There was no one to be seen in the place, for at the moment Laotzse was at the God of Light's abode, talking to him, and with him were all his servants, listening. Since he found no one at home the Great Saint went as far as the inner chamber, where Laotzse was in the habit of brewing the elixir of life. Beside the stove stood five gourd containers full of the pills of life which had already been rolled. Said the Great Saint: "I had long since intended to prepare a couple of these pills. So it suits me very well to find them here." He poured out the contents of the gourds, and ate up all the pills of life. Since he had now had enough to eat and drink he thought to himself: "Bad, bad! The mischief I have done cannot well be repaired. If they catch me my life will be in danger. I think I had better go down to earth again and remain a king!" With that he made himself invisible, went out at the Western Gate of Heaven, and returned to the Mountain of Flowers and Fruits, where he told his people who received him the story of his adventures.

When he spoke of the wine-nectar of the peach garden, his apes said: "Can't you go back once more and steal a few bottles of the wine, so that we too may taste of it and gain eternal life?"

The Ape King was willing, turned a somersault, crept into the garden unobserved, and picked up four more barrels. Two of them he took under his arms and two he held in his hands. Then he disappeared with them without leaving a trace and brought them to his cave, where he enjoyed them together with his apes.

In the meantime the seven fairies, whom the Great Saint had banned to the spot, had regained their freedom after a night and a day. They picked up their baskets and told the Queen-Mother what had happened to them. And the cup-bearers, too, came hurrying up and reported the destruction which some one unknown had caused among the eatables and drinkables. The Queen-Mother went to the Lord of the Heavens to complain. Shortly afterward Laotzse also came to him to tell about the theft of the pills of life. And the Bare-Foot God came along and reported that he had been deceived by the Great Saint Who Is Heaven's Equal; and from the Great Saint's palace the servants came running and said that the Saint had disappeared and was nowhere to be found. Then the Lord of the Heavens was frightened, and said: "This whole mess is undoubtedly the work of that devilish ape!"

Now the whole host of Heaven, together with all the star-gods, the time-gods and the mountain-gods was called out in order to catch the ape. Li Dsing once more was its commander-in-chief. He invested the entire Mountain, and spread out the sky-net and the earth-net, so that no one could escape. Then he sent his bravest heroes into battle. Courageously the ape withstood all attacks from early morn till sundown. But by that time his most faithful followers had been captured. That was too much for him. He pulled out a hair and turned it into thousands of Ape-Kings, who all hewed about them with golden-clamped iron rods. The heavenly host was vanquished, and the ape withdrew to his cave to rest.

Now it happened that Guan Yin had also gone to the peach banquet in the garden, and had found out what Sun Wu Kung had done. When she went to visit the Lord of the Heavens, Li Dsing was just coming in, to report the great defeat which he had suffered on the Mountain of Flowers and Fruits. Then Guan Yin said to the Lord of the Heavens: "I can recommend a hero to you who will surely get the better of the ape. It is your grandson Yang Oerlang. He has conquered all the beast and bird spirits, and overthrown the elves in the grass and the brush. He knows what has to be done to get the better of such devils."

So Yang Oerlang was brought in, and Li Dsing led him to his camp. Li Dsing asked Yang Oerlang how he would go about getting the better of the ape.

Yang Oerlang laughed and said: "I think I will have to go him one better when it comes to changing shapes. It would be best for you to take away the sky-net so that our combat is not disturbed." Then he requested Li Dsing to post himself in the upper air with the magic spirit mirror in his hand, so that when the ape made himself invisible, he might be found again by means of the mirror. When all this had been arranged, Yang Oerlang went out in front of the cave with his spirits to give battle.

The ape leaped out, and when he saw the powerful hero with the three-tined sword standing before him he asked: "And who may you be?"

The other said: "I am Yang Oerlang, the grandson of the Lord of the Heavens!"

Then the ape laughed and said: "O yes, I remember! His daughter ran away with a certain Sir Yang, to whom heaven gave a son. You must be that son!"

Yang Oerlang grew furious, and advanced upon him with his spear. Then a hot battle began. For three hundred rounds they fought without decisive results. Then Yang Oerlang turned himself into a giant with a black face and red hair.

"Not bad," said the ape, "but I can do that too!"

So they continued to fight in that form. But the ape's baboons were much frightened. The beast and planet spirits of Yang Oerlang pressed the apes hard. They slew most of them and the others hid away. When the ape saw this his heart grew uneasy. He drew the magic giant-likeness in again, took his rod and fled. But Yang Oerlang followed hard on his heels. In his urgent need the ape thrust the rod, which he had turned into a needle, into his ear, turned into a sparrow, and flew up into the crest of a tree. Yang Oerlang who was following in his tracks, suddenly lost sight of him. But his keen eyes soon recognized that he had turned himself into a sparrow So he flung away spear and crossbow, turned himself into a sparrow-hawk, and darted down on the sparrow. But the latter soared high into the air as a cormorant. Yang Oerlang shook his plumage, turned into a great sea-crane, and shot up into the clouds to seize the cormo-

LITERARY FAIRY TALES 323

rant. The latter dropped, flew into a valley and dove beneath the waters of a brook in the guise of a fish. When Yang Oerlang reached the edge of the valley, and had lost his trail he said to himself: "This ape has surely turned himself into a fish or a crab! I will change my form as well in order to catch him. So he turned into a fish-hawk and floated above the surface of the water. When the ape in the water caught sight of the fish-hawk, he saw that he was Yang Oerlang. He swiftly swung around and fled, Yang Oerlang in pursuit. When the latter was no further away than the length of a beak, the ape turned, crept ashore as a water-snake and hid in the grass. Yang Oerlang, when he saw the water-snake creep from the water, turned into an eagle and spread his claws to seize the snake. But the water-snake sprang up and turned into the lowest of all birds, a speckled buzzard, and perched on the steep edge of a cliff. When Yang Oerlang saw that the ape had turned himself into so contemptible a creature as a buzzard, he would no longer play the game of changing form with him. He reappeared in his original form, took up his crossbow and shot at the bird. The buzzard slipped and fell down the side of the cliff. At its foot the ape turned himself into the chapel of a field-god. He opened his mouth for a gate, his teeth became the two wings of the door, his tongue the image of the god, and his eyes the windows. His tail was the only thing he did not know what to do with. So he let it stand up stiffly behind him in the shape of a flag-pole. When Yang Oerlang reached the foot of the hill he saw the chapel, whose flagpole stood in the rear. Then he laughed and said: "That ape is really a devil of an ape! He wants to lure me into the chapel in order to bite me. But I will not go in. First I will break his windows for him, and then I will stamp down the wings of his door!" When the ape heard this he was much frightened. He made a bound like a tiger, and disappeared without a trace in the air. With a single somersault he reached Yang Oerlang's own temple. There he assumed Yang Oerlang's own form and stepped in. The spirits who were on guard were unable to recognize him. They received him on their knees. So the ape then seated himself on the god's throne, and had the prayers which had come in submitted to him.

When Yang Oerlang no longer saw the ape, he rose in the air to Li Dsing and said: "I was vying with the ape in changing shape. Suddenly I could no longer find him. Take a look in the mirror!" Li Dsing took a look in the magic spirit mirror and then he laughed and said: "The ape has turned himself into your likeness, is sitting in your temple quite at home there, and making mischief." When Yang Oerlang heard this he took his three-tined spear, and hastened to his temple. The door-spirits were frightened and said: "But father came in only this very minute! How is it that another one comes now?" Yang Oerlang, without paying attention to them, entered the temple and aimed his spear at Sun Wu Kung. The latter resumed his own shape, laughed and said: "Young sir, you must not be angry! The god of this place is now Sun Wu Kung." Without uttering a word Yang Oerlang assailed him. Sun Wu Kung took up his rod and returned the blows. Thus they crowded out of the temple together, fighting, and wrapped in mists and clouds once more gained the Mountain of Flowers and Fruits.

In the meantime Guan Yin was sitting with Laotzse, the Lord of the Heavens and the Queen-Mother in the great hall of Heaven, waiting for news. When none came she said: "I will go with Laotzse to the Southern Gate of Heaven and see how matters stand?" And when they saw that the struggle had still not come to an end she said to Laotzse: "How would it be if we helped Yang Oerlang a little? I will shut up Sun Wu Kung in my vase."

But Laotzse said: "Your vase is made of porcelain. Sun Wu Kung could smash it with his iron rod. But I have a circlet of diamonds which can enclose all living creatures. That we can use!" So he flung his circlet through the air from the heavenly gate, and struck Sun Wu Kung on the head with it. Since he had his hands full fighting, the latter could not guard himself against it, and the blow on the forehead caused him to slip. Yet he rose again and tried to escape. But the heavenly hound of Yang Oerlang bit his leg until he fell to the ground. Then Yang Oerlang and his followers came up and tied him with thongs, and thrust a hook through his collar-bone so that he could no longer transform himself. And Laotzse took possession of his diamond circlet again, and returned with Guan Yin to the hall of Heaven. Sun Wu Kung was now brought in in triumph, and was condemned to be beheaded. He was then taken to the place of execution and bound to a post. But all efforts to kill him by means of ax and sword, thunder and lightning were vain. Nothing so much as hurt a hair on his head.

Said Laotzse: "It is not surprising. This ape has eaten the peaches, has drunk the nectar and also swallowed the pills of life. Nothing can harm him. The best thing would be for me to take him along and thrust him into my stove in order to melt the elixir of life out of him again. Then he will fall into dust and ashes."

So Sun Wu Kung's fetters were loosed, and Laotzse took him with him, thrust him into his oven, and ordered the boy to keep up a hot fire.

But along the edge of the oven were graven the signs of the eight elemental forces. And when the ape was thrust into the oven he took refuge beneath the sign of the wind, so that the fire could not injure him; and the smoke only made his eyes smart. He remained in the oven seven times seven days. Then Laotzse had it opened to take a look. As soon as Sun Wu Kung saw the light shine in, he could no longer bear to be shut up, but leaped out and upset the magic oven. The guards and attendants he threw to the ground and Laotzse himself, who tried to seize him, received such a push that he stuck his legs up in the air like an onion turned upside down. Then Sun Wu Kung took his rod out of his ear, and without looking where he struck, hewed everything to bits, so that the star-gods closed their doors and the guardians of the Heavens ran away. He came to the castle of the Lord of the Heavens, and the guardian of the gate with his steel whip was only just in time to hold him back. Then the thirty-six thunder gods were set at him, and surrounded him, though they could not seize him.

The Lord of the Heavens said: "Buddha will know what is to be done. Send for him quickly!"

So Buddha came up out of the West with Ananada and Kashiapa, his disciples. When he saw the turmoil he said: "First of all, let weapons be laid aside and lead out the Saint. I wish to speak with him!" The gods withdrew. Sun Wu Kung snorted and said: "Who are you, who dare to speak to me?" Buddha smiled and replied: "I have come out of the blessed West, Shakiamuni Amitofu. I have heard of the revolt you have raised, and am come to tame you!"

Said Sun Wu Kung: "I am the stone ape who has gained the hidden knowledge. I am master of seventy-two transformations, and will live as long as

Heaven itself. What has the Lord of the Heavens accomplished that entitles him to remain eternally on his throne? Let him make way for me, and I will be satisfied!"

Buddha replied with a smile: "You are a beast which has gained magic powers. How can you expect to rule here as Lord of the Heavens? Be it known to you that the Lord of the Heavens has toiled for eons in perfecting his virtues. How many years would you have to pass before you could attain the dignity he has gained? And then I must ask you whether there is anything else you can do, aside from playing your tricks of transformation?"

Said Sun Wu Kung: "I can turn cloud somersaults. Each one carries me eighteen thousand miles ahead. Surely that is enough to entitle me to be the Lord of the Heavens?"

Buddha answered with a smile: "Let us make a wager. If you can so much as leave my hand with one of your somersaults, then I will beg the Lord of the Heavens to make way for you. But if you are not able to leave my hand, then you must yield yourself to my fetters."

Sun Wu Kung suppressed his laughter, for he thought: "This Buddha is a crazy fellow! His hand is not a foot long; how could I help but leap out of it?" So he opened his mouth wide and said: "Agreed!"

Buddha then stretched out his right hand. It resembled a small lotus-leaf. Sun Wu Kung leaped up into it with one bound. Then he said: "Go!" And with that he turned one somersault after another, so that he flew along like a whirlwind. And while he was flying along he saw five tall, reddish columns towering to the skies. Then he thought: "That is the end of the world! Now I will turn back and become Lord of the

Heavens. But first I will write down my name to prove that I was there." He pulled out a hair, turned it into a brush, and wrote with great letters on the middle column: "The Great Saint Who Is Heaven's Equal." Then he turned his somersaults again until he had reached the place whence he had come. He leaped down from the Buddha's hand laughing and cried: "Now hurry, and see to it that the Lord of the Heavens clears his heavenly castle for me! I have been at the end of the world and have left a sign there!"

Buddha scolded: "Infamous ape! How dare you claim that you have left my hand? Take a look and see whether or not 'The Great Saint Who Is Heaven's Equal,' is written on my middle finger!"

Sun Wu Kung was terribly frightened, for at the first glance he saw that this was the truth. Yet outwardly he pretended that he was not convinced, said he would take another look, and tried to make use of the opportunity to escape. But Buddha covered him with his hand, shoved him out of the gate of Heaven, and formed a mountain of water, fire, wood, earth and metal, which he softly set down on him to hold him fast. A magic incantation pasted on the mountain prevented his escape.

Here he was obliged to lie for hundreds of years, until he finally reformed and was released, in order to help the Monk of the Yangtze-kiang fetch the holy writings from out of the West. He honored the Monk as his master, and thenceforward was known as the Wanderer. Guan Yin, who had released him, gave the Monk a golden circlet. Sun Wu Kung was induced to put it on, and it at once grew into his flesh so that he could not remove it. And Guan Yin gave the Monk a magic formula by means of which the ring could be tightened, should the ape grow disobedient. But from that time on he was always polite and well-mannered.

Note: This tale, like "The Pilgrim's Progress," is an allegory, the ape symbolizing the human heart. Yet despite its allegorical character, a number of mythological and fairy-tale motives are incorporated in it. The ape himself suggests Hanumant, the companion of Rama. Yo Huang is the Lord of the Heavens. The stone ape is the stone heart of natural man. The Buddhas, blessed spirits and gods, represent the ideals of Buddhism, Taoism and Confucianism. Sun Wu Kung: In Chinese apes are called Hu Sun, but the word Hu having an unlucky meaning, the Master chooses Sun as a family name, while at the same time the letter-sign is freed from the radical indicating an animal. Wu Kung—"the magic awaking to nothingness" (Nirwana). The different ways: magic, the way of raising spirits: the sciences: The three faiths are: Confucianism, Buddhism and Taoism; to these are added six "schools": the Yin-Yang School, the Mo-Di School, Medicine, War, Law, Miscellaneous, so that nine directions in all are represented. Quiescence is the Taoism for nonactivity, while Action is the Taoism for care of the body, as inaugurated by We Be Yang. The Devil-King of Chaos, i. e., sensuality, whose seat is supposed to be in Kidneys. "Red garments," colors, here all have an allegorical meaning. Death, i. e., Yama. The Evening Star is the star of metal; Sun Wu Kung also personifies a metal, hence the Evening Star appears as his apologist. As regards Li Dsing and Notscha see No. 18. As regards the Queen Mother of the West, see No. 15. As regards Yang Oerlang, see No. 17. Guan Yin is generally worshipped throughout China as the Feminine goddess. The motive of the magic flight is found frequently in fairy-tales the world over. Guan Yin is often represented holding a vase, Bau Ping. Laotsze's circlet or ring is the Tao. The eight elemental powers, i. e., Ba Gua. Buddha: while Sun Wu Kung is equipped to struggle against all external powers, he is conquered by Buddha, who does not combat him, but subdues him by his omnipresence. The Monk of the Yangste-Kiang is Huan Dschuang, see No. 68. The circlet or ring which can be made tighter when the ape does not obey, reappears in Hauff's fairy-tale of "The Young Englishman," as a cravat.

THE END